Women writers
and Georgian Cornwall

Women writers
and Georgian Cornwall

Charlotte MacKenzie

Cornwall History

2020

First printing: 2020

ISBN 978-1-716-33922-6

Published by Cornwall History, 1 Cornwall Terrace, Truro, TR1 3RT

Contents

Acknowledgements

As a historian I rely on primary sources. The research for this book was completed partly through visits to access these. Thanks are due to all those who facilitated on site access to materials held at Kresen Kernow Archives and Cornish Studies Service, the Morrab library, and the Royal Institution of Cornwall Courtney library. And I would particularly like to thank Jan Trefusis for access to family owned materials related to Elizabeth Trefusis which are at Trefusis in Cornwall.

The research was completed mostly online or reading digitised images. My thanks to those publishing digitised images of manuscripts and print publications, and those who made digital images for me or replied to queries. These included Ancestry, Bedfordshire Archives and Records Service, British Library, East Sussex Record Office, Family Search, Find My Past, Genealogy Bank, Hertfordshire Archives and Local Studies, Kresen Kernow, London Metropolitan Archives, Morrab library, National Archives, Nottingham University Library, Oxford University Press Scholarly Editions Online, Plymouth Libraries, National Library of Scotland, Library of the Religious Society of Friends, National Library of Wales, Wedgwood Museum, and Worcestershire Archive and Archaeology Service. Andrew Pool kindly retrieved and copied missing pages from one of Peter Pool's publications online. In researching and writing what follows I relied partly on published editions of letters and other documents not all of which include digitised images of the original manuscripts, and on published memoirs. Eliots of Port Eliot kindly agreed use of the cover image.

On 11 December 1948 the Times Literary Supplement published a letter from Fannie Ratchford of the Rare Book Collections, University of Texas in which she noted that

> I have in my keeping, on loan, a group of letters written by Elizabeth Jane Kingston, of Penzance, a first cousin of the young Brontës, to her brother-in-law Joseph Burgster in America

My thanks especially to Elizabeth L. Garver of the Harry Ransom Center, University of Texas at Austin for latest check of Fannie Ratchford papers held there and ongoing correspondence by email; it has not been possible to conclusively establish whether there are any extant letters at this time. I am grateful to Simon Roberts of Bonhams for information related to their sale of a collection of letters of John Lewis Guillemard (Lot 423, Oxford, 7 April 2009); at the time of writing it has not been possible to establish the current location of these letters.

Alan Kent, Isobel Grundy, Jacqui Howard, John Beddoes, John Lenton, Lissa Paul, Lisa Ann Robertson, Lucasta Miller, Melissa Hardie, Nick Holland, Peter Forsaith, and Sharon Ruston reminded me that I was not alone in my interests in Cornwall and women writers, or seeking to rediscover some relatively forgotten Georgian individuals, manuscripts, material objects, and printed texts.

Everything that follows is based on extant and accessible primary sources as referenced, and the interpretations are my own.

Charlotte MacKenzie

Cornwall, December 2020.

Women writers and Georgian Cornwall

Mary Wollstonecraft's youngest sister Everina was appointed in 1797 as governess to the family of the second Josiah Wedgwood. The events which followed affected the lives of five women writers three of whom had close family associations with Cornwall. In February Everina stayed with Mary in London before travelling to the Wedgwoods. During her visit Everina went out for the day with the poet Anne Batten Cristall.[1] Mary was three months pregnant and married William Godwin in March. After Mary gave birth to her second daughter the placenta failed to deliver; the novelist Eliza Fenwick nursed Mary, and Godwin then asked Eliza to write to Everina with the news that Mary had died.[2] Everina made plans with her sister Eliza Bishop to adopt Mary's two daughters Fanny Imlay and Mary Godwin; after visiting her sister in Ireland Everina did not return to the Wedgwoods. In October the Wedgwoods arrived at Mount's bay in Cornwall where they had taken a house for the winter and their daughter Charlotte was born; by the spring they were searching for a new governess, and appointed Thomasin Dennis who later wrote and published a gothic novel. Fanny Imlay and Mary Godwin, the future author of *Frankenstein*, continued to live with William Godwin.

Fifteen years later the families of a Cornish Admiral's widow and a banker who was a widower were part of the same social circle in Truro. These families included at least four female members who later published novels or verses. Two of the banker's daughters, Charlotte Champion Pascoe and Jane Louisa Willyams, published a novel together in 1818 after Walter Scott sent their manuscript to his publisher.[3] Louisa and Charlotte both later separately published their individual writing. The Michell family had returned to Truro after living in Portugal.[4] Charlotte's friend Anna Maria Michell, whose married surname was Wood, published verses in magazines and in 1838 printed a volume of verse including some of her translations from Portuguese and Italian. The youngest and most prolific writer was Emma Caroline Michell, who had been born at Lisbon, and who many years later when aged in her 60s and 70s wrote and published thirteen sensation novels which were mostly set in Cornwall; initially using the pseudonym 'C. Sylvester' and later in her own married name Lady Wood. She also published a volume of verses with her daughter Anna Caroline Steele who was a writer; as was another of her daughters Emma Barrett-Lennard who was also a composer who set songs to music.

Why did women write? Three factors influenced the behaviour and decisions of most Georgian women: their financial circumstances, employment and other opportunities; their education and upbringing; and their family and other relationships. For Georgian women from a range of backgrounds writing was an accomplishment. Publication and earning a living as a writer could be a viable economic choice. Some women wrote to make money, sometimes alongside caring for children or other family members. The proceeds of successful publication might be invested in other enterprises such as a girls' school. Some who wrote to make money stopped writing when there was no pressing financial need. Other women wrote for non-financial reasons. To communicate their beliefs or opinions; to tell stories or experiences; to express their feelings; to engender appreciation within their social circle. Some published their written compositions, anonymously or in their own name, only after being prompted and encouraged to do so; and others were published posthumously by their friends, family, or editors.

For some women writing was a route to increased financial security. The success at the Haymarket theatre of Sophia Lee's drama *The chapter of accidents* in the summer of 1780 partly funded the girls' school in Bath which Sophia opened with her three sisters. The Lees continued their school for 23 years. The publication of Charlotte Smith's *Elegiac sonnets* (1784) raised money to settle her husband's debts and free him from the King's Bench prison. A shoemaker's daughter Elizabeth Bentley invested the proceeds of subscriptions to her *Genuine poetical compositions* (1791), opening a boarding school in Norwich. Three decades later she republished a volume of her verses including others which had appeared occasionally in the *Norfolk Chronicle*; in the interim her only book publication had been some verses for children. A shoemaker's widow Charlotte Richardson briefly opened a school with the subscriptions to her *Poems on different occasions* (1806); after closing the school due to her poor health she raised funds from her *Poems chiefly composed during the pressure of severe illness* (1809).

The families of professionals, farmers, traders, creatives, and artisans included some women who wrote for publication alongside working in family businesses; and many women writers spent some years earning their living as educators. Some women became writers with the active support of their families. Jane Taylor (1783-1824), best known as the author of the ubiquitous children's poem 'Twinkle, twinkle little star', was educated at home; her mother and sister also wrote for children. When Jane was a teenager she and her sister Ann assisted their father in his engraving workshop; this did not prevent Jane and Ann forming a writers' club called the Umbelliferous Society with other young women in Colchester, in which each member wrote and shared some original writing once a month. The sisters' first publications were jointly produced and included some verses and engravings by other members of the Taylor family. In 1812-16 Jane Taylor travelled with her sick brother Isaac, on his doctors' advice, to Devon and Cornwall. Settling at Marazion in 1814 Jane continued to write and publish, and completed her novel *Display. A tale for young people* (1815) which remained in print through thirteen editions until the 1830s. Jane later returned to her widowed mother's home in Essex where they published *Correspondence between a mother and daughter at school* (1817). Isaac Taylor recovered, and he published Jane's unpublished writing after her death.[5]

As a teenager Eliza Fenwick, whose paternal relations were employed in the Mount's bay fisheries, worked alongside her mother in the family's hosiery business in London. Eliza published a novel *Secresy* in 1795, in which she contrasted two young women. One who had been sheltered from life with little education who gives way to her feelings, and another who spent her childhood in India and thinks for herself, explicitly rejecting 'unexamined obedience'.[6] Eliza later worked in the Penzance drapery of Thomas James Fenwick, before returning to London where she wrote and published several children's books, briefly managing Godwin's juvenile library. Eliza's writing was not sufficiently profitable to provide a reliable income for her family. She abandoned writing in favour of being a governess in London and Ireland, before operating a school with her daughter in Barbados, later moving to America and Canada where she ran or was employed in several educational institutions.[7]

Mary Wollstonecraft's *Thoughts on the education of daughters* (1787) observed of women's experience of teaching that being

> A governess to young ladies is equally disagreeable. It is ten to one if they meet with a reasonable mother; and if she is not so, she will be continually finding fault to prove she is not ignorant, and be displeased if her pupils do not improve, but angry if the proper methods are taken to make them so... In the mean time life glides away, and the spirits with it.[8]

The demands and expectations of employers meant that it was rarely practicable to combine being a governess with writing for publication. Nonetheless many women writers spent some time employed as governesses.

Without education women could not write, teach, or manage accounts. In Cornwall Truro grammar school was the preferred choice for many sons of the gentry, professionals, and prosperous traders providing a sound foundation for university; the Latin and grammar schools of other Cornish towns, including those newly opened in Lostwithiel and Penzance, also educated boys some of whom later qualified as doctors, lawyers, or clergymen. At Bodmin this included the medically qualified writer John Wolcot, who published pseudonymously as Peter Pindar. His schoolmaster Mr Fisher was said to be 'fond of poetry' and his younger relations later included a bookseller and printer, and a published poet.[9] There were private schools for girls in Cornwall but these did not have academic reputations comparable to those of the grammar schools. In the 1790s the schools listed in the *Universal British directory* included Grace Wills' in Bodmin, Liskeard Boarding School run by the 'Miss Lewises', and the 'Miss Warrens' in Truro which became known for its pupils' sewing. In 1802-3 Eliza Fenwick sent her daughter to a boarding school in Falmouth; rather than Penzance where 'Miss Stone' and the 'Miss Branwells' later opened schools.[10]

Many Cornish parents either opted to home educate their girls or sent them to boarding schools elsewhere. In the 1760s, when the vicar of St Gluvias Reverend John Penrose went to Bath for his health, he and his wife took the opportunity to personally check out boarding schools for their girls, later sending 15 year old Dolly Penrose to Mrs Aldworth's boarding school in St John's Court.[11] The merchant and smuggler John Copinger and his wife Mary were Catholic and educated their children partly at convent schools in France; in the late 1770s they placed several of their daughters in a girls' boarding school near London, from which they collected them when the family moved into Trelissick House.[12] Susan Mein, the daughter of a naval surgeon, spent her first 12 years living at Fowey in Cornwall before being sent with her two sisters to the Bath boarding school operated by

Sophia Lee and her sisters. The actress Mrs Siddons' daughter Cecilia also attended the Lees' school where she was a contemporary of Jane Louisa Willyams from Truro.[13]

Women who ran schools successfully were relatively independent. With several Lee sisters jointly operating their school Sophia and Harriet Lee continued to write for publication or performance. The educators had not necessarily had sound educational experiences themselves, as their parents moved between theatres in Bath, London, Manchester, Dublin, and Edinburgh in the 1740s-70s occasionally completing seasons in separate locations. Nonetheless the Lee sisters had commercial sense as well as fashionable appeal. The Lees employed a master who taught writing and arithmetic, as well as a 'Mam'selle' to teach French; with other regular lessons from dancing, drawing, and music masters with established reputations in Bath. The Lees' school was initially marketed in newspaper advertisements, and through Harriet's private tutoring of girls in Bath 'in reading and grammar at their own houses', bridging the gap between home education and school.[14]

The Lee sisters' fashionable and literary social networks, and occasional royal dance performances by their pupils at the Assembly rooms in Bath, later ensured that parents and guardians received favourable impressions of the school when they were planning their daughters' education. Dr Mein asked Mrs Gambier, a naval widow living in Bath, to recommend a school before he placed Susan at Belvedere House. Hester Piozzi was an influential literary friend of Harriet Lee; Hester commented in letters on the education of her goddaughter Cecilia Siddons at the Lees' school.[15] The Truro banker James Willyams and his wife Anne Champion enjoyed the creative arts, and a boarding school in Bath was conveniently placed for Anne's relations in Bristol; three of their children later wrote for publication, including Louisa and Charlotte, and a fourth who was a banker acquired a substantial collection of European art at Carnanton in Cornwall.[16]

As a farmer's daughter living at Trembath near Mount's bay Thomasin Dennis was initially educated at home. She was later tutored by Reverend Malachy Hitchins, the vicar of St Hilary, who was a keen astronomer; and became friends with his daughter Josepha. Thomasin had access to books. She became friends with Davies Giddy, who lent her books from his library at Tredrea; and Charles Valentine le Grice, a former school friend of Charles Lamb and Samuel Taylor Coleridge, who from 1796 was the family tutor at Trereife near Penzance. It was Davies Giddy who recommended Thomasin as governess to the family of the second Josiah Wedgwood.[17]

Cornish education and literacy in mathematics underpinned mining, navigation, and trade. Girls as well as boys were educated partly in arithmetic and learned how to keep household or trading accounts. The itinerant lecturer and scientific instrument maker Benjamin Martin, who published a natural history of Cornwall, commented in the late 1750s that he 'never but once saw an Eclipse calculated by a Lady' and she was a Cornish woman.[18] Mary Love, whose husband Thomas was a Penzance fish curer and shipowner, was related by marriage to Charles Valentine le Grice and later bequeathed her cipher and other books to his son Day Perry.[19] Blanche Harris contributed poems, enigmas, and rebuses to the mathematical periodical *The Ladies' Diary or Woman's Almanac*. In January 1777 Blanche married Joel Lean of Gwennap a mine captain who contributed to a similar periodical *The Gentleman's Diary*. During the next six years Blanche continued to contribute to *The Ladies' Diary*. The Leans had nine children. In 1810 Joel started *Lean's Engine Reporter* which published regular technical reports on the performance of mine engines in Cornwall and helped to raise efficiency; *Lean's Engine Reporter* continued to be published by the family until 1904.[20]

Georgian women writers with Cornish connections had varied interests, beliefs, and opinions, and their writing was heterogenous. In the 1770s-80s it ranged from Blanche's contributions to *The Ladies' Diary or Woman's Almanac* to Dorothy Enys' 'Address to simplicity' which was published in the *Gentleman's magazine* in 1785.[21] Over 300 subscribers supported the printing in Plymouth of *Poems on various subjects* (1784) by Ann Thomas of Millbrook in Cornwall; she dedicated the volume to Lady Catherine Eliot of Port Eliot.[22] A decade later, with a similar dedication and subscribers, Ann Thomas published the anti-Jacobin *Adolphus de Biron. A novel founded on the French Revolution* (1794).[23] Ann Thomas was a common name. It seems unlikely that this was a pseudonym given that she identified herself as a naval widow, had numerous local subscribers, and dedicated her work. Nonetheless identifying anything further about her biography as an historical individual proved elusive. Catharine Phillips travelled widely as a Quaker minister before marrying a Cornish copper agent; after being widowed she published pamphlets on a range of social and economic issues in Cornwall including the tin trade and food shortages, and a poem calling for the abolition of the slave trade *The happy king* (1794). Some of her letters and her memoirs were also published.[24]

The daughters of Cornish gentry families, like Dorothy Enys and Elizabeth Trefusis, might be educated to compose verses as a social accomplishment; just as they might learn to dance, draw, embroider, sing, or play a musical instrument. There were many similarities in the family circumstances and life experiences of Elizabeth Trefusis and Dorothy Enys (1746-84).[25] Both were the eldest daughters in their families and may have been educated at home; if they were placed in school details of these are not known. Each experienced bereavement in childhood when their mother died. As young women both formed female friendships. As adults each had personal relationships which continued over many years but neither married or had children. Their financial circumstances as adults were determined by the arrangements made in their fathers' wills.[26] Each established and lived in their own separate household; neither chose to live in Cornwall.

The Enys family in Cornwall acquired substantial assets trading as merchants in the seventeenth and early eighteenth centuries. An engraving of 'Enys house in the parish of Gluvias' was included in William Borlase's *Natural history of Cornwall* (1758).[27] Dorothy Enys (Dolly) was born in 1746, the eldest of eight children of John Enys and Lucy Bassett; two of her younger siblings died in childhood. Dolly was aged 11 when her mother died in 1758; Dolly's younger brothers and sisters were Samuel (Sammy) aged 8, Francis (Frank) aged 5, Catherine (Kitty) aged 4, Mary (Molly) aged 3, and a baby John. The widowed John Enys did not marry again. John Enys employed Frances Penrose (Fanny), who was aged 18 in 1758, and whose uncle Reverend John Penrose was the vicar of St Gluvias. Fanny may have been initially employed as a governess to care for the children; and was identified as a 'companion' when she continued to be part of later Enys households.

John Enys introduced his children to fashionable society through extended visits to London in 1766 and 1767, and to Bath during the three winters 1766-9; his personal accounts itemised their activities and expenditure.[28] The family initially took lodgings in London, and then a house in Richmond. Dolly was 20 in 1766 and John Enys may have wanted to extend her social connections; his sons and two younger daughters were placed in schools, and Sammy matriculated at Oxford in 1768. In London and Bath Dolly's father bought her jewellery, silk, and clothing, on one occasion paying a milliner's bill of over £40; he frequently gave Dolly £21 or 10 guineas, a total of 50 guineas in their first two months in London in 1766. Dolly appreciated decorative arts, went to the theatre and Vauxhall gardens where there were musical entertainments, and had access to books; in July 1767 Dolly took lessons from a Mr Southwell in the fashionable accomplishment of painting on silk cut paper.

Fanny was in her late 20s when she accompanied the Enys family to London and Bath. The Enys accounts of spending from that time show Fanny was frequently reimbursed for domestic payments in a way which suggests that she was organising and running their household; and she accompanied the family on some outings. By coincidence Fanny's uncle Reverend John Penrose was in Bath in May 1766 where Mr and Mrs Mundy from Cornwall told him that they had recently seen 'Mr. Miss, Mast. Sam, three Misses Enys, and Coz: Fanny all very well' at Vauxhall gardens in London.[29] The Enys family visited the foundling hospital. They toured historic buildings including Westminster abbey; took walks in 'Mr Pope's' garden, which included a grotto with minerals from Cornwall, and Kew gardens while they were staying in Richmond; went shopping, had their hair dressed, and had their portraits taken. They went to the theatre in London, Richmond, and Bath. When they arrived in Bath John Enys paid subscriptions for the balls, to Leake's circulating library, and to a coffee house on the Parade.

In 1771 Sammy married the daughter of the vicar of Newbury Sarah Penrose; the Penrose family at Newbury were of Cornish descent. Sammy and Sarah had three children one of whom died in infancy. In the early 1770s there were four adult deaths in the Enys family: of Dolly's recently married sister Kitty Collins in 1772, her father in 1773, her sister Molly in 1775, and brother Sammy in 1776. A commission in the army was purchased for Dolly's youngest brother John, who fought on the British side in the

American war of independence, and whose journals of his extensive military travels overseas have been partly published.[30] Enys continued to be the home of Sammy's widow Sarah, son John, and daughter Lucy; but Sarah soon returned to Berkshire where she made two later marriages and had further children. Frank assumed responsibility for managing the Enys family's estate which was later inherited by his great nephew John Samuel Enys.

In his will John Enys bequeathed an annuity of £150 to his daughter Dolly plus £200 to furnish a house of her own 'to live in when and where she pleaseth'.[31] These arrangements enabled Dolly to lead an independent life; she established her own household with her companion, servant, and friend Fanny. They lived mostly in Bath with a prolonged stay in Exmouth from the summer of 1781. Dolly was assiduous in ensuring the payment of annuities by the Enys' agent Thomas Warren in Truro to former servants of her father, and to herself, writing four letters to him concerning these in 1778-81.[32]

Sammy's marriage developed the Enys family's literary connections. Sarah's brother Thomas Penrose wrote poetry which was published from the mid-1770s with some immediate success; and her sister Ann was married to James Pettit Andrews who later published translations of French and German literature, wrote histories, and edited a posthumously published volume of poetry by his brother-in-law. Dolly's pastoral verse 'Address to simplicity' was light and carefree, imitating John Milton's 'L'Allegro' which ended 'Mirth, with thee I mean to live'. In stark contrast to Thomas Penrose's verse 'Madness' the innovations of which had prompted many reviews and divergent responses from critics a decade previously.[33]

Charlotte MacKenzie

Dolly's interest in writing and the arts is probably best defined as dilettante. She nonetheless attracted the attention of individuals in Cornwall who were interested in writing and literary culture notably Reverend Richard Polwhele the vicar of Manaccan. It is likely that the 'Cornubiensis' of Truro who sent her 'Address to simplicity' to the *Gentleman's Magazine* in 1785 was Polwhele who established his own reputation as a writer partly by providing regular contributions to periodicals in the 1780s-90s. The 'Address to simplicity' was polished; it may have been Dolly's party piece and composed at the time when she was being urged to develop social accomplishments.

Many years later when Richard Polwhele reminisced about visiting 'Miss Enys' in Bath it was Fanny's conversation and writing which he recalled to memory. Fanny's letters to the Truro lawyer Edward Collins of Truthan, who was Dolly's brother in law, were described by their recipient as 'the *best I ever read*!'. Polwhele noted that decades later when he called on Fanny in Penryn 'her conversation was in a high degree interesting'.[34] Polwhele's account drew on a letter from Collins in appreciative remembrance of Fanny which was published by the *Royal Cornwall Gazette* in July 1835. Nonetheless evidence that Fanny or Dolly wrote or anonymously published novels, poetry, or plays is lacking.

Polwhele neatly encapsulated Dolly and Fanny's domestic relationship when he noted, possibly with an unfulfilled editing or printing instruction, 'Fanny was ... a *servant* [say *companion*] to Miss Enys'. When Dolly died in 1784 she bequeathed her 'dear friend and faithful companion' Fanny £50 a year.[35] Fanny lived a further half century and was in her 90s when she died. Polwhele and Collins found Fanny an entertaining social companion and correspondent. Neither Fanny's letters, nor any other literary compositions by Dolly or Fanny appear to be extant, with the exception of Dolly's 'Address to simplicity'.

Several of the women writers considered here sustained a life long correspondence with one friend. Eliza Fenwick with Mary Hays, Thomasin Dennis with Davies Giddy, and Charlotte Champion Pascoe with Anna Maria Wood. Half a century after Dolly's 'Address to simplicity' was published, Maria privately printed some of her translations of sonnets from Portuguese and Italian, and shared a copy with her friend Charlotte noting 'The book, as you imagine, has been very far from being advertised (you see there is no publisher's name)... There is nothing in the book but truth and simplicity, but one does not like to have feelings published against one's will...'. Later it was Maria who chose to have a volume of her letters to Charlotte printed.[36]

The London publication of Anne Batten Cristall's *Poetical sketches* (1795) was supported by subscribers including Mary Wollstonecraft and other well known writers.[37] In the same year Eliza Fenwick published her novel *Secresy* (1795).[38] Eliza Fenwick may have met Thomasin Dennis in Mount's bay, although if the two writers did meet neither mentioned it in their letters which are extant today. By coincidence Thomasin's father Alexander Dennis mortgaged the Penzance shop premises occupied by Thomas James Fenwick, in which Eliza worked, and which later transferred to the Brontës' grandfather Thomas Branwell.[39] Following Thomasin's return to Cornwall one of her verses appeared over her name in a periodical in 1803; she wrote and anonymously published her novel *Sophia St Clare* (1806) with the well known London publisher Joseph Johnson.[40] Elizabeth Trefusis' two volume collection of *Poems and tales* was published in 1808.[41]

These four authors were acquainted with other contemporary writers or asked for their opinions on unpublished drafts; these acquaintances included Anna Letitia Barbauld, Anna Seward, Charles Lamb, Charles Valentine le Grice, Charlotte Richardson, George Dyer, Helen Maria Williams, Hester Lynch Piozzi, John Wolcot, Mary Hays, Mary Lamb,

Charlotte MacKenzie

Mary Robinson, Samuel Taylor Coleridge, and William Gifford. Eliza Fenwick established

friendships with several other women writers and corresponded for decades with Mary

Hays; in 1803 Mary Lamb told Dorothy Wordsworth 'I have a great affection for Mrs

Fenwick'.[42] Thomasin Dennis was friends with Charles Valentine le Grice, and during the

time that she was employed by the Wedgwoods was sufficiently self-confident to discuss

her poetry with John Wolcot, and writing with Samuel Taylor Coleridge.[43]

In 1798 Richard Polwhele published an anti-feminist poem *The unsex'd females* in which

he repudiated the views of some women writers and artists and named others whom he

found acceptable.[44] The latter included Anna Seward and Hester Piozzi who were

associates of Elizabeth Trefusis. Polwhele criticised Barbauld, who later read and

commented on Thomasin Dennis' poetry; Hays, Smith, Robinson, and Wollstonecraft,

who were all well known to Eliza Fenwick, and Helen Maria Williams another associate of

Elizabeth Trefusis. At the same time Polwhele was probably the 'Cornubiensis' of Truro

who sent Dorothy Enys' 'Address to simplicity' to the *Gentleman's Magazine* for

publication. Polwhele might have been expected to know of the poems and novel

published by Ann Thomas of Millbrook. Nonetheless when Polwhele wrote a short

overview of Cornwall's literary history the only woman writer he included was Thomasin

Dennis whom he identified as a poet; his later *Biographical sketches in Cornwall* (1831)

included Elizabeth Trefusis as a person eminent in poetry, about whom he had also

written a complimentary memorial verse.[45]

Charlotte Champion Pascoe corresponded with Walter Scott for more than eleven years

from 1811.[46] Charlotte was married to the vicar of St Hilary and her later writing,

including letters which were published posthumously by her friends and relations,

observed and recorded life in west Cornwall.[47] Charlotte's sister Jane Louisa Willyams published other books including French protestant histories, made donations to organisations assisting British emigrants, and probably wrote the poem signed 'J. L. W.' in the *Emigrants' penny magazine* published in Plymouth in 1850. The Brontës, Thomasin Dennis, Eliza Fenwick, Charlotte Champion Pascoe, and Jane Louisa Willyams, all initially published their novels anonymously and Charlotte used a pseudonym in 1861.[48] It is not impossible that some of the women writers considered here may have similarly published other works which have not been identified as written by them. The Tory *Cornwall Gazette* edited by Thomas Flindell anonymously published poems written 'by a lady' before 1810; it is not known who wrote these.

All of the writers considered here had close family or other connections with Cornwall. Their parental families included two Cornish farmers, a Truro bank manager, the daughters of two Penzance merchants, and an itinerant Wesleyan preacher who had been a Mount's bay fisherman; two were of Cornish gentry families. Ann Thomas may have spent her childhood on Shetland, which was the subject of one of her poems, in which Greenwall, which at the time was the property of a family of merchants named Scott, was described as her 'guardian'. As adults many of these women writers lived partly or entirely in Cornwall; this included Ann Thomas who described herself as the widow of a naval officer, and Catharine Phillips who was married to a Cornish copper agent. All of their families were affected by the Georgian transformations of Cornwall's economy and culture.

The eighteenth century was a turning point in Cornwall's history. Cornish mine adventurers were early participants in the technological developments of the industrial revolution. Cornish mariners and shipowners were active in the expansion of global communications and maritime trade; some Cornish gentlemen held appointments or had

Charlotte MacKenzie

commercial interests overseas. The wars at sea, recurrent conflicts with France, and diversification of religious and political opinions drew participants from Cornwall and influenced opinions at home. Coastal traders and coaches regularly transported passengers to and from London; migration from Cornwall to live and work in London was not uncommon. Georgian Cornwall drew in travellers: visitors interested in mining developments; mariners and passengers on packet and other ships calling at Cornish ports; itinerant preachers and traders some of whom sparked the development of Methodist societies and other faith communities; and patients whose doctors had advised them to winter in Cornwall's mild coastal climate. The impacts of all these interchanges were cultural as well as economic.

The extent and impacts of some new influences in Georgian Cornwall have been exaggerated or underestimated. In 1791 2.8 per cent of Cornish residents were members of Methodist societies; these numbers derive from the reports to Methodist conference. That was a larger proportion than in most other communities in Georgian Britain, but confirms that Methodism's initial participation and impact in Cornwall was less than later when it became a predominant influence in mining communities. The level of participation explained widespread Georgian observations that Cornish communities continued practices proscribed within Methodist societies including hurling, wrestling, and accepting smuggled or wrecked cargoes. The Georgian Methodist participation in Cornwall was comparable to the estimated 3 per cent of mariners sailing British ships who were black, a noticeable presence in many maritime paintings of crews at the time. Georgian communities of Cornish mariners were similarly diverse as was partly noted in parish registers and other records.[49]

Ann Thomas' poems included descriptions of major sea battles in which Cornish mariners participated. Dorothy's brother John Enys was remembered for his journals of military campaigns in America and Canada. In London in 1790 William Godwin noted that he had met 'Miss Trefussis' (sic) with the army officer Henry Barry when he went to have tea with Helen Maria Williams;[50] these four individuals were all creative writers. The protagonist of Ann Thomas' novel Adolphus de Biron was the son of a Scot and a French man, who rejects his paternal heritage because of the revolution choosing to identify himself as a British subject. Adolphus de Biron blamed enlightenment philosophy, the decline of religion, and French support for the American war of independence for the revolution in France. Ann Thomas was critical of women who involved themselves in politics, not least women writers:

> The Revolution has made not only the Men, but the Ladies also profound Politicians, and to those whose Minds are tinctured with Spleen, Ill-nature, and with that sort of malicious Pleasure which delights in human Miseries, it affords the finest Opportunity to vent the Rancour of their Hearts. Some in a verbal Manner point out to you the Necessity of all this Murder and Carnage: Others snatch the Pen, and write, as if one of the Furies dictated every Line.[51]

Thomasin Dennis, who might have read Ann Thomas' novel, was socially hierarchical and chose to set her novel in ancien régime France.

Eliza Fenwick and Anne Batten Cristall were part of the radical political and literary circles in 1790s London which included some well known writers. Both knew Mary Wollstonecraft. John Fenwick was a close friend of William Godwin and advocate of political reform who supported the revolution in France. The Fenwicks were part of the circle of radical writers in 1790s London some of whom wrote novels, plays, or poetry to

Charlotte MacKenzie

communicate political messages. Eliza's novel *Secresy* can be read as supporting Jacobin

opinion when the rationalist Caroline Ashburn asserts that

> obedience has almost driven virtue out of the world, for be it unlimited
>
> unexamined obedience to a sovereign, to a parent, or husband, the mind yielding
>
> itself to implicit unexamined obedience, loses its individual dignity, and you can
>
> expect no more of a man than of a brute.[52]

Human dignity was central to Catharine Phillips' advocacy in support of the abolition of

slavery, and interventions in the market to manage Cornish food supplies. Her objective

was social cohesion rather than the political cause of liberty; she feared, and wrote to

counter, social unrest when there were food shortages in Cornwall.

Great Cornish landowners, gentry, traders, farmers, and their families were participants

in the expanding Georgian markets for books, musical and theatrical entertainments,

decorative objects including ceramics and portraits, textiles, imports, legal and financial

services. Georgian artisans established workshops in Cornish towns as gold and silver

smiths, watch and clock makers, joiners and cabinet makers. John Enys' subscriptions on

arrival in Bath to a circulating library as well as the balls and a coffee house, and his

family's theatre attendances, were characteristic of his Cornish contemporaries. There

was a vigorous Georgian market in Cornwall in which stationers, booksellers, and

printers responded to and built growing demand for newspapers, periodicals, and books.

The London bookseller James Lackington noted in his autobiography of 1792 that during

the previous two decades

> The poorer sort of farmers, and even the poor country people in general, who
>
> before that period spent their winter evenings in relating stories of witches,
>
> ghosts, hobgoblins, &c. now shorten the winter nights by hearing their sons and
>
> daughters read tales, romances, &c. and on entering their houses you may see

Tom Jones, Roderick Random, and other entertaining books stuck up on their

bacon racks[53]

In Cornwall those who enjoyed reading and were among the participants in these new

markets continued to have a knowledge of Cornish folklore.

In May 1801 the popular publisher William Lane of the Minerva Press placed a large

advertisement in the recently established *Cornwall Gazette* boasting that books from his

circulating library were available through booksellers and stationers in eight Cornish

towns including Penzance 'and by all the distributors of this paper'. Enabling the families

of farmers, traders, and some miners as well as gentry to read for entertainment,

information, or self-education. Many of the novels on Lane's list were written by women

and intended for women readers.

In late Georgian Cornwall booksellers, circulating libraries, book clubs, and subscription

libraries occupied an increasingly overcrowded market place where by 1806 Richard

Polwhele could declare that 'Our circulating libraries, under the conduct of stationers, are

almost annihilated I think, in Cornwall, or very little regarded; from the circumstance of

so many book clubs being instituted in our different towns'.[54] Polwhele exaggerated the

extent to which circulating libraries were displaced by local book clubs and subscription

libraries including the Cornwall Library and Literary Society from 1792. Circulating

libraries were commercial retailers responding to demand for cheap entertainment; clubs

and societies used subscriptions to purchase selected titles, and many had specified

religious, educational, or utilitarian purposes and affiliations which defined and limited

their readership.

One of the booksellers with a Lane's circulating library was the shop of Cornwall's first woman printer Elizabeth Elliot in Falmouth. She continued the Falmouth printing, bookselling, and stationery business for forty years after her husband Phillip's death in 1787; extending the shop's stock to include musical instruments and music, and going into partnership with her niece Sarah Cornish by 1811. When the future Prime Minister Benjamin Disraeli passed through Falmouth in 1830 he was delighted to discover Sarah's son the doctor James Cornish had annotated copies of most of his father's books. James Cornish explained that he had also read Isaac Disraeli's other books which he had borrowed from a subscription library.[55]

Some readers became writers. Many individuals in Georgian Cornwall who acquired an education were cultural participants and producers. Some of these were widely known as having moved from Cornwall to London where they were employed as actors, writers, and painters. The actor and playwright Samuel Foote, the satirist Peter Pindar (John Wolcot), and the artist John Opie. More recently there has been considerable interest in the black musician and composer Joseph Antonio Emidy who lived in Cornwall for most of his life from 1799 to 1835. The Victorian bibliographers George Clement Boase and William Prideaux Courtney described the *Bibliotheca Cornubiensis* as listing the books and manuscripts 'of Cornishmen' but were inclusive in their decision making; listing people of Cornish origin who had lived and worked elsewhere, residents in Cornwall who originated from other places, and women as well as men. Boase and Courtney listed Foote, Opie, and Wolcot, as well as the published musical compositions by one of Emidy's sons. Boase and Courtney's entries for Georgian Cornish women included many published recollections of the lives of early Methodist society members. They also listed most of the women writers considered here.[56]

The west Cornish cultural milieu which produced the poetry writing innovative scientist Humphry Davy was home to the families of most of these women writers. Davy grew up alongside families of traders, professionals, and farmers some of whom enjoyed writing, sketching, or music and were part of the audiences for each other's work. Joseph Batten was a published poet as well as an independent minister; it was probably this Joseph Batten of Penzance who was a subscriber to Ann Thomas' *Poems on various subjects* (1784), as well as to his niece Anne Batten Cristall's *Poetical sketches* (1795). Charles Valentine le Grice, a published writer and translator who wrote verses, and Thomasin Dennis were friends.

In 1802-3 Eliza Fenwick became friends with John and Fanny Vigurs; the latter kept a milliner's shop and John was the son of a victualler. Eliza found him to be 'a tall pleasing young man who reads much, draws well from Nature, & writes agreeable verses'. John's brother Thomas Vigurs had the bookshop and printers which was also the Lane's circulating library in Penzance. His shop was a few doors away from the Chapel Street home of Maria Branwell, who later married Patrick Brontë. Joseph Batten published a poem about Penzance in 1815, and Thomasin's father Alexander Dennis published a journal of his travels in Britain in 1816. Both were printed by Thomas Vigurs.[57]

Current interest in Cornwall's cultural distinctiveness is paramount. In Georgian Cornwall it is possible to identify individuals who were interested in recording the Cornish language and vernacular English, folklore, feasts, processions, dances, hurling and wrestling; to read the letters and journals of those who described the organisation and working practices of Cornwall's fisheries and mines; as well as visitors' accounts of rides and walks to explore Cornish landmarks or antiquarian remains. A number of Cornish

Charlotte MacKenzie

gentlemen with antiquarian interests extended the documentation of Cornwall's language, manuscripts, and archaeology.

Individuals identified and described themselves or others as Cornish. Some Georgian identifications of a place of origin were of course entirely fictional. The London attorney and armchair adventurer Robert Poltock subscribed to the coffee table volume *A new general collection of voyages and travels in Europe, Asia, Africa and America* (1745) before writing and anonymously publishing *The life and adventures of Peter Wilkins, a Cornish Man* (1750). This narrative was a mix of surreal visions, such as a woman who could fly, and utopian aspiration which enabled the eponymous Peter Wilkins to abolish slavery through conversations with the King.[58] The latter possibly Poltock's reply to the anonymously published pamphlet by the Cornish man and Governor of Jamaica Edward Trelawney, who personally profited from plantations which he later bequeathed to his widow; Trelawney's pamphlet dialogue between a planter and a military officer included the argument that there was an economic imperative for slavery to continue, while acknowledging it to be morally indefensible and 'contrary to the Law of God and Nature'.[59] Thomas Pitt of Boconnoc wrote to his aunt Hester, Lady Chatham, in 1775 to affectionately announce the 'Birth of our little Cornishman' his first son Thomas. In 1791 the abolitionist poet Richard Williams, who was a mines captain, chose to present his work as the 'most humble Address' of a 'Cornish man'.[60]

The St Ives attorney Fortescue Hitchins, son of the vicar of St Hilary, wrote and published verses; the printing of *The seashore and other poems* in 1810 was dedicated to Samuel Stephens MP of Tregenna Castle and attracted many subscribers. His father Reverend Malachy Hitchins was remembered by one parishioner as 'A free-spoken, merry-spirited man, kind to the poor after his way, neither grudging them meat, clothes,

22

nor smuggled brandy'.[61] Fortescue Hitchins' commemorative verse *The tears of Cornubia*, on the sinking of the *HMS St George* with the loss of hundreds of men's lives in December 1811, revealed that consciousness of a distinctive Cornish identity and relationship with Georgian Britain continued to be present during the quarter century of conflicts and loss of life which comprised the French revolutionary and Napoleonic wars.[62] The acute awareness of national identity as a French man, Scot, and what it meant to be a British subject by choice were central to Ann Thomas' *Adolphus de Biron*. Fortescue Hitchins lost schoolfriends in the 1811 disaster and knew 'the dark maze of comfortless despair'. Before news of this sinking reached Penzance a drenched, exhausted, and sand covered Lieutenant Thomas Branwell RN, who was one of those drowned, was reported to have appeared to his bed-bound father, the innkeeper Richard Branwell, who told his daughters to make food for their brother who was just changing his clothes.[63]

Charlotte Champion Pascoe gained the initial attention of Walter Scott in 1811 when she sent him a Cornish folktale of fairies. Scott observed that this folktale accorded 'singularly with the Highland tradition' in a reply which revealed more discursively that Scott recognised and valued the cultural distinctiveness of Cornwall.[64] Charlotte later wrote about life in west Cornwall. Charlotte's friends posthumously published her letters from the 1830s-40s as *Walks about St Hilary chiefly among the poor* (1879). These included frank accounts of women's experiences living in west Cornwall including domestic violence. The letters showed that Charlotte valued and consciously curated Cornish identity, and recorded the 'Cornishisms' she heard in conversation. In 1861 she pseudonymously published *Wan an Aell, a Cornish Drawel, as Zung, Zold, and Spauken by Barzillai Baragweneth, proving to Juniversal Zatizfaction that Coarnwall is held the fust county in Ingleland* (more 'special by those as enters it from the Westard, - and tarries there).[65]

Charlotte MacKenzie

Alan Kent has delineated a Cornish literary tradition in which the cultural transitions of the eighteenth century were seen as pivotal in the construction of later Cornish identities. Although Kent wrote about the relationships between this literary tradition, female characters, and women's writing he did not consider any of the women writers included here.[66] As writers each had their own aspirations and chosen literary and other points of reference. The connections between their writing, and the cultural characteristics and topophilia which were present or formative in constructions of Cornish identity, are considered here.

Each of the following chapters focuses on women writers whose biographies included family or other associations with Georgian Cornwall: Catherine Phillips, Elizabeth Trefusis, Anne Batten Cristall, Eliza Fenwick, Thomasin Dennis, the Brontës through their mother's Cornish relations, and Charlotte Champion Pascoe. To these names might be added the published writers Dorothy Enys, Blanche Lean, Jane Taylor, Ann Thomas, Emily Trevenen,[67] and Jane Louisa Willyams; and many more who followed later. I made an initial decision to include published writers of fiction, poetry, and non-fiction intended for adult readers; the individual chapters focus on those for whom most biographical as well as bibliographical information was available. Two of Elizabeth Trefusis' verses are published here for the first time. Most of the less well known women writers' publications are digitised online or reprinted; and some have received limited scholarly attention. This has not included discussion of what these writers can tell us about women's lives or literary culture in Cornwall. Most wrote partly about women's societal position, family and other relationships. The purpose of this book is to rediscover their lives and writing, and what it can tell us about Cornwall's history, culture, and literary traditions.

'Cogency, perspicuity and love' Catharine Phillips

Catharine Phillips (1727-94) wrote a memoir of her life which was published posthumously. She was born at Dudley in Worcestershire to the Quakers Henry Payton and his second wife Ann Fowler. As a young man Henry Payton had been a ministering Friend who travelled to attend Quaker conferences; and when Catherine was a child other Quaker ministers stayed with the Payton family. In 1743 at the age of 16 Catharine attended a boarding school in London run by Rachel Trafford, whom Catherine described as a Quaker 'minister as well as mistress', and her sister. A year later Catharine returned to live at home where her vocation developed with the support of her mother. In her *Memoirs* Catharine recalled that her mother 'was desirous that some one of her offspring might be called to the ministry, which was fulfilled in me'. In her ministry Catharine supported the organisation and representation of women within the Society of Friends which led to Women's Yearly Meetings being held from 1784.

Throughout her adult life Catharine was a writer. After receiving positive attention for some early poems which were published Catharine decided when starting her ministry to give up the accomplishment of composing 'verses' which she thought might appear frivolous. She also consciously redirected her reading to matters she regarded as of greater consequence than poetry.[68] It was realistic for Catharine to consider the impact which her conduct had on how others saw her, and to recognise that her clear sense of purpose might engender mixed reactions in her time. Many years later James Jenkins recalled that a woman Friend in Dudley observed of Catharine that 'Even in her juvenile days she assumed a great deal of consequence; often asserting, and maintaining authority to which she had no rightful claim, and which was in some instances unusual for women to exercise'.[69] From 1749 Catharine travelled in the Quaker 'ministry'.

Charlotte MacKenzie

Throughout her life she defended her belief in the equal merit of men's and women's callings writing in an early 1790s poem 'Nor age, nor sex, did them excuse, From their appointed share Of Gospel labours; God did chuse'.[70]

Catharine's first tour as a 'public Friend' in the summer of 1749 was in Wales. Where Catharine met William Phillips a Cornish copper agent who was a widower with two young children and whose parents lived in Swansea; William was attracted to Catharine who stopped communication with him at that time because she feared it might be a distraction from her ministry. In the winter of 1749-50 Catharine toured the westcountry and held Meetings at Penzance and Truro; she was accompanied on different sections of her journey by her brother and two women Friends. In the following three years Catharine returned to Bath, Bristol, and Wales, as well as travelling in Ireland, the north of England, and Scotland.

In 1753-6 Catharine completed a tour of colonial America. Her outward voyage in September 1753 was from Portsmouth on the *Alexander*, Captain Curling, bound for Charlestown in south Carolina; she was accompanied on this journey by a fellow Quaker Mary Peisley who was also travelling to minister. The circumstances the two women encountered in the Quaker community at Charlestown were not without challenges. Mary wrote in a letter to her uncle at the time that 'It seems like a city of refuge for the disjointed members of our Society, where they may walk in the sight of their own eyes, and the imagination of their own hearts, without being accountable to any for their conduct, and yet be called by the name of Quaker, to take away their reproach'.

Travelling through the Carolinas Catharine observed the circumstances of enslaved Africans on plantations; and discussed their conditions and circumstances with those who accompanied and assisted her as guides. She noted in her *Memoirs* that 'Divers of our Friends were then in possession of some negroes, either by inheritance or purchase'. Mary said that this fact caused them 'considerable pain' because they could not 'reconcile this with the golden rule of doing unto all men as we would they should do unto us'.[71] At the same time 40 years before her abolitionist poem was published Catharine noted that the 'concern arose amongst Friends, to abolish slave-keeping in our Society' and that some Quakers 'employed many of them as hired servants after they had given them their liberty'.[72]

Nonetheless Catharine's *Memoirs* focused in more detail on the unfamiliar physical conditions of her journey traversing swamps and other challenging terrain mostly on horseback and sometimes sleeping in a tent. During these three years Catharine visited most east coast settlements of colonial America travelling north as far as New Hampshire. After staying in Philadelphia Catharine made her return Atlantic crossing on a snow which 'had a very quick but stormy passage' from Chester to Dublin where she arrived on 10 July 1756 having learned in the Irish channel that Britain was by then at war with France.

The Dutch Republic remained neutral during the Seven Years' War when Catharine continued to travel abroad. She travelled by sea but was mindful of the risk from French privateers and opted to sail to and from England on northern routes. In July 1757 Catharine sailed as a passenger on the packet from Harwich to Helvoetsluys. Catharine was assisted by individuals who helped to translate and interpret at Meetings but found this tour difficult because she was not always accompanied by an interpreter. By the end of August Catharine decided to leave the Dutch Republic and returned to Harwich on the packet from Helvoetsluys on 1 September. Catharine completed further tours in England, spent some time with her family, and was in Ireland for three months in 1759 returning to Whitehaven; she continued to travel in England and went to Wales in spring 1762.

Following the end of the Seven Years' War Catharine might have completed further tours abroad. Instead for the first time aged in her late 30s she kept house for her widowed mother following her sister Ann's marriage. In her *Memoirs* Catharine recalled major decisions which she had made with a conscious sense of purpose and intention about her priorities and choices in life. This was less true of the years that she spent as her mother's housekeeper when for the first time she appears to have given way to the demands of personal and family feelings, or based her conduct on Georgian social expectations of unmarried daughters, rather than self-direction and conscious choice. A nine year gap in Catharine's journal, to which she referred in writing her *Memoirs*, reflected the changed demands of her everyday life at that time after 'a load of domestick concerns devolved upon me'.[73]

Catharine's mother had encouraged her to pursue her vocation as a public Friend. While keeping house for her mother Catharine continued to travel occasionally to attend annual and quarterly Quaker Meetings elsewhere in Britain including in Cornwall in 1766; after which Catharine resumed her correspondence with the Cornish copper agent William Phillips, who had not married again, and whose two sons were by then adults. Phillips also had occasion to travel on business to Swansea, where some of his family lived, and to Bristol; and he may also have visited Catharine in Worcestershire as their relationship developed. Catharine and William married at Bewdley in Worcestershire in July 1772. On marrying Catharine left the home of her mother who died two years later. William Phillips respected Catharine's continuing role as a public Friend after they married.

Fifty years later one commentator suggested that Catharine's decision to marry at the age of 45, after meeting William Phillips a quarter of a century earlier, had been a conscious decision and choice not to have children.[74] Some Georgian women may have delayed marrying to avoid childbearing or to have fewer pregnancies and children. In her 20s and early 30s Catharine led an independent and adventurous life; she found everyday domestic responsibilities a burdensome distraction from her other concerns. As a widower with two children William Phillips had established a family home at Redruth in Cornwall. After marrying William and Catharine lived in his family home. By all accounts William was a solicitous husband who provided practical organisation and support to meet the requirements of his wife's activities and physical comfort.

In Cornwall the Quaker community included the Fox family who had acquired substantial influence in mining, shipping, manufacturing, and medicine. In 1780 Catharine's niece Catharine Young married the second George Croker Fox of Falmouth. Catharine Phillips joined the Falmouth Meeting with a testimonial from the Chadwick Meeting in Worcestershire as a Friend whose conduct was characterised by 'cogency, perspicuity and love' and which recommended her role as a minister who had endured 'travils and perils'. Initially while living in Cornwall Catharine continued her ministry travelling in England, Wales, and Ireland; some of her discourses to Friends in the late 1770s and 1780s were later published. In 1785 Matthew Boulton wrote to his daughter that he had heard Catharine Phillips address a large Meeting in Truro 'with great energy & good sence for one hour & a half'.[75] William Phillips continued to travel on business and sometimes travelled with Catharine in her ministry.

William Phillips died in August 1785. His eldest son Richard Phillips continued to live in Redruth where he managed the family's copper trading interests after his father's death.

Charlotte MacKenzie

William's youngest son James Phillips had been apprenticed in 1760 to William Arch a woolman in the City of London; and later succeeded his widowed relation Mary Hinde (born Phillips) as a printer and publisher who lived with his family above his bookseller's shop in George Yard off Lombard Street in the City of London.

In her *Memoirs* Catharine described herself after her marriage as 'settled in Cornwall', where she lived for a quarter of a century, despite regretting that there were not more Quakers.[76] After she was widowed Catharine travelled out of Cornwall less frequently. She lived in Redruth but through her connections with the Fox family her social circle included Friends in Falmouth and at Perran wharf where the iron foundry was established in the early 1790s. In mid-life Catharine had been unable to ride after dislocating one of her elbows in a fall; she continued to have a weakness in her left arm and painful joints. When he died William Phillips made a specific bequest to Catharine of a chaise and horses to enable her to travel from home. Catharine was right-handed and noted in her *Memoirs* that she continued to write despite her physical impairments describing herself in another publication as having an 'active' mind in a 'decrepid' body. It was her stepson James Phillips who published several of Catharine's publications in the 1790s.

Catharine had seen America gain independence and was aware of the revolution in France. Increasingly in the early 1790s Catharine wrote and published on topical social and political issues. She described her abolitionist poem as 'Almost all .... pen'd in the Year 1791' but published prose works before the poem in 1794. The first of these prose works was written in December 1791 and addressed *To the principal inhabitants of the county of Cornwall who are about to assemble at Truro on the mining concerns of this county*; it advocated a reformation of conduct and suggested that mine managers should introduce written expectations for miners' personal and social behaviour.[77] Catharine's next publication written six months later set out doctrinal differences between Methodism and Quakerism which she concluded were *Reasons why the people called Quakers cannot so fully unite with the Methodists in their missions to the negroes in the West India islands and Africa as freely to contribute thereto.* Catharine saw the transatlantic slave trade as an obstacle to the conversion of Africans to Christianity but in this publication she did not call directly for the abolition of slavery despite her family's active support for the abolitionist campaign.[78]

In 1792 Catharine's next topical publication looked at household spending and the price of grain, increases in which frequently prompted food riots including those in Cornwall in 1773, 1789, and 1793. In this publication she briefly criticised Parliament for refusing to end the 'injustice and cruelty' of the 'negro-trade'.[79] This publication might be seen as having a radical and environmental perspective. Catharine criticised the impact of the enclosure of common land and expressed concern that agricultural land was being taken to build factories and canals urging careful consideration of this issue before new canals were built. Among the measures she advocated were: public granaries to store grain in times of plenty and feed the poor in times of dearth; ending parish tithes; more small farms; the continuation of commons; and cultivation of waste and unused land including planting trees. She specifically criticised great landowners in Cornwall for not planting trees; explaining that wood might be a cheap source of fuel and that charcoal 'is the support of all our metal business'. An appendix set out in detail the varieties of trees suited to different conditions including trees native to north America and other foreign countries; asking 'What need have we to import walnuts, if the trees will thus flourish and be fruitful in our barren lands?' and suggesting that vineyards might also be established in Britain. In looking at household expenditure Catharine suggested consumption of sugar was falling, or that imports from the West Indies might be replaced by those from the East Indies, without referring directly to the consumer boycott of West Indian sugar led by abolitionists from 1791 which was reported to have many followers in Cornwall.

Catharine's discussion of land use might be seen as radical but her next publication written in December 1792 confirmed her social conservatism and opposition to revolution. Her address *To the lower class of people in the western part of the county of Cornwall* referred to the recent events in France and warned against being 'led away by the specious cry of Liberty' and 'pleasing but delusive cry of EQUALITY'. In this publication Catharine went so far as to suggest that 'the poor' should 'rejoice' that they were not 'slaves'.[80] This left Catharine with a conundrum: she was an abolitionist who recognised she shared a common humanity with those who were enslaved but she feared and rejected the contemporaneous demands of social and political revolutions.

Two years later in *The happy king* Catharine addressed and endeavoured to answer this conundrum. Catharine had probably read the socially conservative Hannah More's poem on *Slavery* which demanded empathy: 'See the dire victim torn from social life, The shrieking babe, the agonizing wife!'. Writing in advance of the outbreak of revolution in France More distanced herself in the same poem from 'mad Liberty' and 'the unlicensed monster of the crowd' while arguing for 'human rights restored' through abolition. In *The happy king* Catharine sought to advance abolition by showing its compatability with monarchy and the political status quo.

Catharine had been opposed to slavery since visiting colonial American plantations in the 1750s. Participation in the slave trade was identified as a matter for 'discipline' among Quakers in 1761 and this prohibition was said to be effective. The leading abolitionist Thomas Clarkson acknowledged the extent to which the Quakers' constant travel and communication between England and America had been important in obtaining and maintaining the prohibition on Quaker participation in the slave trade; causing Quakers to be well-informed participants in the abolition campaign which was mobilised largely through their national and international communication networks.[81]

Members of Catharine's family and fellow Quakers in Cornwall were active participants in the abolition campaign. Her stepson James Phillips had attended the Quakers' yearly London Meetings from 1773, and in 1784 was identified as a correspondent to Cornwall; a role which his family and their commercial connections made him well-placed to fulfil. William and James Phillips had both signed the Quakers' first abolitionist petition in 1783, and James Phillips was one of 23 members of the Quaker committee which was briefly formed at that time. Both Catharine's stepsons and her niece Catharine Fox were subscribers to the Society for the Abolition of the Slave Trade from 1787; James Phillips was a member of the national Committee for the Abolition of the Slave Trade from the same year and was the Society's printer, while George Croker Fox co-ordinated the 1788 abolitionist petitions from Cornwall. The national committee organised the translation of abolitionist pamphlets into Dutch, French, Portuguese, and Spanish. James Phillips played a vital role printing and distributing abolitionist books and pamphlets within the UK, across Europe, and to America; and maintained the Society's communication with abolitionists in France.[82] In the late summer of 1793 James Phillips was ill; by February 1794 he was well enough to attend a committee meeting but he may not have printed Catharine Phillips' *The happy king* which was described as 'printed for the author' without including the printer's imprint.

Ten members of the Fox family in Cornwall, including five women, were subscribers to the Society for the Abolition of the Slave Trade from 1787; as were three members of the Tregelles family who were also Quakers and merchants at Falmouth. Some other Cornish merchants and professionals emerged as supporters of the Society for the Abolition of the Slave Trade in 1787 including the Cornish Copper Company manager John Edwards, the attorney Charles Rashleigh of St Austell, the grocer Silvanus James of Redruth, the corn and flour merchant Peter Price of Penryn, and the Anglican Reverend Henry Hawkins Tremayne of Heligan. The Fox family members included merchants and doctors, and several of the women members were also traders in Falmouth.

George Croker Fox actively canvassed support in Cornwall for abolition of the slave trade in 1788 and was instrumental in the return of pro-abolitionist petitions to Parliament from Falmouth, Helston, and Penryn. Fox corresponded with James Phillips and said he had requested signatures only from 'creditable townsmen and Inhabitants'. The mayor of Penryn was not a supporter of abolition and briefly delayed submission of their petition.[83] It is unlikely that Fox had the support of Joseph Banfield the successful merchant and banker who was the shipping agent at Falmouth for Camden, Calvert and King one of the largest London slave-trading partnerships; Banfield was also a member of Falmouth corporation and mayor in 1788.

Cornwall's large land-owning families and 44 members of Parliament held a range of opinions against or for abolition of the slave trade.[84] Sir Christopher Hawkins of Trewithen was a descendant of the same family as John Hawkins of Plymouth who had completed the first transatlantic slave trade voyage in the 1560s. Hawkins was a Tory and an MP who controlled up to 12 parliamentary seats elected by the Cornish boroughs. Hawkins had substantial political influence in Cornwall and used this partly to strengthen representation of those with commercial interests in the West Indies who were opposed to the abolition of the slave trade. At Grampound Robert Sewell and Bryan Edwards were elected on Hawkins' interest; Edwards published a *History of the British colonies in the West Indies* and was seen by the leading abolitionist William Wilberforce as a powerful opponent. Sir William Young, MP for St Mawes in 1784-1806, had plantations in St Vincent, Antigua, and Tobago worked by 1300 enslaved Africans which he visited in 1791-2; Young spoke against abolition of the slave trade observing directly on 15 March 1796 that he felt 'for his own property in the West Indies' and was appointed governor of Tobago in February 1807 after the abolition bill was passed. Other MPs for Cornish boroughs including Reginald Pole Carew at Fowey, John Theophilus Rawdon at Launceston, William Praed at St Ives, Scrope Bernard at St Mawes, and Edward Leveson Gower at Truro opposed abolition of the slave trade.

Thomas Wallace the MP for Grampound voted for abolition in 1795 and was elected for Penryn after being displaced at Grampound in the following year by Hawkins' candidates. Other Cornish MPs including Sir William Lemon of Carclew, the MP for Launceston James Brogden who was the son of a Russia merchant, and the MPs for Liskeard and brothers Edward James Eliot and John Eliot of Port Eliot supported abolition. The third Pascoe Grenfell, an MP for Great Marlow who was later elected for Penryn, was a supporter of abolition who spoke and voted for Wilberforce's bill on 7 June 1804.

In Cornwall the popular momentum to end slavery engaged 'a formidable segment of the Cornish population' through petitions and public meetings in the 1820s.[85] After the abolition of slavery in 1833 those granted compensation under the 1837 Act included the heirs of Sir Rose Price of Trengwainton who died in 1834; Eldred Lewis Blight Pearse of Bodmin; William Michell who was later MP for Bodmin 1852-9; as well as other individuals living in Cornwall. The third Pascoe Grenfell's eldest son Pascoe St Leger Grenfell was one of four mortgagees who received £4,121 19s compensation for 216 enslaved persons at the Hazelymph estate, Jamaica; this interest had been purchased in 1821 when Pascoe St Leger Grenfell was of age. The documentation refers to the shares as purchased by 'Pascoe Grenfell'; the third Pascoe Grenfell died in 1838 before compensation was paid.

The number of Cornish subscribers to the Society for the Abolition of the Slave Trade in 1787 and the fact that three towns submitted abolitionist petitions to Parliament in 1788 shows that there was early organised support for abolition in Cornwall. Much of this support came from the non-conformist communities of Quakers and Methodists. In 1791 the Penzance Ladies' Book Club purchased a copy of Olaudah Equiano's autobiography.[86] Women as well as men in Cornwall called for and supported abolition of the slave trade; not least by participating as household food shoppers in the consumer boycott of West Indian sugar. In March 1792 newspapers reported that 'No less than 12,000 persons in Cornwall have ceased to use sugar, in consequence of the continuance of the slave trade, or, more probably, on account of the great price of that necessary article'.[87]

The abolition campaign provided opportunities for a wide range of people in Cornwall to engage with a national political and ethical debate and for some to come forward as writers; Catharine Phillips said she had written her abolitionist poem in 1791. After Catharine gave up writing verses in her early 20s she developed a reputation for 'cogency, perspicuity and love'; these characteristics were evident in Catharine's lucid prose. In her poem Catharine put forward economic, political, religious, and moral arguments for abolition. Catharine may have hoped that communicating these through the light tone of her verses would make her arguments palatable to opponents of abolition. In fact it had the opposite effect of seeming to treat a serious matter frivolously, as Catharine had feared after writing verses in her youth. Catharine's

Memoirs and some of her other prose statements communicated abolitionist arguments more powerfully in plainer language.

The poem was addressed to King George III who was seen as a key opponent to abolition. This placed Catharine in the position of speaking moral truths to power which she may have seen as consistent with her role as a public Friend. Economically Catharine acknowledged 'th'advent'rous Merchant brings Much treasure o'er the main' but argued that if the slave trade was outlawed 'Sources for wealth enough remain, When this just law is made.' Catharine concluded that King George III would be a 'HAPPY KING' if slavery were abolished and peaceful trade and prosperity ensued. Politically Catharine made clear her loyalty to the King. She acknowledged 'Britannia's monarch' as 'My Sov'reign under God' just as she had defended the ministry of women as well as men because 'God did chuse'. Catherine's religious argument was the one she had made previously in prose; she saw slavery and the slave trade as an obstacle to effective Christian missions, and believed abolition would change that.

Popular support for abolition was built on empathy. Catharine's moral argument noted that 'the cruel trade Of Slav'ry' was equally painful to all people, observing that 'Hard is the lot of christian slaves, By piracy obtain'd'; that is the European and other captives seized and enslaved on the north coast of Africa. Catharine may have been aware that earlier in the century British captives like these had been ransomed by King George I, including the crews of two ships from Cornwall.[88] In contrast she only briefly referred to, and did not dwell on, the suffering caused to enslaved Africans by the transatlantic slave trade: 'Enough already has been said, And proofs sufficient been; Respecting this detested trade, I wish to drop the theme'.

Charlotte MacKenzie

Catharine Phillips died in August 1794 not long after *The Happy King* was printed for the author. The testimony of her life from the Falmouth Quakers' Meeting on 6 April 1795 formed the obituary published in the *Gentleman's Magazine*. This testimony stressed Catharine's infirmity and endurance in later life. The fact that Catharine became a more prolific writer during the last decade of her life was not acknowledged. Back at work after his illness, James organised the publication in 1797 of Catharine Phillips' *Memoirs*, together with some of her letters and the testimony from the Falmouth Meeting. James' son William Phillips later published some of Catharine's discourses at Quaker Meetings alongside those of Samuel Fothergill in 1803. Catharine had ended her *Memoirs* with the death of her husband, and her other later writing and publications received scant attention from the first communicators and curators of her legacy.

In contrast Catharine's writing during the last decade of her life is of current historical interest, while her religious letters and discourses now receive less attention. Widely travelled and reflective Catharine voiced opinions on Georgian economic, political, and social matters which have consequences and resonance today. The inhumanity of the transatlantic slave trade; the environmental destruction caused by industrialisation; and the impact of decisions about the use of land on food poverty and security.

The 'orphan adventurer' Elizabeth Trefusis

A contemporary pen portrait of Elizabeth Trefusis (1762-1808) concluded that 'she was left, at a very early age, an orphan adventurer, to find her way, as best she could, o'er unknown seas and regions, and many a pelting did she get from divers pitiless storms'.[89] This vignette drew on the Georgian fictional motif of the orphaned individual making their own way in the uncaring natural world; it was a compelling image of a little known woman writer who had lost both her parents by the age of 16, and whose family's coastal estate in Cornwall near the overseas port of Falmouth was buffeted by seaborne weather. This portrayal of Elizabeth, thinly disguised by her informal name 'Ella', drew credence from the fact that its author William Beloe had been a personal acquaintance of her. Beloe's brief biography praised the 'most romantic sensibility' of Elizabeth's 'tender, elegant' verses but did not place her writing in a literary context.

It is possible to summarise the evolution of Elizabeth Trefusis' writing as broadly similar in outline to that of the Lichfield poet Anna Seward. Elizabeth's early verses included female friendship poems two of which are published here for the first time. These were followed by her work on poetic novels with a range of characters and voices. She had an enduring liking for the sonnet form which some critics rated as Elizabeth's best poetry. Elizabeth's three early verses on female friendship follow next. The first two were unpublished by her, the third appeared in *Poems and tales* (1808). 'The flowers' was 'Addressed to my dear Upwood friends on leaving them to settle at Bletsoe'.[90]

Charlotte MacKenzie

The flowers

When Flora sends her painted train

To deck the gardens and the plain,

And bids the earth her nurselings rear

With all a youthful mother's care,

Then Aura in these nurselings see

Each separate charm that meets in thee!

For with thy sweetness, they unite

Thy glowing red, thy dazzling white,

The violet presumes to vie

With the azure lustre of thine eye!

The rose too emulates thy bloom!

The pea thy fragrant breath's perfume!

The everlasting boasts its name!

And seeks to rival Aura's fame!

Reject sweet maid the forward crew

That vainly strive to equal you

But take the Lily, let it rest

Upon that whiter fairer breast,

It imitates my Aura's skin

It pictures well the mind within

Pure emblem of a purer heart

Unsullied by the stains of art

For Aura's bosom knows no guilt

And innocence is in her smile.

The Roman laurel shall entwine

Around the British head!

Marcellus be that laurel thine!

Mars bids it flourish in thy line,

And round young Marcian spread,

To Jessy let my Aura give

If Jessy will the gift receive

A sprig of Myrtle, let the fair

This emblematic present wear

And tell her that this Ever-green

In spite of winter will be seen

With never-fading verdure crowned

When frailer flow'rets strew the ground:

For tho' its silver blossoms die

When chilling blasts usurp the sky

Yet still midst Nature's wreck it wears

A summer robe, & green appears.

Charlotte MacKenzie

Thus in the winter of her years

The storms of time shall idly rage;

For tho' his tainted breath may blast

Those flowers, too delicate to last

That little Hebe stole from Heav'n

And smiling to the fair hath given;

Tho' all the blooming beauties fade,

That now adorn the favour'd maid,

Yet in her mind will still be seen,

The emblem of this Ever-green.

O Jessy! – Aura – if I grieve

Such sweetness & such worth to leave

What heart such sorrows can reprove

For who can know ye, & not love?

If gentle Aura should intend

A present for an absent friend

Search all the garden, till you see

The Cyclamen – give that to me:

An humble plant that lowly grows

Scarce rears it head & weakly blows.

So doats this flower upon the beams

Of Sol that when he faintly gleams

It closes with the closing day!

Thus Ella droops when you're away!

But soon its languid head it rears

When that returning Sun appears

Restor'd by his all-cheering light

Thus I revive when you're in sight!

For friendship is the Sun whose rays

Give warmth & splendor to my days

Haste then my Aura! Jessy haste!

Ah make no long delay!

The hours of friendship who would waste?

Your Ella blames your stay.

Life's summer is too quickly o'er:

We part perhaps to meet no more.

Say will my Jessy's melting eye

Drop me kind tear? Or will a sigh

Steal softly from her feeling heart,

To tell her friend 'tis pain to part.

Adieu ye hours! When o'er the green

Together we have stray'd

Charlotte MacKenzie

Adieu ye hours! Adieu each scene!

I seek a distant shade:

Far far remov'd from those I love

A sorrowing wanderer I rove

Anne will our last adieu

O best beloved be felt by you?

Be felt! ah did one doubt remain

That dear Anne shares my pain

I justly should deserve her hate

For Ella then would be ingrate.

O thou! Whom I would wish to praise;

But find not words to speak my heart

Anne! in these pensive lays

Affection takes the lead of art.

Unskill'd in all the various rules

Pedantic Book-worms teach in schools

To grace my song the tuneful nine

Refuse their aid to lend

Your Ella would not wish to shine

As poet, but as Friend.

When all the feather'd tribe await

My Aura at the garden gate

Or when the fair at early dawn

Attends her fav'rites on the lawn,

Then let my Aura think on me,

And softly sighing say

Here Ella have I stray'd with thee!

Ah why art thou away?

Lov'd Aura, didst though think on me

As often as I think on thee

The every trifle would retrace

My manners, actions, words & face

"Thus" wouldst thou say "did Ella walk

"Thus did she smile, & thus would talk!

"How often have we wander'd here!

"How often!" - then perhaps a tear

Intrusive on thy words would break

And still more eloquently speak.

How Jessy can I part with you?

Or how receive your last adieu?

Jessy thou darling of my soul

Can Ella in that hour control

The overflowings of an heart

That feels 'tis misery to part

That knows your worth, that shares your love,

And yet is destin'd to remove,

Where no kind friend like Jessy cheers

The prospect of her future years.

Haste then my Aura! Jessy haste!

Ah make no long delay!

The hours of friendship who would waste?

Your Ella blames your stay.

Life's summer is too quickly o'er:

We part perhaps to meet no more.

Ella to Jessy

When to Mount Parnass' I would soar

And gain those heights which few explore,

Should restive Pegasus refuse

To bear aloft the would-be Muse,

And scorn to be the common hack,

Of ev'ry fool that mounts his back;

Without his help I'd rise to fame,

By the dear magic of thy name.

Should Ella Jessy's praise rehearse

Ella would consecrate the verse;

And tho' her metric, accent, pause

Might be condemn'd by critic laws,

In vain might critics blame her song

The world would never think her wrong

The solar ray's diffusive light

Illumes the lesser orb of night

Jessy the lustre of that Sun is thine:

The borrow'd splendor of the moon is mine!

To my own picture, taken by Shelley for Jessy

Haste, little image of an ardent friend,

To Jessy haste, and all her steps attend;

For absent Ella should she heave the sigh,

Let instant rapture gladden in thine eye;

But should the maid, with cold indifference, trace

In thine, the lineaments of Ella's face,

An equal coldness let thy features wear:

Assume a frown – ah no! let fall a tear.

Charlotte MacKenzie

It may have been Elizabeth's mother Anne St John of Bletso who first encouraged her eldest daughter to write verses. Aged 14 when her mother died Elizabeth may already have been reading, and expressing her feelings by writing, poetry; one of her published verses mourned her mother's death in 1776, ending with Christian acceptance like Thomas Penrose's poem 'Madness' which had been published in the previous year.[91]

Anna Seward worked on her poetic novel *Louisa* (1784) between the ages of 19 and 42, and she regarded it as her best work. Elizabeth said that she had completed poetic novels when she was young, which for whatever reason were destroyed; extant verses, songs, and dialogues from these were published in *Poems and tales*. A notebook containing handwritten copies of most of Elizabeth's extant verses is now at Trefusis; this included some unpublished poems.[92] A printed copy of *Poems and Tales* which is in the British Library included handwritten additions of verses most of which were unpublished.[93] Elizabeth's unpublished as well as published verses inform the narrative here. The reason for deciding that these unpublished verses were also by Elizabeth is that they contain biographical context.

Poems and tales was widely and mostly positively reviewed including in *The British critic* for which Beloe was one of the editors.[94] The publication of Elizabeth's first volumes of verse in the year that she died was long overdue. Her interest in literary culture and writing had been sustained throughout her adult life; Elizabeth knew other writers and editors, and encouraged and subscribed to others' first publications. *Poems and tales* included a dedication to the journal editor William Gifford who had encouraged Elizabeth to publish her writing.

Elizabeth probably knew that her paternal grandfather Robert Trefusis had written and published verses in English and Latin when he was a fellow of Pembroke College Cambridge in 1733-7, and before being elected MP for Truro in 1734-41.[95] Elizabeth's father Robert Cotton Trefusis had been 3 years old when his father died. His mother Elizabeth Affleck then married a London physician Charles Carleton. When she died in 1748 her will released Trefusis funds to pay a bequest of £4000 to Charles Carleton, and to provide for her daughter Eliza Cotton Trefusis. She had been the sole executor of Robert Trefusis' will; after her death the stewardship of the Trefusis estate and interests of her 9 year old son Robert Cotton Trefusis, were the subject of a Chancery case.[96]

Aged 22 the untitled and moneyed Robert Cotton Trefusis made a socially advantageous marriage to Anne St John the eldest daughter of Baron St John of Bletso in 1761, and gave their first born daughter his mother's name. Elizabeth's parents had eight children together. As a child Elizabeth probably travelled with her parents between town and country. Initially dividing their time between the Trefusis' houses in London and estate in Cornwall their first four children were christened in London, their fifth at Mylor parish church. Closest in age to Elizabeth was her sister Anne; the next four children were boys, one of whom died aged 5 in 1771. In the same year the Trefusis family acquired Holmes manor (also known as High Cannons) in Hertfordshire where they built a new mansion house; the youngest three children were christened in Hertfordshire.[97]

When Elizabeth's father was widowed in 1776 he returned home to Cornwall. His children probably travelled with him. The family events which followed can only have caused Elizabeth further emotional upheaval. A year after her mother died Trefusis married for a second time to Mary Ann Copinger; his bride was the eldest daughter of the merchant and smuggler John Copinger. In the following year Elizabeth's father died; the only child from his second marriage was born posthumously.

Robert Cotton Trefusis made his will a week before his second marriage.[98] As trustees for his children he appointed Elizabeth's widowed maternal aunt by marriage Susanna St John of Bletso; her maternal uncle by marriage Humphry Hall of Manadon in Devon; and her paternal uncle by marriage Sir Herbert Mackworth, a copper magnate and MP, who was married to Robert's sister Eliza Cotton Trefusis. Elizabeth also remained in contact with her maternal aunt Barbara Countess of Coventry who kept handwritten copies of several of her niece's verses among her personal papers.[99]

Elizabeth's widowed stepmother was not appointed as a guardian to the children of her husband's first marriage. By June 1780 Mary Ann Trefusis was living in London where she married Robert Tuite, a wealthy owner of plantations in the West Indies who was appointed Chamberlain to the King of Denmark, and moved to live in Copenhagen. In Cornwall in 1787 Mary Ann Tuite's mother started church court proceedings to legally separate from John Copinger; the written deposition for her case included allegations of attempted incest by John Copinger with his eldest daughter which Mary Copinger had interrupted and prevented.[100] The Tuites divorced under Danish law and Mary Ann Trefusis returned to live in London, later marrying for a third time in 1798. The will of her son Francis Mackworth Trefusis in 1802 indicated that he was closest to members of the Copinger family, although he received financial support from the Trefusis trust established by his father.[101]

After Robert Cotton Trefusis died in August 1778 his children from his first marriage travelled first to Manadon house near Plymouth the home of their aunt and uncle Jane and Humphry Hall. Two months after Anne Trefusis died a plan and particulars of the property in Hertfordshire had been drawn up; it was sold in 1778, a necessary financial step. The first of several equity cases related to Trefusis inheritances and property management commenced in the same year and it was ten months before Robert Cotton Trefusis' will appointing his children's guardians was proved.[102] Without the Hertfordshire property the trustees were then able to balance the income and costs, to manage the Trefusis estate, and to provide for the children who did not all live together or occupy the family home in Cornwall.

It is possible that the five oldest children were placed in schools from 1778, and they may all have visited their aunts and uncles. The guardians' accounts for the youngest child Louisa showed an annual allowance of £20 a year, which from the age of 5 was mostly spent on boarding school fees paid to a 'Mrs A Gilbert'. This was not a large individual allowance at a time when some traders' families spent £20 a year or more on a child's food, clothing, and education. Paired arrangements were shared by the two eldest girls Elizabeth (aged 16) and Anne (aged 15), and the two youngest daughters Barbara (aged 3) and Louisa (aged 1); a letter describing Louisa's final illness aged 14 at the Channel Row, Westminster home of her aunt Susanna St John referred to Louisa being nursed partly by 'Barbara's maid' who was later admitted to Bedlam.[103]

Elizabeth's unpublished verse 'The flowers' was 'Addressed to my dear Upwood friends on leaving them to settle at Bletsoe' where her aunt Susanna lived.[104] Elizabeth and Anne had been staying in Huntingdonshire, possibly while the financial and legal queries surrounding their late father's property debts and probate were resolved. As the eldest child Elizabeth had most understanding of her family's circumstances; she felt the separation from her brothers, two youngest sisters, and a settled family home keenly.

Charlotte MacKenzie

Upwood House was the family home of the naval officer Sir Richard Bickerton, which had been inherited by his wife Mary Anne Hussey from her widowed aunt. During the American revolutionary and French wars the Bickerton household comprised Mary Anne Hussey and her two daughters Maria and Jane Frances; father and son, both named Richard, were away at sea. Elizabeth and Anne's connection with the Bickertons, and why they were invited to stay at Upwood, is not known. Schoolfriends sometimes visited and stayed with each other's families but Maria was four years younger than Elizabeth, and Jane was four years younger than Anne.

Bickerton received his baronetcy in 1778. However the Trefusis girls' invitation to Upwood came about Mary Anne may have welcomed Elizabeth's companionship, literary interests, and participation in her family's home education, entertainments, horticulture, and rural walks. Mary Anne may have encouraged Elizabeth to cultivate and develop her flair for writing verses; although Elizabeth voiced misgivings about feeling appreciated for her creative talent rather than herself. On leaving Upwood Elizabeth wrote plaintively

> Far far remov'd from those I love
>
> A sorrowing wanderer I rove...
>
> Your Ella would not wish to shine
>
> As poet, but as Friend.

Elizabeth felt vulnerable given her family's situation, and she may have been emotionally labile. Nonetheless she was sufficiently schooled in emotional loss to have learned how to communicate feelings with self-control. Her writing was an impressive teenage accomplishment, for which she gained attention and praise.

'The flowers' can be read as a prettily written thank you note in verse which expressed warm affection for the friends who had been her hosts. It was addressed to 'Aura' as well as 'Jessy' and referred to Elizabeth's sister Anne. 'Ella to Jessy' was identified in another handwritten copy as 'To Miss Bickerton'. As the eldest daughter Maria was 'Miss Bickerton', although 'Jessy' was used more commonly as an informal name for Jane; the Hussey family originated from Scotland where 'Jessy' was a common informal name. As Anna Seward's long lasting, loving memories of Honora Sneyd confirmed age differences were not necessarily a barrier to Georgian friendships which evoked strong emotional attachments between women who were not related to each other. As her mother had died when she was 14, Elizabeth may have formed an attachment to Mary Anne. Her unpublished verse written on leaving Upwood voiced her fears that it was a last goodbye to 'Aura' and 'Jessy', and that she might be for ever left without warm encouragement and support.

The ambiguity about who the object of Elizabeth's attachment was may be one reason why she later felt comfortable publishing one of the three 'Jessy' verses. It is one of few verses in which Elizabeth identified the feelings expressed as her own. 'To my own picture, taken by Shelley for Jessy' explored Elizabeth's self-reflection on gifting her portrait to her female friend after they were separated by circumstances. In the verse Elizabeth humorously instructs her portrait to change facial expressions appropriately as she imagines it being viewed with affection or indifference.

Samuel Shelley exhibited for the first time at the Royal Academy in 1773 and had a studio where he painted miniature portraits in Covent Garden 1780-94. If Elizabeth Trefusis had her portrait 'taken' by Shelley to send to 'Jessy' after she left Upwood to 'settle at Bletso' she must also have visited London. Initially Elizabeth would probably have stayed at her aunt Susanna's house in Westminster.

It is not impossible that Elizabeth first met the Army officer and published poet Henry Barry in the early 1780s, either in London or when Elizabeth was visiting her aunt Barbara Countess of Coventry. Barry was in London, where he had his portrait painted by John Singleton Copley in his Captain's uniform, before being promoted and departing for India. Barry gave this portrait to his mother and probably travelled to Worcester to see his parents, brother, and sister. One of Elizabeth's unpublished verses was 'On a young gentleman going to India' where he hoped to obtain advancement and reverse his family's declined fortunes;[105] Barry was in his mid-thirties when his Army regiment was posted to India. The feelings of 'Volny' as he prepared to depart for India directly echoed Elizabeth's emotions on leaving Upwood. Now it was Volny with whom she empathised as

A wand'rer from his native land,

A wand'rer long from all his soul holds dear.

The ambiguity on this occasion was that Volny meant 'free'.

In 1783 Elizabeth came of age. At some point she moved with her sister Ann to live in rented rooms at 14 James Street in St Margaret's parish Westminster, on which rates had been paid by a Miss Elizabeth Rathbone from 1777. Elizabeth did not know then that James Street would be her home throughout her adult life; she moved house on one later occasion from number 14 to number 27 James Street in the early 1800s.[106]

In the intervening years since Robert Cotton Trefusis' death the trustees may have made arrangements for all or some of the children to spend time at Trefusis. The trustees were party to several property transactions related to the estate. Not long after he came of age in 1785 Robert George William Trefusis married Albertina Marianna Gaulis of Lausanne in Switzerland; for the first five years of their marriage they lived at Trefusis and their first two children were christened at Mylor parish church.

In March 1787 the novelist William Beckford and his travelling companions were delayed at Falmouth before sailing to Lisbon on the packet boat *Julius Caesar*; the spring tides and storms were so forceful that Beckford feared 'our thin pasteboard habitation would be blown into the sea, for never in my life did I hear such dreadful blusterings. Perhaps the winds are celebrating the approach of the equinox ...'. Two visits to Trefusis provided a not unwelcome diversion which Beckford described at the time in vivid letters to his mother.[107] The old fashioned and partly dilapidated mansion house would have been familiar to Elizabeth; her brother Robert, dubbed 'the squire' by Beckford, was very much at home in his boisterous household and coastal country estate.

Falmouth, March 8, 1787.

What a lovely morning! how glassy the sea, how busy the fishing-boats, and how fast asleep the wind in its old quarter. Towards evening, however, it freshened, and I took a toss in a boat with Mr. Trefusis, whose territories extend half round the bay. His green hanging downs spotted with sheep, and intersected by rocky gullies, shaded by tall straight oaks and ashes, form a romantic prospect, very much in the style of Mount Edgcumbe.

We drank tea at the capital of these dominions, an antiquated mansion, which is placed in a hollow on the summit of a lofty hill, and contains many ruinous halls and neverending passages: they cannot, however, be said to lead to nothing, like those celebrated by Gray in his Long Story, for Mrs. Trefusis terminated the perspective. She is a native of Lausanne, and was quite happy to see her countryman Verdeil.[108]

We should have very much enjoyed her conversation, but the moment tea was over, the squire could not resist leading us round his improvements in kennel, stable, and oxstall: though it was pitch-dark, and we were obliged to be escorted by grooms and groomlings with candles and lanterns; a very necessary precaution, as the winds blew not more violently without the house than within.

In the course of our peregrination through halls, pantries, and antechambers, we passed a staircase with heavy walnut-railing, lined from top to bottom with effigies of ancestors that looked quite formidable by the horny glow of our lanterns; which illumination, dull as it was, occasioned much alarm amongst a collection of animals, both furred and feathered, the delight of Mr. Trefusis's existence.

Every corner of his house contains some strange and stinking inhabitant; one can hardly move without stumbling over a basket of puppies, or rolling along a mealy tub, with ferrets in the bottom of it; rap went my head against a wire cage, and behold a squirrel twirled out of its sleep in sad confusion: a little further on, I was very near being the destruction of some new-born dormice - their feeble squeak haunts my ears at this moment!

Beyond this nursery, a door opened and admitted us into a large saloon, in the days of Mr. Trefusis's father very splendidly decorated, but at present exhibiting nothing, save damp plastered walls, mouldering floors, and cracked windows. A well-known perfume issuing from this apartment, proclaimed the neighbourhood of those fragrant animals, which you perfectly recollect were the joy of my infancy, and presently three or four couple of spanking yellow rabbits made their appearance. A racoon poked his head out of a coop, whilst an owl lifted up the gloom of his countenance, and gave us his malediction.

My nose having lost all relish for rabbitish odours, took refuge in my handkerchief; there did I keep it snug till it pleased our conductors to light us through two or three closets, all of a flutter with Virginia nightingales, goldfinches, and canary-birds, into the stable. Several game-cocks fell a crowing with most triumphant shrillness upon our approach; and a monkey - the image of poor Brandoin - expanded his jaws in so woeful a manner, that I grew melancholy, and paid the hunters not half the attention they merited.

At length we got into the open air again, made our bows and departed. The evening was become serene and pleasant, the moon beamed brilliantly on the sea; but the owls, who are never to be pleased, hooted most ruefully.

Good night: I expect to dream of *closed-up doors*, and haunted passages; rats, puppies, racoons, game-cocks, rabbits, and dormice.

Two days later Beckford, whose wealth derived largely from his family's plantations in the West Indies, returned to dine at Trefusis.

Falmouth, March 10, 1787.

... I have little taste for the explanation of fire-engines, Mr. Scott; the pursuit of hares under the auspices of young Trefusis; or the gliding of billiard-balls in the society of Barbadoes Creoles and packet-boat captains. The Lord have mercy upon me! now, indeed, do I perform penance.

Our dinner yesterday went off tolerably well. We had on the table a savoury pig, right worthy of Otaheite, and some of the finest poultry I ever tasted;

Charlotte MacKenzie

and round the table two or three brace of odd Cornish gentlefolks, not deficient in humour and originality.

About eight in the evening, six game-cocks were ushered into the eating-room by two limber lads in scarlet jackets; and, after a flourish of crowing, the noble birds set to with surprising keenness. Tufts of brilliant feathers soon flew about the apartment; but the carpet was not stained with the blood of the combatants: for, to do Trefusis justice, he has a generous heart, and takes no pleasure in cruelty. The cocks were unarmed, had their spurs cut short, and may live to fight fifty such harmless battles.

One of Elizabeth's published verses was an animal fable in which an exuberant female kid ran with sure-footed speed along a rocky, unfenced coastal edge.

On the tall cliff's stupendous head

Where oft the screaming sea-gulls stray

Yon frolic kid, with airy tread,

Wanton takes her winding way

... lightly bounding,

With hoofs resounding,

... From rock to rock with measured leap

The fleet one flies.

Nimbly escaping a predatory wolf who gave chase and fell down a precipitous cliff.

Neither Elizabeth nor her other siblings were mentioned by Beckford who, strolling through Arwenack one evening, spotted 'two young girls beautifully shaped and dressed with a sort of romantic provincial elegance walking up and down the grove by the pyramid. There was something so lovelorn in their gestures that I have no doubt they were sighing out their souls to each other'. Beckford had written *Vathek* after organising a country house entertainment. A homely circle of genteel friends, of the kind she had stayed with at Upwood, was probably the audience and readership Elizabeth had in mind as she started to write narrative stories and dialogues in verse.

William Beloe recalled that Elizabeth 'wrote a great deal', 'wrote with extreme haste, and revised nothing'.[109] Elizabeth may have read Anna Seward's *Louisa* (1784) but her poetic novels were not written in epistolary form. In *Poems and tales* Elizabeth referred to her writing as including at least two poetic 'Novels, written in early life, and afterwards destroyed' excerpts from which formed a substantial part of the verses published in 1808. Writing poetic novels enabled Elizabeth to articulate varied moods and emotions in the voices of her imagined characters; while experimenting with different forms including songs and letters in verse. 'Eudora's second song' was later set to music by Thomas Attwood as the ballad 'Let me die!' (1827).

One of Elizabeth's poetic novels was identified by her as 'my novel of *Claribell*'; this included an elegy, and a character named Constance who died for love. Another novel *The cousins* was described as 'a pastoral romance'. Many of Elizabeth's published verses originated as part of this latter novel, the outline plot of which can be reconstructed with the help of Elizabeth's brief notes introducing individual verses. The male protagonist Edmond has been rejected by Enna whom he loves. The cousins Eudora and Isabel are rivals for Edmond's love. Edmond marries Eudora but he does not grow to love her.

Edmond and Eudora have a baby boy. The novel takes a tragic turn when, fifteen months after Edmond and Eudora's wedding, their baby dies. Eudora realises Edmond still loves Enna; Eudora thinks of suicide and imagines her death will bring Enna and Edmond together.

A third work the *Modern Proteus*, noted as 'M.P.', was the source of other verses; these may have been written partly to further develop the character of Isabel in *The Cousins*. Elizabeth was not a playwright but her published collection of verses included the dialogues 'Gertrude or the heroine - a tale' and 'Sir Hubert – a dramatic tale' which were not part of her novels.

Elizabeth's animal fable in verse 'The kid' formed part of her 'pastoral romance'. For Elizabeth the moral of the kid's escape was that

> ... woman was born to be happy and free
>
> But man, tyrant man, seeks each wish to controul ...
>
> No insolent victor shall fetter thy soul! ...
>
> Woman has wicked wit at will.

It was a fleeting moment of feminist, and possibly personal, insight and caution that Elizabeth failed to heed.

In 1787-91 Miss Rathbone paid the rates on a second house at 10 James Street Terrace which was occupied by Henry Barry after he returned from India. Barry and Elizabeth became engaged to each other by August 1788.[110] Elizabeth and Anne subscribed, without revealing their address, to a volume of verses by two teenage sisters Maria and

Harriet Falconar in 1788; three years later Elizabeth was of 'James Street' when she subscribed to Elizabeth Bentley's *Genuine poetical compositions* (1791). At St Margaret's in 1792, Anne married Thomas Maxwell Adams, of a West Indian planter family who lived on James Street; after marrying they travelled to Barbados but returned to England to live at Duryard Lodge in Exeter with their children. Elizabeth continued to write and became acquainted with London's literary and bluestocking circles.

Elizabeth did not cultivate relationships with other women writers. Henry Barry was related by marriage to Anna Seward who became better known for her writing in the 1780s. Elizabeth does not appear to have sought out contacts with women who shared her literary tastes or had successful experience of publishing their writing. In 1790 Elizabeth went to one of Helen Maria Williams' tea parties, where she met William Godwin, but these introductions to politically radical writers were not pursued on either side.[111] Barry socialised with Hester Piozzi. In Autumn 1792 Hester noted her appreciation of some of Elizabeth's verses. Hester thought Elizabeth's pen portrait of Penelope Sophia Weston and her friend 'Miss Powell' was 'mighty smart' '& true enough of both I believe', but no friendship developed between Hester and Elizabeth.[112] If Elizabeth had published her work sooner she would have received recognition as a writer and this might have eased any social awkwardness caused by the fact that she was perceived as originating from a wealthy and landed family rather than a professional or commercial background.

Beloe recalled that he had met Elizabeth Trefusis after one of his own verses was passed on to her by a friend of his. In 1793 Beloe started a journal the *British Critic* with Revd Robert Nares who had a house on James Street. Beloe had taught at Norwich Grammar School in 1780-3; his sister Charlotte later married the Norwich china dealer John

Harwood, a widower, whose son John Edmund Harwood dedicated his *Select verses* (1793) to 'Miss Trefusis'. Harwood shortly afterwards moved to America where he became an actor and later a bookseller with a circulating library in Philadelphia; he published an American edition of his verses which was not dedicated to Elizabeth. Beloe was one of those who felt that Elizabeth had sometimes been over-generous financially to literary fortune hunters; if that included her subscription to the publication of Harwood's verses it may have been Beloe who first introduced them to each other.

As an adult Elizabeth established friendships with men not women. Elizabeth sent her 'mighty smart' verse to its female subjects, but presented it as though it had come from Barry. On another occasion Elizabeth sent her youngest sister Louisa a valentine which she presented as from a 'bashful boy' and mischievously helped her sister to draft verses in reply. Beloe observed that Theophilus Swift, who was married with children, was strongly attracted to Elizabeth and 'worshipped her as his idol'. If Beloe was correct Elizabeth was characteristically flirtatious towards her male friends whom she approached with 'playfulness and most bewitching familiarity'; but Barry was the only man to whom Elizabeth formed a public attachment and became privately engaged.

The return of the author and poet Major Henry Barry from India in 1787 was welcomed by several women writers who found him entertaining company. Anna Seward passed on Barry's compliments to her friend Penelope Sophia Weston of Ludlow in July 1787. In the same year the young William Wordsworth was moved to compose a sonnet when he saw the author 'Miss Helen Maria Williams weep at a tale of distress'.[113] When Helen told Anna that she had met and liked Barry she learned some of his back story from Anna. Barry was one of the many men who had been attracted to Anna's friend Honora Sneyd before Honora married Richard Edgeworth. Anna considered Barry had 'genius, literature, and a high sense of military honour'; she had recently agreed with Hester Piozzi that if 'Barry was a little less sententious he would be divine'.[114] After Barry had proposed to Elizabeth, who was in her mid-20s, he wrote with her consent to her family.[115] At the same time Barry continued to socialise with Hester and Penelope Sophia; he attended several of Helen Maria Williams' tea parties including the one on 9 February 1790 at which William Godwin and Elizabeth were both present.[116]

Henry Barry's parental family lived in Worcestershire where they were immediate contemporaries of the family of the merchant Edward Weston of Worcester whose widow Mary and daughter Penelope Sophia later moved to live at Ludlow and then London. Henry's parents lived in Bath Row, Worcester; Captain Robert Barry was an officer of the Worcestershire militia and may have been among those who dined at Croome Court on 11 November 1770 at the invitation of the Trefusis childrens' uncle the Earl of Coventry who was Lord Lieutenant for the county. Henry's brother the younger Robert Barry married Rebecca Bird in 1772 and lived at Bretforten where Rebecca's extended family farmed and kept the inn.

Henry's sister Elizabeth shared his interest in poetry; in 1788 they both subscribed to the publication of the verses of Maria and Harriet Falconar.[117] When Henry got to know Elizabeth Trefusis both his parents were still living; Henry's father died in 1791, his brother in 1792. After her husband died Henry's mother Sarah made her will in which she bequeathed the portrait of Henry 'by Copley' to him.[118] Sarah's remaining assets were divided equally between Henry and his sister. Elizabeth Barry was described as of Leopard House in Worcester when she died in February 1822; she was single and her probate included financial assets of more than £2000 confirming that Barry's parental family had not been without means.[119]

Charlotte MacKenzie

Henry Barry's army career can be briefly outlined.[120] He enlisted in the 85th regiment of foot on 22 February 1763 joining his father, who had been in the regiment since 1759, and brother who were both first Lieutenants; all three soldiers were soon on half-pay as their regiment was one of those disbanded following the end of the Seven Years' War. In March 1768 Henry Barry joined the 52nd regiment of foot as an ensign, in which he served for the next eleven years in Canada, America, and India purchasing his first promotion to Lieutenant in 1772. Barry was made a Captain in 1777, and was the deputy judge advocate for three court martials at Rhode Island camp in February 1777 – September 1778.[121] Barry's next appointment was as secretary and aide de camp to Lord Rawdon, whom he may have met when Rawdon visited this camp following the battle of Rhode Island. In September 1781, following the battle of Eutaw Springs, Barry was seized and used as a human shield by Lieutenant Manning of the Continental army;[122] he was exchanged as a prisoner in March 1782 and returned to active service as an adjutant-general in New York.[123] Barry was promoted Major before travelling with his regiment to India where he was given the local rank of Lieutenant Colonel. In India Barry participated in the second Anglo-Mysore war and the transfer of Pondicherry to the French following the Treaty of Versailles. Barry returned home from India in advance of his regiment in 1787; Hester suggested that Barry's health might have been impaired by the hot climate, and Beloe later described Barry as having been wounded during his active service.[124]

In London Barry obtained later transfers and promotions as a Major of the 19th regiment of foot (May, 1789), Lieutenant Colonel of the 71st (Highland) regiment of foot (May, 1790), and Lieutenant Colonel of the 39th regiment of foot (December, 1790). When Lord Cornwallis objected to the way in which these appointments had been made he was advised by the War Office that the second had been made following royal intervention; in

London Barry actively lobbied his contacts including Lord Seymour while letters to and from India travelled too slowly for appointments to wait on recommendations 'by your Lordship' as Cornwallis preferred.[125] In 1791-3 Barry spent some time with his regiment including in Ireland. Barry retired in March 1793. In retirement he was appointed as a Colonel of the 39th regiment of foot from July 1793. Barry's regimental transfers and retirement meant that he was not required to travel again to India, nor to the West Indies. From February 1793 the war with revolutionary France increased Britain's commitments in Europe. Despite being retired Barry joined Lord Moyra's staff and expedition to Ostend in 1794.[126]

In 1822 the American Scot Alexander Garden recalled of Barry that

> in nothing was his conduct regarded as so farcical, as in his claim to delicate and liberal feelings. On one occasion, it has been stated, that reading a Poem, of his own composition, on the blessings of Liberty, a gentleman present asked him frankly "How his actions could be so much at variance with the principles he professed?" "Because, Sir" he unblushingly replied, "I am a Soldier of fortune, seeking a strong and comfortable establishment. My feelings are as delicate as yours, or any other man's; but I never suffer myself to be humbugged by them".[127]

Barry and Garden fought on opposite sides during the American war of independence and may not have been well known to each other. Nonetheless several of the character traits presented by Garden fit with telling observations of other contemporaries on Barry's army preferments, politics, and poetry.

In 1775 Barry had published two tracts, which went through several editions, setting out the advantages for America of remaining British territory.[128] Barry had first hand experience of many British campaign fronts during the American war as independence was won. In London in 1788 Barry met William Godwin and continued to associate with him for more than a decade during the French revolution and revolutionary wars. Their exchange of ideas led Godwin to seek out Barry on several occasions and to invite his comments on the manuscript of his play *St Dunstan* which set out arguments in favour of the enfranchisement of nonconformists through an historical drama. Barry was not a radical or revolutionary but like his army mentor Lord Rawdon he may have continued to identify and describe himself as liberal and politically supported the Whigs.

Barry was sociable, and cultivated a wide range of contacts; on 10 March 1791 he became a member of the Society of Antiquaries in London. Barry probably introduced Elizabeth to some of the men she wrote verses about, including Theophilus Swift who worked as a barrister in Barry's home town of Worcester; and the Honourable John Knox with whom Barry had coincided in India. Barry had family living in Ireland to whom he made visits, and where he was briefly elected as a member of the Royal Irish Academy.

In 1792 Barry provided Wolfe Tone with introductions to Lord Rawdon. One of Tone's associates expressed dislike for Barry whom he described as an obsequious 'orator of Debretts - and lick-spillane of great men';[129] conduct which may have served Barry well in his successful quest for preferment in the Army. Barry's correspondence with Tone was politically nuanced, suggesting that progressive changes would come while making clear his opposition to rebellion or violent revolution.

> I more than think the astonishing success of France must have a general effect in meliorating all the European Governments. Ireland, which has as many grievances to be redressed as any other country, will, no doubt, come into her *peaceable* share of advantages. Your friends, the Roman Catholics (I might

call them my friends, since no man has been more anxious to advance their just cause), must see this and the certainty of *final* success must induce them to *present* tranquillity. Both here and with you, Government must, and that soon, yield much to the general wish of the people, which is becoming so unanimous and manifest that it cannot long be withstood; so that there seems no other mode of preserving the British constitution but by purifying its practice and reverting to its elementary principles. In this, my friend, we have a great advantage over France. She was without a constitution, and had no guides whatsoever to direct her in the road to freedom, and hence the unhappy deviations and excesses which have perplexed and marked her journey; but surely, that must now cease, as she is within view of the city. I am not one of those (of whom there are many, both from ignorance and design) who confound the means with the end, and, because they find the first incidentally bad, conclude that the last must be radically vicious. I detest cruelty (which, by the way, is inseparable from despotism) but I so love liberty as to think it cannot be obtained by a nation at too high a price. And had the loss and calamities in France been treble what they were, the freedom of twenty-four millions of human beings and that of their posterity would not have been dearly purchased. Such are, and ever have been, my sentiments on this interesting subject. I am sure they concur with yours, and I only state them to prove that when I speak, as now, for *firm moderation* (no solecism this, I hope) it is from the conviction that it is not only a safe but certain way of obtaining the object. The wish you kindly have, and it is mutual, for us to meet, I now hope will be soon accomplished, as it is likely some private business will call me to Ireland about Christmas.

In the following year Lord Rawdon became Lord Moyra and inherited an estate in Ireland. In advance of the expedition to Ostend in the summer of 1794 Penelope Sophia wrote lightly to Hester 'I understand Lord Moyra has given Colonel Barry a very lucrative appointment, I have therefore no doubt of a change having taken place in his Political Creed'. Nonetheless a year later, in conversation with Hester, Barry personally defended Helen Maria Williams who had supported the revolution and was living in France.[130]

Barry's reasons for writing and publishing were largely instrumental. He was ambitious and wrote to make himself stand out to an intended audience of the moment including British administrators and senior army officers in colonial America in the early 1770s. Barry's two publications in verse appeared after the American war drew to a close; his interest in poetry was something he mostly used to cultivate his social relationships particularly with women.[131] Hester acknowledged that Barry was 'a Literary Person by Profession, having published many small Performances, none of them disgraceful to a Gentleman or a Scholar'; she nonetheless expressed her disregard for Barry's unpublished poetry in her diary noting that 'he is soon suffocated with his own Plenitude of fragrance; & *strangled in the waste Fertility*.'[132] Alexander Garden recalled that Barry would 'send "his *bettermost* kind of compliments to a lady"; and, in a simple flower, present "the sweetest of all possible flowers"'.[133] Two of Elizabeth's verses revolve around her thoughts and feelings on being presented with a single bloom.

In 1794 Hester's mind teemed with questions when she heard unsettling rumours about 14 James Street. This was Elizabeth's address, from which her sister Anne had married in 1792, and at which Hester's close friend Penelope Sophia Weston lodged for a few months before marrying Mr Pennington in the same year. Hester had heard

> that House of Miss Rathbone's is now supposed to have been but a Cage of unclean Birds living in a sinful Celibàt. Mercy on us! Colonel Barry is with Lord Moyra; he had a good Escape of Miss Trefusis if all be true.

Why was Miss Weston so averse to *any Marriage* I am wondering; and why did Miss Trefusis call Colonel Barry *Hylas* of all names? And why did Miss Weston make such an *Ado* about little Sally Siddons's Wit & Beauty & Stuff? The Girl is just like every *other* Girl – but Miss Weston did use to like *every Girl so*.[134]

These recorded rumours have generated continuing historical uncertainty as to whether Elizabeth Rathbone's commercial activities at 14 James Street entailed more than residential lettings to genteel occupants. Hester's flurry of doubts has been quoted as evidence of gay communities and awareness in late eighteenth century London. It is unclear whether Hester ever asked or got answers to her perplexing questions; her friendship with Penelope Sophia continued.

In Greek mythology Heracles seized the infant Hylas, taught him to be a warrior, and established a sexual relationship with him; one day when collecting water from a stream Hylas encountered water nymphs and – in different versions of the legend – either chose to remain living with them, or drowned. It is not impossible that Barry had sexual relationships with men. And that Elizabeth referred to him as 'Hylas' partly because she was aware of that while believing from her own experience that Barry was attracted to women and loved her. Two of Elizabeth's verses were called 'The inconstant' and 'The libertine'. Each of these were described as forming part of her 'pastoral romance'; they were also written in the first person, and communicated unhappiness caused by the behaviour of a love object who was male.

The Honourable John Knox and Barry knew each other in India in the mid-1780s. Knox came from Ireland, where Barry was cultivating his connections in the early 1790s. On Friday 10 August 1792 Barry wrote to Wolfe Tone that Knox was 'on his passage home' from India. Four weeks later Barry wrote again to Wolfe Tone noting that Colonel Knox was arrived in London and they would be leaving together for Holland and Brussels on Tuesday 11 September; in the event Barry wrote again from London on Wednesday 12 September confirming that they would be setting out next day. Eleven weeks later on Monday 26 November Barry wrote to Wolfe Tone explaining that he and Knox had stayed longer than planned in Europe, but were now back in London. Their travel on Army matters as officers, as Britain prepared for war with revolutionary France, was not remarkable; both were later associated with Lord Moyra's expedition to Ostend. What marks out this correspondence is the preoccupation with Knox, rather than their Army mission, which Barry communicated in his letters to Wolfe Tone. Knox was wealthy, single, and had no children or other family dependents; one of Elizabeth's verses was an 'Advertisement for a wife. In the name of the Honourable General Knox'.

Maidens, here's a heart to sell!

Take the toy, and treat it well.

Knox's bequest to Barry in 1800 of an annuity of 200 guineas was a substantial legacy to an Army colleague and friend.[135] Whatever the specific nature of the rumours heard by Hester in 1794, they appear to have been primarily about the women living at 14 James Street. When Barry returned from Lord Moyra's expedition he resumed his relationship with Elizabeth, and continued to socialise with Hester.

Elizabeth's relationship with Barry lasted for many years. Neither married. Extant letters show that in 1788 and 1797 Barry wrote to Elizabeth's uncle and aunt the Earl and Countess of Coventry with a statement of his financial circumstances.[136] Elizabeth's income evidently relied partly on the continuing goodwill of her relations and it may not have helped that Barry's first letter included a brash assurance that his motivation in wanting to marry her was not 'Pecuniary advantages'. Nonetheless by the early 1790s Barry was sufficiently accepted by Elizabeth's family to be party to her sister Anne's marriage settlement with Thomas Maxwell Adams. He later received a mourning bequest in the will of Susanna St John of Bletso who had been one of Elizabeth's trustees and who was the sister in law of Barbara Countess of Coventry.[137] In the second letter Barry suggested to Barbara Countess of Coventry that after marrying Elizabeth's income should continue to be for her exclusive use; but if money was the social obstacle this was not sufficient. Barry and Elizabeth were both of age but neither seemed willing to marry against her relations' wishes, despite the fact that by 1797 Barry said his annual income was £4000. Not even the death of Elizabeth's brother Robert in 1797, who had inherited their father's estate when he came of age, and the fact that she was then party to the Chancery case of Clinton v. Coventry on behalf of her nieces and nephews, changed Henry and Elizabeth's apparent unwillingness to marry against the wishes of her aunt Barbara.

Barry and Elizabeth each maintained independent addresses. Like Anna Seward and her everyday companion John Saville in 1790-1809 during the many years when Barry was in London he lived on the same or nearby streets a short walk from Elizabeth. If Barry and Elizabeth married in secret or were lovers their relationship appears to have been childless. Beloe suggested that Elizabeth ended the relationship when Barry went to Bath for his health; in December 1800 Hester wrote to Penelope Sophia 'we have seen Colonel Barry who looks very well indeed – tho' Miss Trefusis seems to have forgotten him'.[138] Their separation broadly coincided with Knox's appointment as Governor of Jamaica, shipwreck in the West Indies, and probate bequest to Barry.

Elizabeth later moved to 27 James Street where she paid rates from 1805. Barry may have noticed the publication of Elizabeth's verses but they do not appear to have been in contact with each other. He continued to be friends with Hester Piozzi who occasionally visited Bath. Barry had a chance meeting and conversation with Fanny Burney, who noted in her diary that Barry remembered her brother from India in the 1780s.[139]

The evidence related to Elizabeth's life does not suggest that she continued to be emotionally close to her relations, or sustained the female friendships formed in her teenage years through visits or correspondence. After Sir Richard Bickerton died in 1792 his widow and daughters continued to live at Upwood where Mary Anne died in 1811, and Maria (d 1845) and Jane (d 1827) both remained single. After being widowed in 1807 Elizabeth's sister Anne and her daughters initially continued to occupy Duryard Lodge in Exeter. Anne had an income from her family's plantations in Barbados, despite which she was called to initial bankruptcy proceedings in 1821. By then Anne was living in Bath with her unmarried daughters; she later received £4,400 8s 7d compensation after slavery was abolished.[140]

Elizabeth did not extend her acute consciousness of individual emotions into a political philosophy based on shared humanity and fellow feeling. Elizabeth was conscious of literary trends but her verses drew on personal experience, classical mythology, and observations of nature without reference to Georgian Britain's expanding relationships with Africa, the Americas, or Asia. Her brother in law's father had published a pamphlet in 1788 opposing abolition of the slave trade;[141] Elizabeth must have been aware of abolitionist poetry written from a range of political viewpoints but chose not to write on the matter.

If some of Elizabeth's 'Novels, written in early life' were 'afterwards destroyed' the timing, circumstances, and reasons for this are not known. In 1808 Elizabeth published her verses with guidance from the Tory satirical poet and editor William Gifford. She may not have shown him all of her extant writing at that time. Nonetheless some omissions or selections were made and it is possible that Gifford's taste influenced Elizabeth's choice of which verses to publish.

Beloe claimed that Elizabeth's political opinions were driven by forceful emotions 'almost adoration of our own monarchical government, or her indignation, amounting almost to rage, against the French Revolution'.[142] This was an exaggerated statement of political dislike on his part. Britain was intermittently at war throughout most of Elizabeth's life. Her longest love relationship was with an Army officer who espoused a liberal political outlook. Elizabeth wrote a 'Loyal song written for the Pimlico volunteers', described as sung 'by Mr Hobbes' at the dinner following the presentation of their first colours, which was included in her published verses. During the American revolutionary and French wars Richard Bickerton's successful naval actions taking prizes in the Channel were the subject of newspaper reports which would have been closely followed at Upwood House; nonetheless, unlike Ann Thomas, Elizabeth made no comment on British battles at sea or on land in her verses.

Some of Elizabeth's verses were addressed to or described historical persons most of whom can be identified from the initials or other information provided. These included verses which were singled out for praise by some reviewers when *Poems and tales* was published. The military and administrative individuals, to whom Elizabeth had probably been introduced by Henry Barry, included the Honourable John Knox; and Warren Hastings, whom Elizabeth felt had been unfairly treated, and whom she described meeting at his home in Daylesford.

The unpublished content of the notebook at Trefusis, such as 'A good Plumb Pudding' which was a recipe, suggests it may have been a family copy. At the same time it included a note 'Eudora's letters etc from a novel Miss T. wrote in early life and destroy'd', so if the verses were written into the notebook by Elizabeth it was not that used for their original composition but may be one she made to show or lend to others including Gifford. The handwriting of the verses added to a copy of *Poems and tales* which is in the British Library was broadly similar, but the differences between some individual letters indicated it may not have been the same hand. It was these handwritten verses which included the first person note that 'The flowers' was 'Addressed to my dear Upwood friends on leaving them to settle at Bletsoe'. The handwritten copies of Elizabeth's verses were not made by Barry some of whose original letters are extant.

Beloe's literary biographical memoirs generated controversy and criticism when they were published in 1817. It is unclear that Beloe had any direct acquaintance with Elizabeth's circumstances during the later years of her life. Beloe suggested that Elizabeth had squandered wealth, which she may never have had, and became reliant on ether and laudanum.[143] Both of these were widely available and used at the time, prescribed by doctors and sold by apothecaries. Elizabeth may have been struggling with physical illness as well as emotional distress; the cause of her death is not known. When she died Elizabeth lacked financial resources to the point that, although she made a will, the death duty register index noted simply 'no property' next to her probate entry.[144] Elizabeth's volumes of poetry received positive reviews, some of which she may have read, and others of which appeared after and noted her recent death.

Elizabeth Trefusis' published work and influence were less extensive than Anna Seward's. Nonetheless there were parallels between the evolution of the two women's writing and literary tastes. There were some similarities between their personal emotional histories, despite their very different family backgrounds and circumstances, and the fact that Anna Seward was a generation older. Of her time and place as a Georgian orphan from one of Cornwall's longstanding landed families, Elizabeth's early verses revealed poetic talent and sensibility.

The 'poetess of nature' Anne Batten Cristall

Anne Batten Cristall's *Poetical sketches* was published by Joseph Johnson in March 1795.[145] Anne's mother Elizabeth was the daughter of the Penzance merchant John Batten and his wife Anne whose brother Christopher Nichols was a victualler. One of Elizabeth's brothers Joseph Batten was a dissenting minister and poet who published an elegy on the death of Thomas Vigurs in 1774 which was printed by the Falmouth bookseller Matthew Allison.[146] The formative influence of these family relationships on Anne Batten Cristall's development as a poet and one of her later places of residence are identified here for the first time.

Anne's father Alexander Cristall was a ship's captain when he met Elizabeth Batten of Penzance. Alexander Cristall was born in Scotland in the early 1720s. Following the Jacobite uprising of the mid-1740s Cristall, who was a mariner, moved to London where in January 1754 he married Margaret Gordon in the 'scotch church' at Stepney. During the Seven Years' War Cristall commanded the privateer *British Queen*. The action in which Cristall's ship was eventually captured and taken to St Malo in May 1762 lasted for six hours, three of his ship's crew were killed and five wounded; the *British Queen* had been returning to London from Guadaloupe.[147] By the end of the war Cristall was a widower with a 6 year old son John. Cristall's new ship the *Hunter* was initially sailed in the coastal trade between London and Penzance, and also called at Penzance when returning from the straits of Gibraltar.[148]

In April 1767 Captain Alexander Cristall was described as of Aldgate in London when he married Elizabeth Batten at Penzance. After marrying the Cristalls lived in Alexander's home on Swan Street at the Minories in Aldgate and had three children in 1768-71.

Elizabeth Cristall returned to Penzance in 1769 where Anne Batten Cristall (1769-1848) was born; Elizabeth gave her first daughter her mother's name after the elder Anne Batten died in that year. After the *Hunter* ran aground on the Kent coast in 1770 Alexander Cristall decided to change occupation and established a mast, sail, and block-making business at Hanover Stairs in Rotherhithe in a riverside yard which became known as 'Cristall's wharf' by the early 1800s; the Cristalls moved to live south of the Thames at Lewisham where their two younger sons were christened in 1774-6. Alexander's son from his first marriage John Cristall followed in his father's footsteps and was a mariner who captained East India Company ships. Alexander and Elizabeth's younger sons Joseph and Alexander Cristall worked alongside their father and later continued to occupy commercial premises in Rotherhithe where Joseph Cristall and his sons had a ship breaking business which was still operating in the 1850s.[149]

Aged 14 in 1782 Alexander and Elizabeth's first child together Joshua Cristall was apprenticed to the 'chinaman' William Hewson in Aldgate.[150] From the mid-1780s it is likely that the Cristalls spent time in London with the family of Elizabeth's brother Joseph Batten who was appointed minister of the Independent chapel in Back Street, Southwark in 1786.[151] Reverend Joseph Batten was a widower whose eldest child 8 year old Joseph Hallett Batten attended St Paul's school. Elizabeth Cristall and her two teenage daughters Anne and Elizabeth may have helped with the care and early education of Joseph's family until he married for a second time to Elizabeth Ellis in 1790. Reverend Joseph Batten may have encouraged his niece Anne to read and write poetry. The elegy published by Joseph Batten in 1774 had been for the young man Thomas Vigurs whom he described as 'my darling Friend' while expressing spiritual acceptance of death. One of Anne's verses was an elegy for an unnamed imaginary young woman in which the poetic voice was a musician narrating a tragic myth which also ended with a spiritual acceptance of death.

During the late 1780s Joshua and Anne began to make friends and acquaintances in London's radical and literary circles. By 1788 they had become acquainted with Mary Wollstonecraft, who returned to live in London to establish herself as a writer in 1787. At the end of Joshua's apprenticeship he was offered the opportunity to go into business with Hewson but chose instead to pursue his ambition to be an artist. Wollstonecraft compared Joshua's circumstances to those of her brother Charles and urged him to consider the impact that his decisions might have on Anne

> Pursue your studies, practice as much as you can, but do not think of depending on painting for a subsistence before you know the first rudiments of the art – I know that you earnestly wish to be the friend and protector of your amiable sister and hope no inconsiderate act or thoughtless mode of conduct will add to her cares – for her comfort very much depends on you.[152]

In 1790 Joshua Cristall accepted a position painting china at Thomas Turner's porcelain factory in Shropshire. He travelled and sketched to develop designs for Thomas Turner and visited Cornwall in the early 1790s where he painted St Michael's Mount.[153] Although Wollstonecraft had expressed concern for Anne's well being to Joshua she did not seek Anne's company during his absence noting kindly but disapprovingly that

> I have seldom seen your Sister since you left town I fear her situation is still very uncomfortable I wish she could obtain a little more strength of mind I am afraid she gives way to her feelings more than she ought to do.[154]

Joshua's departure to work for Turner coincided with Reverend Joseph Batten's marriage which may have had an impact on Anne's relationship with her uncle and his family.

When the merchant John Batten died at Penzance in 1792 his will made a bequest to his daughter Elizabeth Cristall and then to her children which he stipulated should not be subject to the control of her husband.[155] At the same time the death of his father may have been one of the factors which led Reverend Joseph Batten and his family to return to live in Cornwall where his eldest son Joseph Hallett Batten attended Truro Grammar School before going to Cambridge University. Reverend Joseph Batten of Penzance and his eldest son were later listed as subscribers to Anne's *Poetical sketches*. In 1815 Joseph Batten wrote a 78 line poetic 'sketch' of Penzance which was published anonymously by a later Thomas Vigurs who was a bookseller and printer in Penzance; this poem revealed Joseph Batten as someone who accepted the science of geology which had emerged in his lifetime as well as the education of girls including in science.[156]

Joshua, Anne, and the younger Elizabeth Cristall all developed their talents with the aspiration of earning their living in creative industries. Joshua returned to London where he studied part time at the Royal Academy schools from 1792, Anne wrote poetry, and Elizabeth developed skills as an engraver. Some women exhibited at the Royal Academy from its inception in the 1760s but women's access to training at the schools was in practice restricted by cultural barriers and only Joshua Cristall trained there. The Cristalls had friends who were Jacobins and supporters of the revolution in France from 1789. These included George Dyer, the politically radical Cambridge educated son of a London shipwright, who was a Baptist minister and published poet who earned his living partly by teaching. Elizabeth Cristall's engravings included a portrait of George Dyer drawn by Joshua Cristall which is now in the National Portrait Gallery.

Charlotte MacKenzie

It may have been George Dyer who introduced Anne to the publisher Joseph Johnson who held regular dinner parties for his authors. Anne Batten Cristall's *Poetical sketches* was published by Johnson and shared the same title as William Blake's first book of poems. In her preface Anne revealed her admiration for the 'poetic energy' of Robert Burns and the 'simple elegance' of some of Dyer's verses. The final poem of Anne's *Poetical sketches* was addressed directly to Dyer. Anne's verses were mostly not political but the 'Ode on truth' acknowledged Dyer's calls for 'Pity, Liberty, and Peace' as well as his personal ambition.

Anne's *Poetical sketches* included a frontispiece engraving by Joshua Cristall. The volume was a substantial collection of 24 verses some of which contained several parts or songs. The book appeared with a list of culturally influential subscribers including John Aikin who shortly afterwards became the first editor of the *Monthly magazine*; the writer Amelia Alderson who married the Cornish painter John Opie in May 1798; the poet and abolitionist Anna Barbauld; George Dyer; the writer Mary Hays; the writer and political reformer Anne Jebb; the poet Samuel Rogers; Dr John Wolcot who had fostered and promoted John Opie as an artist in Cornwall and London; and Mary Wollstonecraft and her sister Everina who was a friend of Anne Batten Cristall. The Cristalls remained on friendly terms with the china salesman William Hewson and his wife who also both subscribed to the *Poetical sketches*.

The publication and distribution of *Poetical sketches* was advertised in newspapers; it received attention and was reviewed in England and America. Three of Anne's verses were published in the *Gentleman's Magazine* in April and October 1795. Other magazines republished one of the verses with their reviews which initially welcomed a new poetic voice perceived as having 'genius, and warmth of imagination' or 'genius, sentiment, and pathos' alongside critical concerns about the occasional irregularities of form which made her poetry more directly expressive of feeling.[157] Opinion was divided on the fact that Anne animated, personified, and emoted elements of the natural world. This led the *Critical Review* to define Anne positively as a 'poetess of nature'; while a later critic in the *Monthly review* prosaically itemised several instances of unnaturalistic descriptions or mixed metaphor.[158] Periodical reviews were generally anonymous and Anne may have felt disappointed or hurt at the critical comments which might have been written by one of her literary acquaintances.

In 1796 when Mary Wollstonecraft was in London after her relationship with Gilbert Imlay ended she once again socialised with Anne. In June 1796 Anne met the radical political philosopher William Godwin when they both had tea at Mary Wollstonecraft's. On another occasion, as Wollstonecraft's relationship with Godwin developed, she sent him a note saying that her sister Everina was spending the day with Anne, and she would dine with him 'If you please'.[159]

Following publication of the *Poetical sketches* Mary Hays and George Dyer provided further introductions for Joshua and Anne. In April 1796 Mary Hays held a tea party attended by William Blake and Joshua Cristall amongst others.[160] George Dyer considered Anne had 'a very fine talent for poetry' which merited cultivation and urged Mary Hays to collaborate with her in writing 'an excellent *poetical novel*'.[161] The suggestion that Anne might have a talent for storytelling in verse was understandable since, as the *Annual Register*'s reviewer noted, many of her poems blended 'the narrative and the descriptive'. The poetic narratives ranged from a conversation in which a father eventually forgave his unmarried daughter for allowing herself to be seduced to tales of invented mythological characters. Nonetheless unlike Anna Seward and Elizabeth

Trefusis this encouragement to write a novel in verse was not taken up by Anne, nor by Mary Hays.

In March 1797 Dyer introduced Anne Batten Cristall and Mary Hays to Robert Southey who then made his friend the Bristol bookseller Joseph Cottle aware of Cristall's poetry:

> But Miss Christall have you seen her poems? – a fine, artless, sensible girl, now Cottle that word sensible must not be construed in its dictionary acceptation. ask a Frenchman what it means and he will understand it tho perhaps no circumlocution explain its French meaning. her heart is alive. she loves Poetry – she loves retirement – she loves the country. her verses are very incorrect & the Literary Circle say she has no genius. but she has Genius, Joseph Cottle! or there is no truth in physiognomy.[162]

Two years later Dyer promised Southey that both Amelia Opie and Anne Batten Cristall would write for Southey's *Annual Anthology* but only Amelia Opie did so.

Reading between the lines of the comments made by Wollstonecraft and Southey as well as the *Poetical sketches* it is possible that Anne had an unhappy love affair or unrequited attachment. In the late 1790s Anne would have been aware of the mixed reception of Mary Hays' novel the *Memoirs of Emma Courtney*. Hays openly described her unreciprocated attraction to William Frend, and her conduct was then satirised by Charles Lloyd in his novel *Edmund Oliver* (1798) and by Elizabeth Hamilton in her novel *The modern philosophers* (1800). In 1796 Hamilton had ended her friendship with Mary Hays because of the way in which Hays had reviewed Hamilton's fictional *Translations of the letters of a Hindoo Rajah* (1796). George Dyer withheld some of his verses from publication in 1802 so that 'Every thing of personal encomium is here suppressed, except of persons now no more. No name of individuals now living is made free with

...'.[163] In this literary environment it is possible that if Anne Batten Cristall wrote for publication after 1795 she chose to do so anonymously and was careful in her choice of editors or publishers to ensure her privacy was respected.

There were similarities between the family backgrounds of Anne Batten Cristall and George Dyer who became close to each other in the 1790s. Anne addressed one of her published verses directly to George who wrote a light and carefree verse *To a lady* named Anna. In contrast *The padlocked lady* is a narrative verse by Dyer in which the image of a woman with a sealed mouth, named 'Azza', was used to represent the liberties lost under the British government's politically repressive measures during the wars with revolutionary France.

Anne may have loved George and wanted to marry him. Many years later Robert Southey was perplexed when Dyer confided in him about his former relationship with Anne, whom Southey had met on the single occasion when Dyer introduced them. On two separate occasions Dyer went out of his way to tell Southey the only reason he had not allowed his relationship with Anne to develop further was 'that he did not think it prudent to marry' confessing on the second occasion 'that he was very sorry he did not marry Miss Christall; but really it would have been exceedingly imprudent'.[164] If Dyer regretted that he had not developed his relationship with Anne it is not impossible that he might have contacted her and told her himself as she was by then living at Lewisham.

Dyer had married for the first time in his late sixties to Honour Mather who was a widow. Dyer shared his personal regrets with Southey after the death of his friend Charles Lamb who had said that if he outlived Dyer he would write a novel based on Dyer's life. By the time Dyer spoke to Southey he was writing his memoirs by dictation having lost his sight; Dyer's obituary in the *Gentleman's magazine* briefly quoted from these manuscript memoirs which are not among the extant papers deposited in archives. If Dyer voiced his regrets about his relationship with Anne in his dictated memoirs it may be one reason why, after his death, they were not published as he had intended.

Joshua Cristall succeeded in pursuing a career as an artist. He took lodgings at 28 Surrey Street with his sister Elizabeth and was one of the artists helped by the London physician Dr Thomas Monro who provided open house materials and meals for aspiring artists in exchange for gifts of paintings. Joshua received a legacy after his parents died in January and February 1802, and travelled in Wales where he completed landscape paintings. From 1803 Joshua exhibited at the Royal Society; he was one of the founding members of the Watercolour Society in the same year. He was unwell in the mid-1800s but enjoyed success with the large paintings he completed while recuperating on the Sussex coast. Joshua's financial circumstances improved after he married Elizabeth Cossins, who had an independent income, in 1812. Elizabeth Cossins had operated a girls' school in the Manor House on Paddington Green. Joshua renewed the lease of the Manor House where they lived for the first ten years of their marriage, and later moved to live in the Wye valley in 1722-39. After Joshua was widowed he initially continued to live at Goodrich where he was listed in the 1841 census but later returned to live in London where he died in 1847.

Alexander Cristall's will in 1802 left half his estate to his two daughters and half to his four sons.[165] The will did not include Alexander's reasons. Men sometimes sought to provide a sufficient income for daughters whom they considered might remain single or to improve their daughters' future marriage prospects by ensuring they had assets. Alexander may have wanted to ensure 'Nancy' and Elizabeth's independence from their brothers given his executor John was married with children and sailed long-distance routes, Joshua was pursuing an uncertain career as an artist, Joseph was already married with children, and Alexander may have intended to marry as he did in the year following his father's death. Joseph and Alexander continued their father's commercial activities at Rotherhithe.

Anne was noted in Godwin's diary, in the letters of Mary Wollstonecraft, and by George Dyer as present at social gatherings in London up to and including 1797; and she was described by Dyer as possibly writing for publication in 1799. She may have left London in the late 1790s or following her parents' death. Anne Batten Cristall's probate described her as formerly of Maidenhead Thicket in Berkshire; then of Haileybury in Hertfordshire; and lastly of Lewisham Hill, Blackheath where her parental family had lived from the 1770s.[166] Maidenhead Thicket on the Bath road from London was notorious for its highway robbers and atmospheric ancient woodlands. After Anne received her parental inheritance if she had wanted tranquillity and solitude to write in the countryside, while living near a coach road to London, a cottage at Maidenhead Thicket might have met her requirements.

Aged 30 in 1799 Anne may not have been confident of earning her future income as a writer, and she may have taken a position as a family governess or schoolmistress. By 1810 *Cary's new itinerary* identified the main properties in Maidenhead Thicket as

> near the entrance of the Thicket on l. Miss Lowndes; and at a distance from the Road is Heywood Lodge, – Sawyer, Esq.; and at *Maidenhead Thicket*, on l. see the Spire of Shottesbrook Church, near to which is a Seat of Arthur Vansittart, Esq. Near the End of the *Thicket* on l. Pinke Lee, Esq.; and Woolley Hall, Rev. Mr. Palmer; and opposite Stubbins, Lord Dorchester.[167]

Charlotte MacKenzie

Among the subscribers to Anne's *Poetical sketches* was the Hackney independent minister Samuel Palmer, a Mr J. Palmer of America, a Mrs Palmer, and a Miss Palmer of Bedford which was Samuel Palmer's home town; from 1780 Samuel Palmer kept a boarding school in London and one of his sons is known to have been a schoolmaster at Chigwell in Essex. It is not impossible that there might have been a connection between one or more of Cristall's subscribers named Palmer and the ordained occupant in 1810 of the mansion house Woolley Hall near Maidenhead Thicket; Woolley Hall was advertised as available to let in 1815. By the time of the 1841 census if not before there was a private school at Maidenhead Thicket.

Members of Anne's family later obtained influential positions in education. In 1819 Anne witnessed the Rotherhithe wedding of her niece Mary Cristall to John Charles Tarver who later taught French at Eton College. Reverend Joseph Batten's two sons were ordained. In 1820 Reverend Samuel Ellis Batten married Caroline Venn whose father Reverend John Venn was an influential member of the evangelical Clapham Sect and abolitionist; Reverend Joseph Hallett Batten was employed for over thirty years at Haileybury College, initially as a professor of classics in 1806-15 and then as principal in 1815-37.

Many future senior officials of Britain's expanding empire were trained at the East India Company College in Haileybury which opened in 1806; the College stood in open countryside and landscaped grounds designed by Humphry Repton. Haileybury College was an intellectual and cultural community organised like an Oxford or Cambridge college. Before being appointed as a professor at Haileybury College Batten had been elected as a Cambridge fellow. During his time at Haileybury College Joseph Hallett Batten was made a Doctor of Divinity by royal mandate and was elected as a Fellow of the Royal Society. The professors at Haileybury College were specialists in their subjects which included non-European languages, classics, history and political economy, and some arts. Some professors combined teaching at the College with substantial intellectual or creative output. The drawing tutor Thomas Medland was an engraver and watercolourist who produced prints, including pictures of Haileybury, and exhibited at the Royal Academy where he would have been known to Joshua Cristall.[168] All of the students, teaching, and administrative staff of the College were men; only their family households and the College's domestic staff included women.

By the 1830s the teaching staff at Haileybury included individuals with an interest in the potential of descriptive economic and social sciences and their application to policy and administration. The population theorist Thomas Malthus taught there; he invited Harriet Martineau to visit Haileybury College where she found the prolific contributor to and later editor of the *Edinburgh Review* William Empson was also a professor. Aged in her early 30s Harriet Martineau found the College congenial and her visit to Thomas Malthus and his wife was the first of several she made there. Recalling her first stay at Haileybury College in her autobiography written over forty years later Martineau described an institutional environment which in August combined the rural recreations, 'summer evening parties', and domestic services of a country house with tranquil time to work and study:

> the families of the other professors made up a very pleasant society ... every facility was indeed afforded for my work. My room was a large and airy one with a bay window and a charming view; and the window side of the room was fitted up with all completeness with desk, books, and everything I could possibly want ... Almost daily we went forth when work was done – a pleasant riding party of five or six.[169]

This working environment was not open to women in universities at that time.

Charlotte MacKenzie

Joseph Hallett Batten and his family initially occupied half of the 'old manor house' at Haileybury and then lived in the Principal's house. Batten was married to Catherine Maxwell who had been born in Quebec to parents who were Scots; the Battens had five sons and five daughters. Their sons were educated at boarding schools and went to university; four later entered the employment of the East India Company. After Joseph Hallett Batten died in 1837 his widow and some of his children, daughters in law, and grandchildren lived in Paddington in London, and in several cases remained in London while their fathers were working overseas in postings for the East India Company.

At Haileybury Anne probably lived with her cousin's family and may have done so for almost three decades. Anne would have been an adult female companion for Catherine Batten, as well as at College social gatherings, and may have assisted with the education at home of the Battens' children the youngest of whom was aged 10 when his father died in 1837. Anne may have found the opportunities, social milieu, and ethos of Haileybury conducive to writing; if she continued to write for publication she did so anonymously or using a pseudonym.

After leaving Haileybury Anne lived on Lewisham Hill with her sister Elizabeth to whom Anne bequeathed her estate a decade later. Elizabeth had not developed a career as an engraver although some of her engravings are extant. In the 1841 census both sisters were described as of 'independent' means. The sisters' home was listed between 'White Cottage' occupied by the schoolmistresses Christiana and Mary Burn and boarding schoolchildren, and Reverend Joseph Prendergast the headmaster of Colfe's School in Lewisham in 1831-57. Colfe's school was illustrated in a print c.1830; 'White Cottage' was a white painted timber boarded property adjoining the headmaster's house.[170] Anne and Elizabeth's home may have been part of, or near to, the same group of buildings. Elizabeth Cristall was listed as occupying a separate household next to Reverend Joseph Prendergast's residence which was identified as 'Lewisham Hill Grammar School' in the 1851 census. Neither census listed any pupils or domestic servants as resident in the Cristalls' household. In 1853 Elizabeth Cristall's estate included savings of over £600 which was not inconsiderable at the time.[171]

'A Woman of talents' Eliza Fenwick

Eliza Fenwick's novel *Secresy or the ruin on the rock* 'by A Woman' was printed twice in 1795; by the author with an identified list of booksellers, and also by 'G. Kearsley'.[172] The gothic setting and plot of the novel both incorporated elements derived from the author's knowledge of Cornwall. Eliza's father Peter Jaco was an itinerant Methodist preacher whose family had interests in the Newlyn pilchard fisheries and trade with southern Europe.[173] In 1802 Eliza travelled to Cornwall with her two children, on the advice of her daughter's doctor, and worked in the Penzance linen drapers owned by their uncle Thomas James Fenwick. The influence of Eliza's Cornish connections on her writing is explored for the first time here.

Eliza's father Peter Jaco was born in 1728 the fifth of six children of Nicholas Jacka and Honour Downing. Jaco became one of the Wesleys' early followers while working for his family's concern in the Mount's bay pilchard fishery. By 1753 Peter Jaco had been identified by the Methodist local society as an 'exhorter' or lay preacher and he then travelled widely from the mid-1750s.

Jaco may have met the elder John Fenwick when Fenwick visited Cornwall as a Methodist itinerant preacher. In 1756 Fenwick married Priscilla Mackariss in London. Their eldest son John, who later had a long relationship and children with Eliza, was born in London in 1757. It was common for Methodist preachers to participate in trade. The elder John Fenwick subsequently established himself as a merchant in Newcastle on Tyne where he lived for two decades with his wife and family before travelling again as a Methodist preacher from 1777. Fenwick was briefly dismissed as an itinerant preacher for

drunkenness in 1785 before being reappointed to Epworth in 1786.[174]

Jaco's itinerancy as a preacher make his family circumstances more difficult to trace. It

is possible that Jaco was appointed to the Staffordshire circuit or travelled in advance of

John Wesley who preached there in March 1764. Eliza's birthday was in February and her

christening was probably that recorded at Lincoln cathedral on 21 February 1764. In the

following decade Jaco was appointed to circuits in Sheffield; Lancashire; London for two

years in 1767-8, and Kent in 1769; then Newcastle for two years in 1770-1 when Jaco

probably renewed his connection with the elder John Fenwick who was an active

Methodist society member, and John and Eliza may have met as children; and finally

Dublin in 1772-3. Peter Jaco was in London from 1774 where his health gradually

declined before he died in July 1781.[175]

Peter Jaco's wife Elizabeth travelled with him and it is possible that their daughter Eliza

spent some time staying with relations, including in Cornwall, or attended boarding

school before the family settled in London. When Eliza Fenwick (1764-1840) was living

and working in Penzance in 1802-3 she wrote to the novelist Mary Hays

> I have on my father's side a host of relations in this Country some rich and some
>
> poor; my Aunt & her daughter live in this town & it is curious that Lanno
>
> [Orlando, Eliza's son] exceedingly resembles this cousin & many others. They are
>
> I think the handsomest set of people I have seen. My father & eldest Uncle (who I
>
> saw some years ago in London) I well remember to be both in person & face
>
> uncommonly handsome & the same characteristicks of fine & bold beauty are to
>
> be seen in the whole of them except myself & another Miss Jaco who is however
>
> married to a Captain Burgess of the Navy a man of considerable property.[176]

91

In his will Peter Jaco bequeathed his daughter Eliza £100 on condition that any marriage she made was with her guardians' agreement.

Jaco's will described him as a 'hosier' and it is likely that his wife and daughter worked alongside him. One of Jaco's letters said that his wife and daughter were in business together and confirmed that this was important to the family's income. After her father died Eliza probably initially continued to live at home, on Artillery Lane near Spitalfields market, with her widowed mother who later received financial support from the Methodist widows' fund.[177]

It is unlikely that Elizabeth Jaco would have objected to her daughter marrying a man who was the son of a fellow itinerant Methodist preacher. Nonetheless it is possible that John and Eliza were not married; John's brother Thomas James Fenwick later had five children without being married to the Helston born woman he identified in his will as 'Catherine Pascoe known and reputed as Catherine Fenwick now and for many years past residing with me'.[178] Eliza and John Fenwick's first child Eliza Ann was christened at St Dunstan and All Saints Stepney on 28 June 1789 when Fenwick was described as a gentleman. By October 1792 John and Eliza Fenwick were living at 7 Apollo Buildings on East Street near Walworth Common. In the early 1790s John Fenwick released funds through a series of property transactions related to Norris farm in Enfield in which he had received an interest from the estate of his maternal grandfather Robert Mackariss.[179]

The younger John Fenwick was a political radical who was a member of the London Corresponding Society which advocated universal adult male suffrage. He was a friend of the philosopher and novelist William Godwin whose diaries show that he met regularly with Fenwick for at least 35 years from 1788 when his diaries start until Fenwick's death in 1823. John Fenwick joined the Society for Constitutional Information, which published

radical political literature, in October 1792.

Unlike Mary Wollstonecraft who had left England in December 1792 John Fenwick

travelled to France after the execution of Louis XVI and after France had declared war on

Britain on 1 February 1793. Godwin's *Political Justice* was published the same month. In

January Godwin had taken a copy of his work to the French ambassador in London with

a letter to the National Convention in which Godwin declared himself 'un des admiratuer

les plus zélés de la révolution française'.[180] The purpose and intended destination of John

Fenwick's journey was almost certainly known to Godwin who wrote to Fenwick on 15

February that

> You will remember the terms upon which the inclosed copy of my book is sent. It
>
> is to be given to General Miranda, provided you are likely to live upon terms of
>
> easy access to him; otherwise to any Frenchman of public importance & personal
>
> candour to whom you have access: that at all events there may be an additional
>
> chance from your influence, to gain a hearing & if possible a translation for the
>
> work.

This suggests that Fenwick intended to travel to France's northern front where Miranda

commanded the Army of the North. It was a dangerous time to travel in French territory

given that British citizens were subject to arrest as prisoners of war, and cross Channel

post was soon largely interrupted. By April France had withdrawn from Belgium, Miranda

was arrested, and the Committee of Public Safety had been established.

By October 1793 John Fenwick returned to London where he worked as a translator and

political writer. In 1794 Fenwick published a translation of the *Memoirs of General*

Dumourier; he wrote an anti-war *Letter to the people of Great Britain, respecting the present state of their public affairs* published by James Ridgway in 1795 who was a prisoner in Newgate at the time; and he translated and edited a play *He's much to blame* in association with the dramatist Thomas Holcroft. In 1798 Fenwick wrote and published highly critical *Observations on the trial of James Coigly for high treason*. In 1799 he wrote the first biography of his friend William Godwin; and in 1800 Fenwick's play *The Indian* was staged. Fenwick's political opinions were not in doubt but he was not one of the 1790s radicals who were arrested. It is possible that Fenwick had other employment alongside his political activities and publications. Fenwick may have worked as a journalist before being editor of the unsuccessful *Albion* and *Plough* in 1801-2, and his family may have lived partly on the proceeds of his transactions related to Norris farm.

John and Eliza Fenwick were both part of the circle of radical writers in 1790s London some of whom wrote novels, plays, or poetry to communicate political messages. In these circles Eliza met other women who earned their living from writing. It may have been during John's absence from London in February to October 1793 that Eliza started to write her novel. In the same year Eliza was probably organising or providing care for her sick mother; Elizabeth Jaco died of 'consumption' in January 1794.

When *Secresy or the ruin on the rock* by 'A Woman' was published in 1795 a positive review described the author as having 'studied and imbibed the principles and spirit of *Anna St Ives*' by Thomas Holcroft; while another reviewer lambasted the novel's sexual relationships outside marriage as 'a morality, worthy enough of modern France, but far removed (we trust) from the approbation of Englishmen'.[181] Eliza's epistolary novel was partly intended to illustrate the benefits of educating girls by contrasting the mistakes of an uneducated heiress Sibella Valmont with the rational conduct of her educated friend Caroline Ashburn.

Eliza paid for the printing of her novel which included a cryptic dedication to 'Eliza B.' who 'had paid me for it beforehand'. The identity of 'Eliza B.' whose subscription may have helped to fund the printing is not known. After the novel was published the identity of the author was not kept secret among the Fenwicks' friends and Eliza established stronger relationships with other women writers in their circle.

After Mary Wollstonecraft gave birth to her second daughter in August 1797 the placenta did not deliver. John and Eliza Fenwick stayed with the Godwins for two weeks. Eliza nursed Mary and organised the baby's wet nurses. After Mary died it was Eliza who, at William Godwin's request, wrote to Mary's sister Everina to inform her family noting 'I was with her at the time of her delivery, and with very little intermission until the time of her death'.[182] This experience may have brought John and Eliza closer together; their son Orlando was christened on 3 May 1798. The Fenwicks continued to see William Godwin regularly and became acquainted with Mary Jane Godwin who he married in December 1801; she was the grand-daughter of the Exeter merchant Samuel Tremlett and had children from her previous relationships. Eliza became close friends with the novelist Mary Hays who she saw regularly in London and with whom she confided and corresponded for thirty years 1798-1828.

At the turn of the century John and Eliza Fenwick became friends with Charles Lamb; he later recalled writing for the *Albion* newspaper in the summer of 1801:

> *Fenwick* resolutely determined upon pulling down the Government ... Our occupation now was to write treason ... Blocks, axes, Whitehall tribunals were covered with flowers of so cunning a periphrasis ... that the keen eye of an Attorney General was insufficient to detect the lurking snake among them.[183]

Charlotte MacKenzie

As children Charles and Mary Lamb had lived with their parents at the London address of one of the MPs for Liskeard and Inner Temple bencher Samuel Salt by whom their father John Lamb was employed as a factotum. In 1783 a meeting of the Society for Constitutional Information which was attended by 60 landowners in East Cornwall had identified the interests controlling or influencing the 44 parliamentary seats in Cornwall. This list included the six MPs elected at Liskeard, Grampound, and St Germans in the interest of 'Mr Eliot'.

In 1702 Daniel Eliot bequeathed Port Eliot to his cousin's son on condition that his chosen heir Edward Eliot married Daniel's daughter Katherine; in the event Katherine Eliot instead married the historian Browne Willis. The later Eliots of Port Eliot derived much of their eighteenth century wealth from the merchant James Craggs which had been made partly from the transatlantic slave trade.[184] Craggs was a director of the South Sea Company established to deliver the British government's obligations to supply enslaved workers within the Asiento contract. Craggs had one son and three daughters. The younger James Craggs had one daughter Harriot outside of marriage by the actress Hester Santlow. Two of the elder James Craggs' three daughters were married to great Cornish landowners: Elizabeth to Edward Eliot of Port Eliot, and Margaret to Samuel Trefusis of Trefusis. Following the collapse in share prices of the South Sea Company the government imposed a fine of £64,000 on the elder Craggs. Nonetheless after the younger Craggs died shortly before his father the elder Craggs' remaining legacy of £1.5 million was shared between his three married daughters. In 1724 the third daughter Anne made a second marriage to the Cornish landowner John Knight, MP for St Germans in 1710-22, who was also briefly elected at St Mawes in 1727. At the age of 13 Harriot was married to her uncle Richard Eliot who was managing in trust and later inherited his brother Edward's estate.

In due course it was Edward Eliot (1727-1804), the son of Richard and Harriot, who inherited Port Eliot. Two of his sons were MPs and early supporters of the abolition of the slave trade. Of these two sons Edward James Eliot was a university friend of William Wilberforce and William Pitt. Edward James Eliot was one of the subscribers to Charlotte Smith's *Elegiac sonnets* (1784) published while her husband was in debtor's prison. In 1785 Edward James Eliot married William's sister Harriot Pitt against the wishes of his father who wanted his son to make a more financially advantageous marriage. Edward James Eliot was known to 1790s radicals as a political reformer who was also an evangelical Anglican and member of the Clapham Sect. In advocating the abolition of slavery Edward James Eliot did not acknowledge that his family's wealth had derived partly from the slave trade.

In Cornwall in the early 1790s the elder Edward Eliot was not concerned with political or religious reform. In 1792 he commissioned Humphry Repton to draw plans to remodel Port Eliot, which is a waterside property and former priory. Earlier works commissioned by Edward Eliot removed tombstones outside the church. Edward Eliot provided replacement land for burials on which he built a new and substantial family vault. After this work had been completed an unknown artist painted the house and church at Port Eliot in the late 1770s or early 1780s. Repton produced a 'red book' of designs with written explanation one page of which was headed plainly 'Of Gothic'; Repton's plans included a proposed gothic walkway linking the house to the church.[185]

Eliza Fenwick's novel revealed an inner imagination which drew on places in Cornwall, and the stories she had heard of some great Cornish landowners, notably the Eliots of Port Eliot, as well as her personal experience. By the end of the novel the secrets have been revealed. Mr Valmont of Valmont Castle tells Clement Montgomery that he is his father. Mr Valmont's niece Sibella discovers she is an heiress and need not depend on Valmont in future. Clement is revealed as leading a dissipated life and having had an affair with Mademoiselle Janetta Laundy. Arthur Murden, the nephew of a nabob, confesses that he disguised himself as a hermit and lived in 'the ruin on the rock' to be close to Sibella whom he loves; nonetheless Arthur is shocked when he realises that Sibella is pregnant by her childhood friend Clement, who has by then married a wealthy widow. The passageway between Valmont Castle and the hermitage is discovered.

The setting of Eliza's novel in the moated Valmont castle may have derived from her knowledge that the Enfield property in which John Fenwick had a family interest had been a moated farmhouse. Other elements of the novel's setting echoed dimensions of Port Eliot, and the actual or proposed changes by Edward Eliot, including: the wooded, waterside location; the building of a new family vault; the 'wild and rocky' scenery adjoining the park which Repton's plan labelled 'the Craggs'; and the passageway which, in the novel, joins the castle to the eponymous ruined hermitage clinging to a dramatic outcrop. During visits to Cornwall it is likely that Eliza had seen the hermitage at Roche. The first description of Sibella Valmont in the novel was of her seated, dressed all in white, nursing a pet fawn Nina; there was a deer park at Boconnoc, the Pitt family's home in Cornwall, not at Port Eliot.

The plot of *Secresy or the ruin on the rock* turned on the secret intention of Mr Valmont to engineer the marriage of his niece and heiress Sibella to Clement Montgomery so as to secure the future fortune and inheritance of Valmont castle for his son who had been born outside marriage. The Eliot family history included foiled intentions to arrange the marriage of an heiress to an Eliot cousin. As well as the marriage of James Craggs' and Hester Santlow's daughter Harriot to Richard Eliot.

The character of Clement Montgomery may have incorporated Eliza's personal doubts about John Fenwick. John was seven years older than Eliza but they probably met as children when both their families were in Newcastle. John and Eliza were, to echo Thomas James Fenwick's phrase, 'known and reputed' as married, but they may not have been; John Fenwick had probably had relationships with other women of which Eliza was aware. John Fenwick acquired a reputation for mismanaging money and heavy drinking; he provided the inspiration for Charles Lamb's character 'the excellent toss-pot' Ralph Bigod in the *Essays of Elia*.

On a visit to Cornwall in September 1776 Eliza's father Peter Jaco wrote happily from Mount's bay that

> I have two neat chambers, built upon the extreme margin of the shore ... so that at this moment I can see nearly twenty sail of ships, and upwards of a hundred large fishing-boats ... Nothing on earth can be more agreeable to me.

For Peter Jaco returning to Newlyn was a homecoming; he saw his family including his father Nicholas.[186] Eliza was aged 12 when her father wrote this letter. Perhaps because of her father's influence or childhood visits to her relations Eliza thought of Cornwall as a place to which she could escape.

In the summer of 1800 Eliza considered leaving her relationship with John Fenwick and 'totally' separating herself and her children 'from his bad or good fortunes'. Eliza's relations in Cornwall included her 'brother' – in fact, John's brother - Thomas James Fenwick who had opened a linen draper's shop on the market place in Penzance.[187] In a letter to Mary Hays in July 1800 Eliza noted that she had 'written to Cornwall & urged them immediately to enable me to come there'; but she did not travel to Cornwall at that time. On 26 July Charlotte Smith, who had retrieved her family's financial situation by writing for publication, wrote reassuringly to Mary Hays that Eliza was 'not only a Woman of talents, but of great sweetness of temper, and an excellent heart'. In a reverie in September 1801 Eliza had 'half a mind to jump on a little vessel now in the river & sail away to Cornwall'; but she was still living with John, and waited until the following summer to travel to Cornwall.

The circumstances in which Eliza finally moved to live at Penzance were not carefree. In June 1802 John and Eliza's daughter Eliza Ann was unwell. Eliza's mother had died of consumption and Eliza, fearing for her daughter, noted with relief that 'Carlisle', one of the doctors who had attended Mary Wollstonecraft, called Penzance 'the Montpellier of England & that were she in London & money were no object he should order her hither'. By the autumn Eliza Ann was well enough to attend school in Falmouth while her mother 'could bear a gallop of 25 miles to Falmouth for dinner very well'. When she was not in the shop or occupied with her children Eliza roamed the coast and countryside in west Cornwall noting contentedly that even in winter 'a fine day here has all the warmth & clearness of Spring'.

Cornwall in 1802-3 did not inspire Eliza to work on the second novel which she had considered writing in 1800. Despite Charlotte Smith's optimistic expectations of Eliza, she wrote from Penzance to Mary Hays that 'my barren imagination & still more barren situation, will not furnish any hint towards a second work'. Eliza had companionship but missed her creative friends. She had relations in Penzance but does not appear to have made new connections in Cornwall through the Fenwicks' London friends; Valentine le

Grice, a schoolfriend of Lamb and Samuel Taylor Coleridge, lived at Trereife near Penzance from 1796 but Eliza does not appear to have known him.

In Penzance Eliza made friends with Fanny and John Vigurs writing to Mary Hays that Fanny was 'An elegant pleasing and accomplished woman' who had established herself as a 'Millener'. This was Fanny Clansie who opened a milliner's shop at Penzance in partnership with Grace Davy who was Humphry Davy's widowed mother. Fanny Clansie's father had been in partnership at Roscoff with the merchant and smuggler John Copinger; members of the Clansie family had settled at Penzance after bankruptcy proceedings commenced against John Copinger and the French revolutionary wars disrupted trade with France.[188] John Vigurs was the son of a victualler who kept the *Seven Stars* in Penzance; Eliza found him to be 'a tall pleasing young man who reads much, draws well from Nature, & writes agreeable verses but whose parents while they made his dolt of a brother a bookseller & printer made him a *tallow Chandler*'. Eliza learned that Fanny was socially ostracised and attributed this to the Vigurs' social status; it may also have been due to the fact that the Vigurs' recent wedding had been celebrated with a Catholic mass at Lanherne following the Anglican ceremony, which was legal within the Roman Catholic Relief Act in 1791 but not common in Cornwall at the time. All three spent Sundays hiking in west Cornwall and sharing picnics together rather than in church.

Thomas James Fenwick's shop in Penzance was initially successful. Eliza worked in the shop with Thomas and two 'shop women'; the shop was so busy 'on Market days' that she did not eat between 'an early breakfast till about 7 in the evening'.[189] Nonetheless by June 1803 Thomas James Fenwick was declared bankrupt. Mary Lamb wrote to Dorothy Wordsworth on 9 July

You saw [John] Fenwick when you was with us – perhaps you remember his wife and children were with his brother, a tradesman at Penzance. He (the brother), who was supposed to be in a great way of business, has become a bankrupt; they are now at Penzance without a home and without money; ... I am distressed for them, for I have a great affection for Mrs Fenwick.[190]

In Cornwall Eliza may have turned to her father's relations for help. Thomas James Fenwick's creditors continued to meet and receive dividends for the next two years, and he was eventually able to establish a new business.

By the autumn of 1803 Eliza had returned to London where she established herself as an author of books for children producing ten titles in 1804-12. The Godwins opened a children's booksellers and publishing house M. J. Godwin & Co, also known as the Juvenile Library, which Eliza briefly managed from November 1807. Early in 1808 Eliza travelled with her daughter who had an acting engagement in Ireland. The Fenwicks continued to have financial problems and in 1808 Charles Lamb wrote to a friend that 'Little Fenwick' or John was in Fleet prison for debt. In 1811 Thomas James Fenwick told Eliza he would pay his brother 'an income sufficient for his wants' suggesting that John should move to live in Cornwall. There were occasional later references to writing and publication plans of Eliza Fenwick, and some of her books for children published later editions including translations, but her last new publication was her English grammar schoolbook in 1812.

From 1812 Eliza earned her living mostly by teaching in Ireland, Barbados, America, and Canada. For two years from June 1812 Eliza was a governess to the Honnor family at Lee Mount near Cork in Ireland. In 1811 John and Eliza's adult daughter Eliza Ann Fenwick who was an actress had moved to Barbados where she met, and in August 1812 married, William Rutherford; he was an actor and the son of a Methodist lay preacher Thomas Rutherford who had known Eliza Ann's grandfather the elder John Fenwick. In Barbados William Rutherford established a newspaper and opened a reading room while Eliza Ann Rutherford opened a school. William and Eliza Ann Rutherford had four children together and in July 1816, on the day that their fourth child Orlando was born, William Rutherford left Barbados for London and never returned to his wife and children.

In August 1814 Eliza Fenwick had travelled to Barbados where she helped her married daughter to operate the school that she had opened at Bridgetown. After they left London for Barbados John Fenwick did not see Eliza or either of his two children again, nor did he meet any of his four grandchildren. In November 1816 Orlando Fenwick died of yellow fever aged 18. Nonetheless Eliza continued to live in Barbados and work with her daughter; and also helped to care for her four grandchildren after William Rutherford left for London and her son died. Initially employing free black servants in Barbados Eliza's school and household later relied on five enslaved workers.

Seven years later in September 1822 Eliza Fenwick and Eliza Ann Rutherford moved to New Haven, Connecticut. The school they opened there was not successful and two and a half years later they moved to New York where Eliza Fenwick ran a boarding house. In March 1827 Eliza Ann Rutherford died at New York and, as William Rutherford was living in London, Eliza Fenwick became the sole guardian of her grandchildren William aged 14, Thomas aged 12, Elizabeth aged 10, and Orlando aged 9.

In 1829 the family relocated to Niagara on the Lake where Eliza ran a seminary with her friend Mary Baldwin Breckinridge; and then in 1833 to York, renamed Toronto in 1834, where Eliza took charge of one of the boarding houses of Upper Canada College.

Charlotte MacKenzie

Tragically her two eldest grandsons William and Thomas Rutherford died in 1834 after taking a boat out on lake Ontario. In the late 1830s Elizabeth Rutherford was employed as governess to the family of the American Scot and businessman Alexander Duncan; they were friends of Eliza who also lived at the Duncan family's home on the shores of lake Ontario before moving with them to Providence, Rhode Island. Eliza Fenwick died at Providence in December 1840.

.

'Unequal to the situation' the Wedgwoods' governess Thomasin Dennis

Thomasin Dennis (1770-1809) was the eldest daughter of Alexander and Catherine Dennis who farmed Sawah in St Levan; not long after Thomasin was born the family moved to Lower Trembath near Penzance which included a mill. While Thomasin was growing up her extended family lived in west Cornwall where they were farmers, merchants, and shopkeepers; including some financially independent women. Thomasin was initially educated at home, and later tutored by the vicar of St Hilary Reverend Malachy Hitchins. As an adult Thomasin greatly extended her reading and studied classics. She became friends with Davies Giddy and Charles Valentine le Grice. The first of these relationships had a formative influence on Thomasin's choices and life experience; for that reason Giddy's biography and long friendship with Thomasin is explored here. le Grice's intellectual companionship and conversation were valued by Thomasin, and their friendship continued after le Grice married.

Aged 23 in July 1794 Thomasin witnessed the wedding of her cousin Anne Weymouth to Richard Symons a saddler of Redruth. Of Thomasin's four siblings who did not die in infancy Elizabeth lived at home and may never have been employed; Alexander died aged 16 in 1792; and John was apprenticed to the surgeons Moyle and Paul of Marazion in 1797, later joining a partnership with John Bingham Borlase and William Berryman as 'surgeons, apothecaries, and men-midwives' in Penzance.[191] When Thomasin's youngest brother Richard Dennis was aged 15 and considering his future prospects Thomasin adversely compared 'the too often narrow-minded and illiberal business of shopkeeping' with the 'amiable and independent occupation' of farming; Richard later worked in partnership with his father as cornfactors and farmers of Trembath.[192]

Thomasin's uncle John Dennis was a draper in Penzance who established a woollen manufactory with his son John, who later started a bank with his brother William; Thomasin's female cousins Mary and Ann Dennis married the brothers Thomas and Joseph Rock who were factors in Birmingham. Their kinswoman Grace Dennis was a mercer who managed large retail premises at Penzance for over 20 years retiring in 1804; she was a Quaker.[193] The Penzance market place shop premises letting by 1800 to Thomas James Fenwick, and mortgage of Alexander Dennis of Madron, was a property and financial investment of Thomasin's father.[194]

Farmers and cornfactors like Thomasin's father Alexander Dennis were sometimes the target of economic protests. Following winter shortages letters were circulated in six west Cornwall parishes in March 1795 urging people to prevent grain being shipped out of Penzance. Crowds containing hundreds of people drawn mainly from the mining districts around St Just assembled in Penzance on 10 and 11 March and were dispersed.[195] Thomasin's contact with and views on these protests are not known. Alexander Dennis was a socially conservative and religious man who attended church up to three times on Sundays. When visiting the Rock family in Birmingham Alexander Dennis went twice on the same Sunday to hear Edward Burn, a renowned orator who had controversially argued that the radical politics of Joseph Priestley were partly to blame for the 1791 Church and King riots in which Priestley's house was destroyed.[196]

Thomasin had access to books through local circulating libraries and bookshops. From the late 1790s Thomasin's reading was guided by the Oxford graduate Davies Giddy who gave her access to his library at Tredrea; she learned Greek and read classical literature. Thomasin's social circle included Charles Valentine le Grice, who was three years younger than she was. In 1796 le Grice had been appointed as the Nicholls' tutor at nearby Trereife; he was an Oxford graduate, published author, and classical Greek translator who had been at school with Charles Lamb and Samuel Taylor Coleridge. By the late 1790s Thomasin was in her late twenties, an educated single woman who had access to the social, scientific, and cultural circles in west Cornwall. She was already writing poetry which had not yet been published; and she was self-confident in her contacts with the published writers whom she met.

Davies Giddy was three years older than Thomasin; he was the only son of the curate of St Erth Edward Giddy, who was an active magistrate, and his wife Catherine Davies of Tredrea. Giddy had attended Penzance grammar school and been tutored by Malachy Hitchins before attending Benjamin Donne's Mathematical Academy at Bristol, and then completing his education at Pembroke College Oxford. At Oxford Giddy studied chemistry with the socially radical physician Thomas Beddoes, and considered training in medicine. After graduating in 1789 Giddy returned to Cornwall where he continued to pursue his scientific interests and applied his mathematical skills to mining and steam technology closely following the innovations of Jonathan Hornblower and Richard Trevithick. As the 1790s unfolded Giddy chose no profession.

Giddy was a reliable man entrusted by his friends. As an adult who continued to live with his parents at Tredrea Giddy sometimes socialised and shopped with his sister Philippa; in his twenties and thirties Giddy established communicative and caring friendships with at least four women, extricating himself from any unwelcome romantic attachments by explaining that his feelings were like those of a brother. In 1800 Giddy undertook to purchase items for Thomas Wedgwood in Cornwall and send them out to him on the West Indies packet. When Giddy met his future wife in 1805 the opportunity to be in contact with each other was provided by Giddy agreeing to deliver a letter for her. Giddy was later appointed as an executor and trustee by Thomas Beddoes, and by the surgeon William Millett of Marazion.

In Cornwall in 1790 Giddy supported the election of Francis Gregor who promoted himself as independent; once Gregor was elected as an MP he generally supported Pitt's Tories including voting for the laws against sedition. Sufficiently swayed by liberal enthusiasm to wear a French revolutionary cockade in 1791 and hand them out to his friends, as the revolution unfolded Giddy was appointed to hold public offices and his actions were consistently conservative. Giddy gave his attention to Cornish politics and administrative matters as Sheriff of Cornwall in 1792-3 and deputy Lieutenant in 1795, and followed his father by accepting appointment as a magistrate. In 1795 one of the Cornish magistrates commented on the large crowds of protestors in Penzance and the lack of arrests that 'Almost every individual in the mining parts of the Country where the riots happened, was more or less concerned in them, so that each man feels it his own cause'.[197] That was not how Giddy felt. In December 1800 Christmas stores were stolen from the mill at Nancledra which was a property of the Giddy family after thieves gained entry through the roof.[198] There were Cornish food riots in the months that followed. As a magistrate Giddy supported the decision of 15 April 1801 that workers' incomes might be subsidised by parishes and boroughs when necessary to enable them to buy food and subsist.[199] In his next letter to Thomasin, Giddy echoed Hannah More's political ballad *Half a loaf is better than no bread*.

> The whole country, for I am sorry to say the malady is far from being confined to
> the common people, seems seized with a fit of insanity ... The people cry the

talisman of factors has been 'Is not a large loaf better than a small one' the real dilemma should thus be stated 'Is not a small loaf better than no loaf'.[200]

Giddy was elected a Fellow of the Royal Society in 1791. In the same year Beddoes spent the summer in Cornwall collecting geological specimens for a planned lecture series. While staying with Giddy at Tredrea Beddoes addressed a poem 'An ode to night' to Giddy's sister Philippa; he also wrote a paper setting out his opinion that a combination of distributed 'Houses of Reception' in mining districts and dispensaries in towns would provide the most effective access to medical treatment as 'Cornwall is rendered by its geography peculiarly unfit for an Infirmary'.[201] Nonetheless after successful fundraising the infirmary was built at Truro and opened in 1799; local dispensaries followed.

In 1793 Beddoes dedicated his *Observations on the nature of demonstrative evidence* to Giddy. Beddoes drew on new technology to conceptualise and communicate human physiology suggesting that 'animal motion' derived from changes in gases produced by electricity and that 'our nervous and muscular system may be considered as a sort of steam engine: this hypothesis, though not perhaps at this moment capable of strict proof, is extremely probable'.[202] Beddoes' medical research focused on inhalation of gases which he believed might have curative potential. The engineer James Watt produced equipment for Beddoes; both were interested in the applications of engineering to obtain medical advances.

Five years before Humphry Davy suggested nitrous oxide might be used for anaesthesia Giddy wrote to Beddoes: 'The power of heavy inflammable air, as I take it, to diminish ... excitability in the brain may possibly be applied to many useful purposes. May it not be used before painful operations?'.[203] It was Giddy who later gave Davy a book by Beddoes

and Watt with an appendix by Samuel Latham Mitchill on nitrous oxide or 'the gaseous

oxide of azote', and made the introductions which led Davy to work with Beddoes in

Bristol. In February 1799 Giddy wrote excitedly to Thomasin 'I really believe Chemistry

will date a new era from the labours of a young man under twenty at Penzance'. Davy's

decision to quit his medical apprenticeship to Borlase and work with Beddoes in Bristol

opened the way for Thomasin's brother John to join Borlase's partnership in Penzance.[204]

In 1797-9 Beddoes and Giddy corresponded about the illness and treatment of Lydia

Veale Baines of Penzance.[205] Lydia was the eldest daughter of Captain Cuthbert and

Lydia Baines of Penzance; her father was a Royal Navy Commander who had completed

twenty years at sea from the age of 12 before he settled in Cornwall where he was

employed in the impress service. Giddy was a friend of the Baines family and sometimes

stayed at their house when he was in Penzance. Lydia was 20 years old and in Bristol

with her paternal aunt Lady Mary Knightley, the wife of Sir John Knightley of Fawsley,

when she first asked Beddoes' advice about whether to take the 'hot well' water at

Hotwells which had been associated in the mid eighteenth century with reports of

recovery from 'consumption'. Beddoes became concerned that Lydia and her family

underestimated the seriousness of her condition, and told Giddy that there would be

little chance of recovery if Lydia did not act immediately and follow medical advice.

In January 1798 Beddoes told Giddy that he had recommended a sea voyage for Lydia,

and found a couple in Bristol who were willing for her to sail with them to Madeira

despite the wartime conditions at sea, but Lydia refused. When Lydia breathed the

'factitious airs' tried next by Beddoes her cough worsened. On 10 February Beddoes wrote to Giddy asking him to explain to Lydia's parents that he would try everything to ameliorate her condition which he nonetheless now considered hopeless.

Beddoes was empirically testing whether the emissions of cows might contain healing properties; Lydia stayed for a time in a room with an open window into a cow barn but by March Beddoes confirmed that the experiment with 'cow dung' had not improved her condition. Beddoes told Giddy that it might be best for Lydia to return to Penzance. Lydia was now of age and she continued to be treated by Beddoes in Bristol who confirmed to Giddy in April that she refused to 'go west'. Later that year it was agreed that Lydia should return to Cornwall for the winter. Beddoes again recommended a sea voyage during which she should take no medicines and eat only figs and French plums; and then to take a half grain of opium three times a day with rhubarb. In Cornwall while Lydia was presumably following Beddoes' prescription of opium and rhubarb Giddy visited Lydia regularly before she died in March 1799.[206]

In the late 1790s war with France made travel to southern Europe more hazardous; some physicians who had previously advised patients to winter abroad instead recommended the mild climate of Cornwall. Arriving at Marazion on 11 November 1797 Reverend John Skinner noted that

> the mildness of the western climate renders this vicinity singularly inviting, and often beneficial to valetudinarians, and were it not for the frequent rains that occur in this part of the country, the invalid would have little occasion to travel to Italy, or the South of France for a mild and salubrious atmosphere.[207]

The Birmingham physician Dr William Withering provided medical advice to several fellow members of the scientific dining club the Lunar Society. In 1797 Withering advised James Watt to send his son Gregory to winter in Cornwall; where Watt acknowledged that his son was also able to pursue his interests in geology and mining technology 'At the same time that he is securing his health he is acquiring knowledge in his business'.[208] On Giddy's advice Gregory Watt lodged in Penzance with Grace Davy and met her son Humphry the future chemist. Together the two young scientists roamed the Cornish countryside collecting rocks, accepted Giddy's invitation to make use of his library at Tredrea, and conducted experiments in the laboratory of the Cornish Copper Company manager John Edwards.

Possibly receiving similar medical advice another Lunar Society member Thomas (Tom) Wedgwood spent the autumn of 1797 in Cornwall before travelling to London in December. Tom's brother and sister in law Josiah (Jos) and Elizabeth (Bessy) Wedgwood took a house at Mount's bay from October where their third daughter Charlotte was born on 10 November 1797; later the same month Jos, Tom, their younger sister Kitty Wedgwood, and Bessy's younger sister Kitty Allen all dined with the Giddy family at Tredrea.[209] Giddy's diary recorded the Wedgwoods' active social engagements as they attended balls at the Penzance Assembly Room and completed excursions to Prussia Cove and Land's End, sending their carriage for Giddy and his sister, or stopping by at Tredrea to collect them, and dining together in Penzance. In February 1798 Giddy went with Gregory Watt and Jos Wedgwood to visit Copperhouse.

Bessy Wedgwood was the eldest of 11 children; her mother had died in 1790 and she was close to her father and siblings. Jos was sole owner of the Wedgwood pottery which he left under the everyday management of his cousin Thomas Byerley who had been managing their London showroom since 1780. Jos regularly saw his brothers Tom and John who was married to Bessy's sister Louisa Jane (Jenny). Tom's life was marked by recurrent health problems including headaches and rheumatism. In his early twenties

Tom's physical pain was said to be 'so severe that he would sometimes throw himself to the ground screaming'.[210] Jos was close to Tom and often stepped in with practical support. Jos and Bessy saw Jos' mother and younger sisters, who also had a house at Cobham, and his eldest sister Susannah Darwin who lived in Shrewsbury and whose father in law the physician and author Erasmus Darwin was living in Derby. While living with the Wedgwoods, by whom she was employed as a governess, Thomasin observed to Giddy that 'This House is perpetually changing Inhabitants, and I think none of them can be happy in the same place a week together.'[211]

The Wedgwood family had strong scientific, literary, and political connections. The Wedgwoods, Beddoes, Darwin, and Giddy all read and engaged with late eighteenth century debates about education; as did Thomasin. The Wedgwoods' interest in education was sincere and active. Children of the first Josiah Wedgwood and of Erasmus Darwin had been partly educated together at Etruria. In addition to arithmetic, writing, drawing, and Latin the boys' daily activities included 'two hours Riding or other exercise which will include gardening, Fossiling, experimenting etc' in the morning and French taught partly through 'conversation ... in the fields, garden or elsewhere as it may happen' in the afternoon; while the education of the younger girls included English and music as well as 'exercise'.[212] Jos became a robust outdoor sportsman who enjoyed shooting and encouraged his nephew Charles Darwin to do the same; Tom developed an active interest in experimental science, and enjoyed shooting and other outdoor sports when his physical health allowed. The Allen sisters Bessy and Jenny also received an education in music; when Samuel Taylor Coleridge stayed at the Allens' home in Pembrokeshire in 1802 he enjoyed 'plenty of music and plenty of cream'.[213]

Charlotte MacKenzie

After his first wife died Erasmus Darwin had two daughters with his children's governess Mary Parker but they did not marry; in 1794 Darwin helped his daughters Susan and Mary Parker to establish a boarding school for girls, and published *A plan for the conduct of female education in boarding schools* in 1797. Jos later provided a loan and financial advice to two Byerley cousins who had opened a girls' school in Warwick; and he built a school at Etruria.[214] Beddoes married Anna Edgeworth whose father and sister's *Practical education* (1798) promoted Beddoes' idea that 'rational toys' might combine amusement with instruction. Tom endeavoured unsuccessfully to bring together Beddoes, William Godwin, Coleridge, and Wordsworth to conduct research and operate a school in London which he would fund.[215] Beddoes commissioned artists to make working models of his rational toys; he established a committee to develop plans for a manufactory which included John Wedgwood, and that issued a prospectus inviting subscriptions in 1800.[216]

Jos and Bessy intended to home educate their children. Tom's notebooks included extensive reflections on associationist psychology and child development. His reflections were based on observations of himself and of his nieces and nephews, partly with a view to understanding and improving his experience living with chronic health problems.[217] It is possible that Tom's observations and conversations influenced Jos and Bessy's initial decision to employ a governess. Tom's conclusion that attention to the health and emotional well-being of children was of prime importance in enabling their development into happy and benevolent adults was later echoed by Jos in a letter to a prospective governess in which he referred to the importance of 'steady attention to the health, disposition, and manners of our children'.

Early in 1797 Jos and Bessy recruited Everina the youngest sister of Mary Wollstonecraft as their children's governess. When Godwin stayed with the Wedgwoods at Etruria near

Stoke on Trent in June the same year he told Mary that Everina seemed happy.[218] In September Mary died; Everina visited her sister Eliza Bishop in Ireland, and did not return to the Wedgwoods. Everina's choice at that time opened the way for Thomasin to be recruited by the Wedgwoods as their next governess.

In Cornwall Jos asked Giddy's advice about a new governess for their young family; at the time they had four young children Sarah Elizabeth (B.) aged 4, Josiah (Joe) aged 3, Mary Anne aged 1, and the new baby. Giddy promptly recommended Thomasin noting in his diary on 17 March 1798 'I found a note in Marazion Post Office. Rode on to Penzance and talked with Mrs Wedgwood. Rode on to Miss Dennis. The whole business settled. Walked back with Miss Dennis. Slept at Mrs Wedgwoods.'[219] Two months later Thomasin travelled with the Wedgwoods when they returned to their home at Stoke house near Cobham in Surrey where she lived for the first 15 months of her employment. Thomasin was the eldest of eight children and aged 13 when her youngest brother Richard was born; she had been educated mostly at home and through individual reading.

Most governesses lived as part of the household. When Godwin stayed at Etruria he complained that the widowed Mrs Wedgwood held a dinner party which lasted eight hours; Everina did not attend. Five years later a letter from Jos to a 'Miss Webster' explained at some length the Wedgwoods' expectations of a new governess and how they preferred to organise their household

> I returned home yesterday, and I am happy to find that Mrs Wedgwood had not entered into any engagement in my absence. We shall therefore be happy if you accept our situation after I have given you a fuller account of it, than I could do, when I had the pleasure of seeing you.

Our family consists of five children, of whom the eldest is not quite nine years old. We have wished for a governess, not so much for the sake of the accomplishments that are often a principal object in education, as to secure the constant superintendence of a respectable person on whom we may rely for a steady attention to the health, disposition, and manners of our children, and to prevent the necessity of their being much with servants. We have consequently made it a point that the children should live as much as possible with the governess, when not with ourselves, and she has breakfasted and drunk tea with the children. She has taken her dinner with us, except when we have had parties; and we have always been desirous that she should join our family party whenever it was agreeable to herself. Our situation is very retired, and I am afraid the very little society it might afford you would not prevent you being very sensible of the difference between it and a lively town.

Some of the disagreeable feeling which will, in almost all cases, attend the undertaking such a situation, especially for the first time, might perhaps be prevented, if mutual confidence could be at once established, and the parties rely on the candour and liberal disposition of each other. Allow me then to assure you that you would on every occasion be treated with respect and consideration; and that if anything should at any time wear a contrary appearance it would be the effect of misapprehension on your part, or inadvertence on ours. I believe I may refer you with confidence to the lady who is leaving us, as to this point and another connected with it, and equally desirable for you to be assured of: I mean our habit of expressing our wishes without reserve on every subject relative to the children, being convinced that a good understanding cannot be preserved without openness, and a freedom of communication.[220]

Thomasin was initially 'charmed with their [the Wedgwoods'] candour and politeness, and experience from them increasing kindness and confidence' and wrote happily to

Giddy that she already felt 'an affection for the children'; then in July that 'Joe is particularly fond of me', was learning French words through play, and that his favourite story was *The town mouse and the country mouse* from Aesop's fables.[221]

While Thomasin was employed as the Wedgwoods' governess Giddy's letters to Jos and Thomasin included discussion of educational philosophies. Bessy admired Rousseau's principles of home education. Thomasin necessarily agreed to follow the Wedgwoods' preferred system although she thought that both Darwin's *Plan* and the Edgworths' *Practical education* were more realistic than Rousseau's *Émile*. In September 1798 Thomasin told Giddy she thought Rousseau's system 'as romantic as it is impracticable' while the character of Émile was 'a composition of artificial sentiment and mad philosophy' rather than a 'child of nature'.[222] Jos was also a realist not an idealist; noting in a letter to Bessy in July 1800 that Rousseau had placed his own children in foundling homes and that the upbringing of Mary Wollstonecraft's daughters now depended on Godwin.[223] Jos and Bessy were aware that after her sister's death Everina Wollstonecraft had sought to adopt Mary's two daughters which Godwin refused.

Tom observed and noted the 'dejection of spirits & frequent fits of peevishness' of Jos and Bessy's eldest child B., which he attributed partly to physical factors such as being hungry, and partly to her education 'with Bessy Wedgwood'; Tom thought that the remedy was to frequently change the toy that B. was playing with to counter her robust notion of private property which Tom wanted to curb.[224] By August 1798 Thomasin noted that, as they became more familiar with each other, 4 year old B. 'becomes daily more petulant, peevish, tormented with an incessant desire for new pleasures'; saying to Giddy that she thought B. needed different toys which would occupy all of her mind.[225] Thomasin persevered and 15 months later wrote to Giddy that the 5 year old 'B. is really

Charlotte MacKenzie

an outstanding child her conduct for two or three months past has been absolutely

perfect and many of her observations are worthy of being recorded'; possibly an oblique

criticism of the impact of Tom's interventions on B.'s earlier behaviour.[226]

In January 1798 Tom and Jos offered to pay an annuity to Samuel Taylor Coleridge to

enable him to write full time which he accepted; after the Wedgwoods returned from

Cornwall Coleridge visited them in June 1798. Thomasin wrote enthusiastically to Giddy

that Coleridge was 'entertaining beyond anything I could have imagined, but I was

surprised to hear him say that Burns and Cowper were the only modern writers that

deserve the name of poet'; Coleridge's frequent use of figurative language in

conversation amused Thomasin and reminded her of Burns' *A song of similes*. This was

Coleridge's first meeting with his patron Jos since the publication of Charles Lloyd's

Edmund Oliver; Thomasin felt Coleridge was 'excessively angry' about the fact that the

novel's flawed, eponymous character was a thinly disguised portrait of him. Nonetheless

Thomasin admired the independence of Coleridge's opinions on politics noting that

'Almost all the other persons I have seen since I came here appear to me like people of

another world. Godwin seems to speak from every mouth'.[227] Giddy provided an

introduction for Thomasin to meet the satirical writer John Wolcot when she was briefly

in London in August 1798.

While Thomasin was working for the Wedgwoods she read novels and new poetry.

Thomasin felt the women in the family were sometimes unfriendly towards her and she

may have wanted to find or join in with topics of conversation. The Wedgwoods were

robust proponents of the abolition of slavery manufacturing popular porcelain brooches

and wall plaques in support of the campaign; in 1798 Thomasin read for the first time

the anti-slavery song *The sorrows of Yamba; or, the negro woman's lamentation* (1795) which she described as 'very affecting'. It was probably while Thomasin was working for the Wedgwoods that she first read Ann Radcliffe's novels; as a girl Susannah Darwin had played with Ann Radcliffe whose uncle Thomas Bentley had a retail partnership with the first Josiah Wedgwood. Thomasin also read *The memoirs of Emma Courtney* after Kitty Wedgwood told her about meeting the feminist writer Mary Hays, and she may have read Hays' female biographies and *Appeal to men of Great Britain* (1798).[228]

In the autumn of 1798 Bessy's sister Jessie Allen was staying with the Wedgwoods and they visited their sister Kitty who had recently married the prominent Whig political theorist and widower James Mackintosh. In mid October Bessy wrote to another sister Emma Allen about the plans they all had to attend a 'very grand Ball' in Guildford on 25 October to celebrate Nelson's victory in the battle of the Nile.[229] These plans may have been unexpectedly affected by the illness of Jos and Bessy's daughter Mary Anne who died aged 2 and was buried on 27 October.

Thomasin's efforts to develop shared interests with the Allen and Wedgwood sisters were partly successful. In the spring of 1799 Kitty Mackintosh invited Thomasin to London. Thomasin was in London for two weeks; in addition to the time she spent with Kitty she saw her cousin John Dennis and stayed with a friend of his father. Thomasin and Kitty went to the Drury Lane theatre to see Sarah Siddons in *Isabella or the fatal marriage* and *Macbeth*, and Siddons' brother John Philip Kemble in *As You Like It*. After returning to Stoke House Thomasin went to the Epsom races with Bessy. The Wedgwoods' second son Henry was born in May 1799. Kitty was reported in the same month to have given birth to triplets, probably prematurely; she took several months to recuperate.[230] Jos and Bessy moved their family to Upcott House in Somerset to be closer to Tom whose ill health had worsened and who was being treated by Beddoes in Bristol. Thomasin and the children were the first to arrive at Upcott where Jos and Tom soon joined them; Thomasin encouraged Giddy to visit noting that there might be an opportunity to meet Maria Edgeworth who was visiting her sister Anna Beddoes.[231]

The Wedgwoods' role as patrons gave them substantial influence. Tom's scientific interests and patronage were driven partly by the search for solutions to his ill health. In 1799 Beddoes opened a research centre in Bristol called the Medical Pneumatic Institution. It was funded partly by donations from members of the Lunar Society, and Watt manufactured some of the equipment used by Beddoes. Tom, who was a member of the Lunar Society, became a patient of Beddoes; his donation of £500 enabled the new institution to finally open in March at Dowry Square in Hotwells. Other members of the Wedgwood family also contributed smaller donations. Since October 1798 Humphry Davy had been working with Beddoes on preparations for the new institution where Davy was appointed as the first medical superintendent.

In April 1799 Davy wrote to Giddy confirming that he had found a way to obtain pure nitrous oxide the inhalation of which made him 'dance about the laboratory as a madman, and has kept my spirits in a glow ever since'; he believed it would be a 'valuable medicine'.[232] In the same letter Davy noted that the Medical Pneumatic Institution had over 80 out patients. Invigorated by her recent visit to London Thomasin adopted a light hearted and sceptical tone in relation to the medical benefits of Davy's discovery noting to Giddy that 'one might as well expect Gold from lead as health and youth from airs that produce temporary insanity'.[233]

Davy's experiments with nitrous oxide advanced with the help of those who were willing to inhale the gas and describe its effects on them. After inhaling nitrous oxide in July

120

1799 Robert Southey wrote to his brother 'such a Gas has Davy discovered! the Gazeous Oxyd! It made me laugh and tingled in every toe & finger tip ... I am going for more this evening – it makes one strong and so happy! so gloriously happy!'.[234] In August Giddy 'breathed the airs with Dr Beddoes and Mr Davy'; staying with the Wedgwoods at Upcott House before and after his visit to Bristol.[235] Southey, Coleridge, 'Mr Wedgwood', and others wrote reports of the effects of nitrous oxide on them which Davy published in his research findings in the following year;[236] Tom and Jos both tried nitrous oxide. Davy also worked with Tom to review the latter's efforts to reproduce images on glass using light responsive chemicals which was a pioneering step in the early development of photography; when Davy moved to the Royal Institution in London in 1802 Wedgwood attended Davy's chemistry lectures and Davy wrote up and published the image making method 'Invented by T. Wedgwood, Esq. With observations by H. Davy'.[237]

In August 1799 Jos and Bessy made plans to move their family home to Gunville House in Dorset near the Purbeck clay quarries which supplied the Wedgwood potteries. During the following winter they divided their time between visiting Bath and Bristol where they stayed with John and Jenny Wedgwood at Cote House in Westbury, and with Jos and Tom's mother who had leased Cornwallis House in Clifton. In mid December at Cote House Thomasin was 'the solitary inhabitant of this great house' until Jenny returned from a visit to Devon. Thomasin was looking forward to Christmas when Kitty Mackintosh would be visiting. Humphry Davy called at Cote House while Thomasin was there alone, and 'sat a long time and was very communicative'. Thomasin told Giddy that she intended to 'make the fashionable experiment of the intoxicating air' with Jenny before leaving Bristol.[238]

The Wedgwood family then assembled at Cornwallis House where 'Mrs Wedgwood senior' organised a 'magnificent festival' to celebrate Jos and Bessy's seventh wedding anniversary. This was probably one of the family 'parties' which the Wedgwoods preferred their governess not to attend, and it may have been a traditional long dinner party like that which Godwin attended at Etruria in June 1797. Beddoes was a daily visitor to Cornwallis House to see Tom, and dined there while his wife Anna was in Bath for her health; Beddoes was accompanied by the Lambtons, two boys who were being home tutored by the Beddoes, to whom Thomasin told stories.[239]

On 15 January 1800 Thomasin returned to Cornwall to see her family for the first time in almost two years. Tom had obtained a passport to travel overseas for his health, and sailed from Falmouth on the West Indies packet in February. Jos went to see his brother off, and on 20 February Giddy rode to Falmouth to see the Wedgwoods.[240] Thomasin stayed in Cornwall until 27 March.

Following Thomasin's return Jos and Bessy had plans to spend April and May in London and then go either to Etruria or to visit Bessy's family in Pembrokeshire. As events unfolded the next few months were a difficult time for the Wedgwoods. Thomasin arrived to find Bessy in distress at her younger sister Octavia's acute illness, and this was followed by news of her death. Jos received badly timed and unwelcome advice from Giddy urging the Wedgwoods to allow Thomasin to 'partake constantly of the evening party'; he did not reply immediately to Giddy's letter.[241] When Jos and Bessy went to Pembrokeshire they left Thomasin with the children at Gunville. Thomasin was not happy but she discovered some enjoyable walks and as ever drew on her imagination to amuse herself; she became intrigued by a house occupied by emigré Catholic priests on the edge of Eastbury Park.[242] When Jos replied to Giddy he said that it might be better for his family that Thomasin left. On 16 May Giddy wrote to Jos urging him not to act immediately.[243] Jos returned to Gunville without Bessy for a few days in late May, when Thomasin said he 'seemed as miserable all the time as a hermit just beginning his profession'; but Jos did not speak to Thomasin about her position. The awkwardness surrounding Thomasin's employment was not the only domestic concern the Wedgwoods had at that time. The roof of Gunville needed to be replaced, the upstairs windows were boarded up, and for several weeks Thomasin and the children occupied the ground floor.

In June the Wedgwoods took a cottage at Christchurch. Thomasin moved in with the children in mid June and then Jos, Bessy, and one of Bessy's younger sisters joined them a week later.[244] Tom arrived home early from the West Indies and unexpectedly came to stay during the same month. The Wedgwoods made plans for Tom, their widowed mother Sarah, and younger sisters to occupy nearby properties in Dorset. As events unfolded Jos stayed in Dorset to see more of Tom; and Bessy made an extended visit by herself to her bereaved family in Wales. While Bessy was in Pembrokeshire Jos reassured her about his relationship with Thomasin during her absence

> We seldom meet for five minutes except at dinner, and then with eating, drinking, and helping the children, we manage to pass an hour with a few remarks. I believe if we were to live twenty years together we should make no further progress in intimacy. However, she does exceedingly well in her situation; she did not come here to amuse me. I do not see any signs of melancholy about her. I fancy my sisters visit has cheered her for a while.

Bessy extended her stay at her father's ending her letter to Jos one month later 'love to the children and Miss Dennis'. In addition to the works at Gunville Jos was getting the neighbouring property of Eastbury Park ready for Tom in September, where they were installing a hot room with equipment specially designed and built by James Watt; and his sisters had been to view Chettle House for themselves and their mother. Jos dissuaded Bessy from bringing a woman identified as 'Ridgway' from Pembrokeshire to Gunville because he did not regard 'Ridgeway' as a suitable person to be with their children.[245]

Giddy, Jos, and Bessy had been less than direct with Thomasin and all had a decisive influence on the course of events. Reading between the lines Jos was more amenable to Thomasin's continued employment than Bessy. When they were not with their parents Jos wanted his children to be in the company of an educated governess rather than a servant. Bessy seems to have been less comfortable with Thomasin's presence in her home and family. Thomasin had told Giddy she found her relationships with some of the women in the Wedgwood and Allen families strained at times. Wollstonecraft may have been correct to observe in 1787 that the children's mother could make the experience of being a governess 'disagreeable.... In the mean time life glides away, and the spirits with it'.[246] At the same time Thomasin did not communicate her concerns directly to the Wedgwoods which Jos later acknowledged was necessary to resolve tensions.

After Bessy's return in September, and the family's return from Christchurch to Gunville, Thomasin felt unwell and the question of whether she continued to be the Wedgwood's governess was decided. Thomasin wrote first to Giddy's sister Philippa. In early October Thomasin confirmed to Giddy that she had had a 'nervous complaint with a slight fever', 'difficulty of breathing', and loss of appetite; and noting that her spirits could be 'roused from the deepest melancholy only by hysterics and tears'. Thomasin was advised to travel for her health and told Giddy she wanted to come home to Cornwall.[247] Jos decided to bring Thomasin's employment to an end writing to his friend Thomas Poole, on the same day that Thomasin wrote to Giddy, that it had been amicably agreed she should leave 'on account of her spirits being quite unequal to the situation'; and asking

Poole whether he could recommend someone 'possessing a cheerful sound mind'.[248] On 1 November Samuel Taylor Coleridge wrote to Jos:

> Your late Governess wanted one thing which, where there is health, is I think indispensable to the moral character of a young person, a light and cheerful Heart. She interested me a good deal; she appears to me to have been injured by going out of the common way without any of that imagination, which, if it be a Jack O'Lanthorn to lead us out of that way, is however at the same time a Torch to light us whither we are going.[249]

Thomasin returned home to Trembath as she had said she wanted.

In January 1805 Giddy spent four days at Gunville where the Wedgwoods had changed their governess several times in the four years since Thomasin left.[250] When the position was vacant in the spring of 1803 Southey tried unsuccessfully to persuade Coleridge to recommend his sister in law, the former actress Mary Lovell, to the Wedgwoods.[251] The Wedgwoods ultimately sent their eldest son Joe to the grammar school at Ottery St Mary, the master of which was Samuel Taylor's brother George Coleridge, and then to Eton; and their three younger sons to Rugby and Cambridge. Their elder daughters Elizabeth (B.) and Charlotte later helped with the daily home education of their two younger sisters Fanny and Emma who also spent a year at school in London.

At home in Cornwall in 1806, with her own first novel *Sophia St Clare* at the printers, Thomasin enjoyed reading Godwin's didactic novel *Fleetwood* which criticised Rousseau's educational philosophy.[252] Jos and Bessy's son Joe may have remembered Thomasin and thought about her later when his first children were born. Joe married his cousin Caroline Darwin. They named their first two daughters Sophia, who died in infancy, and Sophy which had not previously been a Wedgwood-Darwin family first name.

Charlotte MacKenzie

The gothic novelist Thomasin Dennis

Thomasin Dennis wrote the first gothic novel known to have been written in Cornwall *Sophia St Clare* (1806) which was published anonymously.[253] The epistolary novel drew on established conventions of Georgian fiction with which Thomasin was familiar as a reader. Set in the imagined kingdom of ancien régime France it can nonetheless be linked to places and people in Cornwall during the French revolutionary and Napoleonic wars. Love, inheritance, and revenge were pivotal to the plot. Initially scheduled for publication in 1805 the two volume novel appeared in the following year after a brief delay and a fire at the workshop of its well known London publisher Joseph Johnson.[254]

In December 1806 the *Anti-Jacobin Review* concluded that the story was 'extremely well told' comparing it to Ann Radcliffe's *The Italian*.[255] Four months later the *Critical Review* praised the novel for 'sufficient intricacy of incident to keep attention on the stretch'; prompting the reviewer to discursively dismantle the machinery of gothic fiction:

> doors turn on their hinges by invisible agents; men and women flit along like supernatural beings; the very light of heaven is altered as it passes through the thickness of intermingling boughs, or through the variegated colours of painted windows: all is hushed and if the stillness be ever broken, the voices appear to come from spirits, who are above, around, or underneath[256]

The *Anti-Jacobin Review* had also commented on the novel's use of stock gothic imagery of gliding figures, flashing eyes, and chilling sighs. The pathetic fallacy was rarely used in the novel although at one point the convent walls seemed to be 'frowning, as it were'. As a first novel it was seen as showing promise; reviewers hoped to read more by the same author. Anna Laetitia Barbauld read *Sophia St Clare*, and later urged Thomasin to continue writing after reading some of her verses, as had the Cornish satirist John Wolcot in 1798.[257]

The plot of the novel unfolded partly through deceptions and disguises which were later revealed to Sophia. The fictional subterfuge and terror involved participation or collusion by individuals within the Catholic church. *Sophia St Clare* was written in 1803-5 as Britain resumed its war against republican France where Napoleon had recently restored the Catholic church; and during the final year of Addington's administration which indefinitely deferred Pitt's promise of Catholic emancipation following the 1800 Act of Union with Ireland. The novel can be read as anti-Catholic; a letter from Thomasin noted that her 'Father thinks Bonaparte in the wrong to invite back such a horde of priests, a class of whom his opinion pretty much resembles Godwin's, that they have no interest in society but only to gratify their love of power'.[258] Nonetheless the choice of St Clare as a surname was a knowing tribute by Thomasin to the first woman who wrote and established a rule of life for a religious order. The novel's critique of credulity included the fact that Sophia was 'ready to fancy myself a companion for sprites and goblins' who would have been familiar to Thomasin from the drolls and superstitions of west Cornwall.

Sophia St Clare has so far received little attention in the vast feminist literary criticism of the gothic genre. Written by a woman who has scarcely been acknowledged as a writer it merits scrutiny from a feminist perspective. Sophia is the most frequent correspondent and main narrator of the novel which tells her life story through 75 letters. Sophia is confined and faces dilemmas structured by patriarchy. *Sophia St Clare* might be seen as a courtship novel in which the realisation of love is revealed; Sophia is rescued by a family friend and they grow to love each other. Nonetheless Sophia's wish for their close friendship and declared love to develop into a companionate marriage does not come to fruition. The malefactors who mistreat Sophia are two female characters with many similar representations in folklore, drama, and courtrooms before and during the eighteenth century; a wicked stepmother, and a vengeful wife who directs her anger at her husband's true love Sophia.[259] The back story of another female character Mlle la Harpe, whose fiancé died on the eve of their wedding, drew on Thomasin's knowledge of the personal life of the feminist author Mary Hays.

When the vicar of Manaccan in Cornwall Richard Polwhele published his anti-feminist poem *The unsex'd females* in 1798 the list of women authors he found palatable included Ann Radcliffe, while those he repudiated included Mary Hays and Anna Laetitia Barbauld.[260] Polwhele's later editions of the *History of Cornwall* included Thomasin Dennis as one of Cornwall's 'literary characters' but described her educational accomplishments and writing of poetry without mentioning that she was a novelist.[261] Thomasin's poetry was largely unpublished; 'To a screech-owl' appeared over her name on 26 September 1803 in *The weekly entertainer* magazine which was published at Sherborne.[262] Polwhele may have been aware that Thomasin had written the anonymously published *Sophia St Clare* but if he knew he did not say. Three decades later the *Parochial history of Cornwall* acknowledged Thomasin's authorship while claiming unfairly that *Sophia St Clare* lacked 'incident … similar to those which are characterized in the drama by producing stage effect';[263] this evaluation would not have prompted Victorian readers to pick up a book in which the character of Lusignan provided a thinly disguised account of Davies Giddy's personality and conduct towards Thomasin whose life and relationships are briefly outlined here.

At the start of the novel Sophia is confined in a Carmelite convent by her widowed stepmother who intends to misappropriate Sophia's inheritance from her father. After her friend Isabella Poitiers intervenes Sophia is rescued by the Count de Lusignan and goes to stay with his cousin Mme Adhemar in Montmorency. Sophia is introduced to society; she goes to the theatre in Paris and visits the French king's court. Lusignan fights and wins a legal action to free Sophia from her stepmother's control. He and Sophia spend time together and realise that they love each other. The Baron de Valmont courts Sophia without success; it is from Valmont that Sophia learns that Lusignan will obey his father's wishes and marry a wealthy aristocratic woman.

Sophia returns to her late father's house. Lusignan is living a few miles away; he is unhappy in his marriage and frequently walks near Sophia's property regretting his mistake but they do not meet. Lusignan's wife is jealous and through a ruse imprisons Sophia in a 'solitary castle'. Unhappy and ultimately chained in a dark room Sophia becomes ill, is bled, and then removed to a cottage. Lusignan has been absent on government business; when he returns he is informed of what has happened and leaves his wife. The Countess is prevented from poisoning herself but dies a few days later. Sophia continues to be nursed in the cottage where she is visited by her friend Isabella, Mme Adhemar, and Lusignan who would now be free to marry her; and then Sophia dies. The gothic incidents, disguises, and deceptions occur during Sophia's two periods of captivity; as in the novels of Ann Radcliffe these were rationally explained by the end.

Historical time is disordered. In the novel the French king's court moves between Versailles and St Germain; historically the latter was occupied by the exiled Stuart court until the descendants of Jacobite courtiers were removed by the French republic in 1793. While Sophia is staying with Mme Adhemar she is introduced to Mlle la Harpe who is educated and interested in natural history. Mlle la Harpe lives alone in a house approached by a path through bowers of roses, honeysuckle, and ivy; wears a peasant

Charlotte MacKenzie

dress and straw bonnet; studies botany; collects dried plants, fossils, minerals, and butterflies; has a cage of singing birds, and a garden grotto made of 'artificial rock'. These fashions and interests place Mlle la Harpe firmly in the eighteenth century enlightenment; as does Lusignan's reference to the study of 'chymistry'. Thomasin's broad knowledge of sciences in her time owed much to her friendship with Giddy; she met Humphry Davy and had read in French the chemistry of Lavoisier who was guillotined during the Terror.

Geographically *Sophia St Clare* is located in Paris and in the rural districts and chateaus at Montmorency, St Denis, St Germain, and Versailles, and in a French convent; places that Thomasin had not visited given the largely uninterrupted wars with France during her adult lifetime. In writing Thomasin was able to draw on her knowledge of the nunnery at Lanherne in Cornwall. In 1619 an English Carmelite order had been established at Antwerp by Mary Roper, Lady Lovel. 175 years later the nuns of this religious order fled to London in June as French revolutionary forces advanced through Belgium during the Terror; occupying Antwerp in July 1794 despite the efforts of coalition forces. At the invitation of the Arundell family who were Catholic the refugee nuns settled at Lanherne.

Writers and illustrators found Lanherne and the Carmelite convent inspiring and evocative. Reverend John Fisher made Lanherne the prime focus of his volume of verses in 1801, and it is likely that Thomasin knew of and read these after she returned to Cornwall.[264] Letitia Elizabeth Landon (LEL) wrote her poem 'St Mawgan church and Lanhern nunnery Cornwall' for *Fisher's drawing room scrapbook* in the early 1830s. This poem explored the universal theme of what it might feel like to live a life secluded from family and personal relationships; it could have been Antwerp or anywhere. LEL wrote

130

four poems about locations in Cornwall; she was a professional writer who followed the same intrinsically colonial approach of writing after seeing prints of places which she had not visited whether these were in India or in Cornwall.

In contrast in 1836 the Truro solicitor and poet Henry Sewell Stokes published *The vale of Lanherne* and other poems with illustrations of the nunnery and St Mawgan church drawn by his wife Louisa Rachel Evans; Stokes' poem included the story of the nuns' 1794 departure from Antwerp. A year later Anna Eliza Bray's *Trelawny of Trelawne; or the prophecy: a legend of Cornwall* (1837) began with an account of the author's stay at Trelawne. Bray described the Trelawny family portraits, read some manuscripts, and tolerated her host taking her guests on an excursion to the 'gloomy vault of the dead' 'under Pelynt church'. At Trelawne Bray coincided with a group of priests who visited 'Llanherne' (sic) and 'gave us an account of the happy condition and hospitality of the Cornish nuns, among whom are many foreigners'.[265]

Wilkie Collins' *Rambles beyond railways* (1851) had a chapter on 'The nuns of Mawgan' which reintroduced gothic imagery. This included the local stories Collins had heard of a priest hole and a priest's skull in Lanherne. Collins' account echoed Thomasin's descriptions of the skull seen by Sophia and a windowless room in which she was later confined; and the private way to the chapel choir where the nuns sat behind a screen. In 1859 Collins published his gothic influenced novel *The woman in white* in which Victorian women's unequal legal status, inheritance, falsified identities, and wrongful confinement were pivotal to the plot.

In Cornwall Thomasin had access to Giddy's library at Tredrea and he borrowed other books for her from the Cornwall Library and Literary Society in Truro. Thomasin may have read novels from the circulating library at Thomas Vigurs' bookshop in Penzance or shared similar copies with her sister or mother at home. In March 1805 when Joseph Johnson agreed to publish *Sophia St Clare* Thomasin wrote to Giddy 'I hope he will not publish the work in a coarse manner like novels for circulating libraries'.[266] The novels published by William Lane's popular, widely distributed Minerva Press included the anonymously published *Lusignan or the Abbaye of la Trappe* in June 1801; the story of which was based on Claudine de Tencin's 1730s novel *Mémoires du comte de Comminge* and stage adaptation *Les amans malheureux* by Baculard d'Arnaud. In 1801 the *Cornwall Gazette* advertisement for Lane's circulating library listed *Lusignan* which Thomasin later used as the name of her main male character. As Thomasin wrote her novel in 1803-5 Lusignan's travels as a French political envoy echoed Giddy's decision to make the transition from local to national politics and his election as MP for Helston in 1804-6.

In her letters from 1801 Thomasin's jibes at the Godwinian opinions of the Wedgwoods and their friends were replaced by her own and her father's political observations on Britain's war and peace with France; not least Alexander Dennis' anti-Catholicism which provided one theme of *Sophia St Clare*. In 1802-3 Thomasin may have met Eliza Fenwick, the author of *Secresy*, who was living at Penzance and working in shop premises mortgaged by Thomasin's father. Since 1789 Mount Edgcumbe family viscounts had adopted the name Valletort; this choice was echoed in *Secresy* as well as *Sophia St Clare* which both included aristocratic male characters named Valmont. It is unclear whether Valtort's courtship of Sophia was based on Thomasin's personal experience. Sophia's married friend Isabella was most probably based on Thomasin's friend Josepha with whom she had corresponded from the Wedgwoods; her fictional name recalled the drama *Isabella or the fatal marriage* in which Thomasin saw Sarah Siddons play the leading role at Drury Lane in 1799.

Thomasin's friendship with Davies Giddy extended over fourteen years of meetings and correspondence with each other. By 1796 Giddy and Thomasin were friends. Their family acquaintance was sufficiently informal for Giddy to stay overnight at Trembath, or call there to have breakfast, before returning home to Tredrea from Penzance. Thomasin and Giddy spent whole days with each other as well as socialising together with Charles Valentine le Grice and Josepha Hitchins who were both regular visitors to Trembath. It is possible that they met more frequently than Giddy's diaries or their letters confirm given that Giddy did not systematically record personal matters in his diaries and neither built shared memories by recalling their meetings in letters.

A fellow student at Oxford recalled Giddy as an intellectually absorbed individual who was 'not attentive to his dress'; confirming almost a decade later when he saw Giddy in Cornwall in 1797 that although 'his dress and address are not very prepossessing' he was 'a good scholar'. In 1800 Anna Beddoes teased Giddy for wearing a red handkerchief around his neck. Charles Williams Winn wrote to Robert Southey in 1805 that he had coincided with Giddy on the Oxford to London coach whose 'conversation was the most entertaining and full of information, his appearance disgustingly mean'.[267]

In 1798 after Thomasin left Cornwall to work for the Wedgwoods Giddy spent time alone with Josepha Hitchins walking together from Newlyn to Marazion, calling on her family in St Hilary, and clambering over rocks on the seashore to collect samphire; Giddy was attracted to Josepha but their friendship was not sustained. This was the first of several other friendships with women which Giddy had during his long association with Thomasin. The other female friends included Beddoes' patient Lydia Baines in 1798-9, and Beddoes' wife Anna from November 1800; Giddy said he 'became great friends' with

Anna's friend Maria Thompson in October 1803; he met his future wife Mary Ann Gilbert in 1805. Giddy's relationships with Thomasin and Anna continued after he married.

In 1804 Giddy's sister Philippa became engaged to John Lewis Guillemard, a Fellow of the Royal Society, who spent some years living in France and America in the 1780s-90s, and who had been part of Beddoes' circle in Bristol after returning from revolutionary France and before leaving for America in 1794. Giddy and Guillemard had many shared scientific interests, and later spent family occasions together including at least one Christmas at Tredrea. Todd says that Giddy initially vehemently objected to Philippa's choice of husband.[268] Nonetheless Giddy attended the wedding at St Erth in December 1804, at which Thomasin would probably have been a guest. In September 1808 Giddy wrote to Thomasin 'I am too much subject to the influence of strong feelings myself, not to make every allowance for their effects on others'.[269] Giddy was not unaware of the feelings he aroused in some of his female friends; nonetheless he was seen by others as a cool headed and circumspect man whose conduct was honourable. He was appointed as an executor and trustee for Thomas Beddoes, and later for Josepha's husband the surgeon William Millet who committed suicide by shooting himself in 1829.

Giddy introduced Thomasin to the Wedgwoods with whom she had tea before they asked Giddy to recommend a governess. The Wedgwoods' offer to Thomasin caused some drama in the Dennis household at Trembath, with Thomasin and her younger sister Elizabeth both in tears at the prospect of separation.[270] Two weeks after Thomasin's appointment was agreed Giddy sent her instructions on propriety, character, and conduct. Giddy's guidance was as informative about his predilections as it was exacting, stipulating that the passions should be directed by 'the aims of reason'; that 'habitual Cheerfulness', gaiety of mind, and playfulness made companions pleasing; and that likeability was also enhanced by assimilating 'in matters of indifference' to 'the manners and even the caprices' of those with whom one associated. He counselled against sharing secrets, both private matters observed in the Wedgwood household, and personal confidences with new acquaintances.[271]

Thomasin entrusted Giddy with personal confidences but the tone and subject matter of her letters to him appear self-consciously crafted and mostly followed his predilections. Giddy was sober minded and preferred the company of buoyant personalities partly because he was anhedonic and self-controlled rather than expressive of feelings. In her letters from the Wedgwoods Thomasin adopted a light-hearted tone. Nonetheless when Thomasin was upset or dispirited she turned to Giddy whose attention could generally be relied on to lift her mood. A decade later writing to Giddy shortly after the deaths of her mother and sister Thomasin still considered Giddy's reaction 'I am afraid this letter is so little calculated to give you pleasure that I had better not have written at all'.[272]

Thomasin's nickname for Giddy was 'Cato' after the Roman statesmen known partly for their stance against corruption. On occasions Giddy was judgemental and intellectually aloof. Noting in letters to Thomasin in July to September 1798 that 'the Merchant of a small town finds his mind perpetually crowded with and indulging in schemes for the ruin of his Neighbours', and that he could not imagine anyone combining intellectual pursuits with 'tending behind a counter, or sedulously posting the ledger in a Merchant's Office'.[273] As Sheriff of Cornwall in 1792-3 Giddy processed creditors' demands and insolvencies of local traders which he may have found a tiresome distraction from his scientific interests. His remarks were tactless given the occupations of many of Thomasin's relations; but Giddy's prejudices did not prevent him from later marrying a small town grocer's daughter, nor from keeping meticulous accounts as a guardian of Thomas and Anna Beddoes' children.

Giddy sometimes characterised his relationship with Thomasin as that of a mentor and protogée. In Cornwall Giddy occasionally dined with Sir Christopher Hawkins at Trewinnard. In the winter of 1797-8, when the satirical writer John Wolcot called on Hawkins in London, Hawkins showed Wolcot an 'Ode to philosophy' written by Thomasin. With swift reasoning and ever ready financial calculation Wolcot observed that

> she seems to prefer things to words, substance to shadow, simplicity to affectation, in short a shirt without ruffles to ruffles without a shirt. I should like to see more of her poetical attempts and, if she wishes, make her known and put money in her pocket. There is on her a head of truly classic taste and if some lines of the Ode belong not to other Authors Miss Dennis will cut no mean figure on Parnassus – one line is particularly happy, viz: "And make the mental desert bloom".

Wolcot initially qualified as a doctor and clergyman but later earned his living writing as 'Peter Pindar'; he discovered and promoted the Cornish artist John Opie taking a share of Opie's initial earnings. Thomasin was sufficiently self-confident to form independent opinions of Samuel Taylor Coleridge, as well as Wolcot, which she shared with Giddy; and to later suggest to Giddy that Anna Letitia Barbauld might be willing to read and comment on her writing.[274]

Wolcot asked his friend and cousin by marriage Thomas Giddy of Penzance, who was Davies Giddy's uncle, whether he could obtain and send him more examples of Thomasin's verses noting

As for heroic measure I would not wish her to cultivate it, it is so difficult to manage in order to keep attention awake ... Bid her hunt nature for interesting objects (for nature abounds) and she can never be at a loss for a subject for her muse to work on – an Ode to Winter – to Summer, etc – to the sea – to the mountain – to the moon – to the sun – to Hesperus – to the bee – to the spider etc etc etc.[275]

It is unclear whether Wolcot's advice on how to cultivate her talent reached Thomasin but Giddy arranged for her to meet Wolcot in London in August 1798. It was the first time that Thomasin had been to London; she told Wolcot that she did not write to make money and that if she ever published any of her writing she would do so anonymously.[276] Some of Thomasin's cousins shared Wolcot's interest in the financial value of her writing, criticising her a decade later for selling the copyright of *Sophia St Clare* to Joseph Johnson; this encouraged Thomasin to explore the possibility of commercially publishing her poetry.[277]

Thomasin followed Giddy's advice on reading. In December 1798 she read Erasmus Darwin's *Zoonomia* (1794) and particularly admired the 'chapters on Instinct Sleep and Reverie'.[278] While Giddy was regularly visiting Lydia Baines in the last months of her life he and Thomasin corresponded about whether Darwin's belief that mental processes had a physical basis led to materialism. This discussion drew them closer but it opened up intellectual, temperamental, and religious differences between them.

Thomasin was interested in Erasmus Darwin's descriptive psychological observations of subjective connections experienced between waking life and dreams. If Thomasin was reading and discussing gothic novels while she was at the Wedgwoods that is not

Charlotte MacKenzie

something she acknowledged directly in her letters to Giddy. Writing to him on 26 December 1798 Thomasin revealed she had a vivid gothic imagination.

> I think the *Zoonomia* a wonderful book the chapters on Instinct Sleep and Reverie particularly pleased me. It appears to me that the incoherence of ideas in dreams is well accounted for by the absence of volition, external stimuli ... I am inclined to believe that Dreams are a species of Temporary Insanity as far as that may proceed from sensation & imagination alone independent of disorder in the system.

> I do not know how it is but I have never met with anything satisfactory in the subject of imagination, though it is infinitely the strongest of our faculties, and probably the parent of many of them. Having suffered it to acquire perhaps too much ascendancy over my mind, I will mention a for instance of its power which have always appeared to me unaccountable. Everybody I fancy at some time has been amused by what is termed Castle Building. At such moments a peculiar turn of mind has led me to picture scenes of grief or horror. A thousand times have I wept over the imaginary funerals of my friends, or from misfortunes happening to them. If I looked at the sea, fancy immediately transported me into a desert country where an exile and a fugitive, a wide ocean rolled between me and home. The sight or thought of a precipice was attended either with the idea of falling over it myself, or endeavouring in vain to save another person. Many times in a dark room I have amused myself with trying to fancy a spirit in a person opposite to me, and in two or three instances wrought up my imagination to such a pitch of fear, as by indulging it a minute longer would have had the effect of reality. I have for a long time discontinued the latter, after experiencing every sensation of the sublime that Terror can excite.

> Conversing on these subjects one evening with some ladies, I chanced to mention my own singular habits, which excited great surprize, at the sort of Pleasure my

Fancy chose to amuse herself with – Mrs Wedgwood wishes to hear your opinion

on a subject which she thinks curious, and what sort of influence indulgence of

such reveries is likely to have on the mind – I confess I feel some reluctance to

disclose these follies to you, and I expect that Cato will look very sternly.[279]

Thomasin had blundered through the barriers of Giddy's guidance on etiquette by

sharing her mental imaginings and conversations with and from the Wedgwoods.

Personally he may have felt Thomasin's imaginings were morbid and found them

distasteful, and wondered whether her 'peculiar turn of mind' reflected any deeper

disorder than a melancholy mood.

Giddy had previously encouraged Thomasin to read the philosophy of Edmund Burke

who associated terror with the sublime. Although Giddy was willing to promote

Thomasin's potential as a writer in his reply to this letter he cautioned her against

indulging her imagination. Returning the focus onto psychology Giddy likened

consciousness to a ship at sea in variable weather conditions.

> I would represent the first by a steady Gale filling the sails and enabling the Pilot
>
> to choose whatever stream best suits his purpose and at the same time to modify
>
> its direction; the second by such Breeze as will keep the vessel in that current
>
> where it happens to be placed, but is yet unable to prevent its being borne down
>
> directly before the stream; the third to a dead calm where the Helm losing all its
>
> influence, suffers the Skiff to be tossed about at the mercy of contending
>
> Torrents. See then Reasoning, Imagination, and Dreams.

It was the first of these which Giddy valued most and believed could be strengthened

through rational education; although he noted that 'The strength of any faculty will vary

in different persons' and acknowledged that imagining played a part in scientific

discoveries and inventions.[280] Giddy knew that Humphry Davy wrote poetry, and may have been aware that Davy valued and cultivated his imagination. Davy reported that

nitrous oxide prompted reveries in which he once noted feeling like a 'sublime being';

and wrote to Giddy on 20 October 1800 to tell him that he had travelled from Bristol for

the sole purpose of seeing Tintern Abbey by moonlight.[281] Nonetheless Giddy was less

welcoming of the role of imagination in scientific and literary creativity. Giddy would have

recognised Thomasin 'trying to fancy a spirit in a person' as reminiscent of the

superstitious belief in appearances, which his scientific education led him to reject.

Some of the reserve between Giddy and Thomasin was swept away. Their letters became

more informal and social with Giddy writing to 'My dear Thomasin' about Lydia's failing

health; and then about the marriage of Josepha's brother Reverend Thomas Hitchins to

Emma Grenfell despite the opposition of his mother Joanna Hitchins. Briefly abandoning

her usual purposeful cheerfulness Thomasin let Giddy know how miserable she was

feeling; blaming the conduct of 'the Ladies' in the Wedgwood and Allen families for

'every mortification, every painful, every melancholy sensation'. In contrast she

confessed 'I have always been satisfied even pleased with the behaviour of the

Gentlemen', and in relation to Giddy's plans to visit her in the summer that 'even the

uncertain prospect of it almost makes me happy'.[282] Giddy, who was regularly calling on

Lydia in the last few weeks of her life, fretted in reply to Thomasin 'Perhaps I have acted

wrong ... taking you from the bosum of your Friends and rendering you unhappy'.[283]

In May 1799 Thomasin told Giddy about her visit to London and seeing Mrs Siddons at

the Drury Lane theatre. She had news from Josepha in Cornwall who said that she had

been made ill because of her parents' disapproval of her brother Thomas' marriage; and

of Charles Valentine le Grice's impending marriage to his employer, his pupil's widowed

mother, Mary Nicholls of Trereife.[284] In the summer Giddy kept his promise to visit

Thomasin breaking his journeys between Cornwall and Bristol to stay at Upcott House in Somerset on 27-30 July and 4-7 August 1799. They spent these eight days as they had so often in Cornwall in conversation, reading, and walking together; all noted in Giddy's diary. On 4 August at Upcott Giddy also met Coleridge for the first time.[285]

Giddy had recommended Thomasin as governess to the Wedgwoods and during the time that she worked for them he occasionally wrote to Jos as well as Thomasin. After his visit to Upcott Giddy's writing with thanks to Jos was delayed until early October while his mother recovered from a severe illness after he returned home. Giddy's letter communicated his unsettled feelings at that time. Of his circumstances living with his parents Giddy noted bluntly 'If my conduct was governed by selfish principles I would immediately marry but under present impressions I should consider it a crime to be accessory in calling others to a station I myself detest'. He then explained to Jos that before his visit whenever Thomasin felt the Wedgwoods' actions towards her were motivated by pity or condescension she experienced their kindness as a 'humiliation'; at the same time Giddy communicated his continuing ambivalence about Thomasin's vivid imagination, and acquired taste for gothic imaginings, when he described her social embarrassment as an 'Hallucination' which was now 'removed'. He urged Jos to continue to extend 'civilities' to Thomasin and to include her in the Wedgwoods' 'domestic circle'.[286] Giddy's interventions may have been well intended but in the months that followed the Wedgwoods did not include Thomasin in their family gatherings as Giddy had hoped that they would.

When Thomasin was excluded from a Wedgwood family party to celebrate Jos and Bessy's wedding anniversary in December 1799 she poured out her heart in a letter to Giddy. Thomasin felt hurt not to have received any reply to her two most recent letters to him, she had a cold, and 'The children sick and cross tease me while I write'. Three days later she wrote to Giddy again. One of Giddy's letters had reached Thomasin after a delay because it had been sent to Cote rather than Cornwallis House; but she was now missing the books which had been packed ready for the Wedgwoods' move to Dorset.[287]

On 15 January 1800 Thomasin returned home to Cornwall to see her family and friends for the first time in almost two years. Giddy called on her three days later and they resumed their days and other meetings together. In mid February Thomasin stayed at Tredrea for four days. On the following Thursday 20 February Giddy rode to Falmouth to see the Wedgwoods before Tom sailed for the West Indies. On Tuesday 25 February Giddy called at Trembath after dinner, stayed overnight, and spent the next morning there. On Saturday 1 March Giddy and Thomasin probably both attended Josepha's wedding to William Millett. During the next four weeks Giddy called at Trembath to spend time with Thomasin on five occasions; and on Wednesday 19 March Thomasin called at Tredrea with her younger brother Richard. A week later Giddy spent the day with Thomasin and they walked together from Trembath to Zimmerman's cottage which was known locally as a place where lovers met. A decade later Josepha's younger brother Fortescue Hitchins published a collection of verses called *The Sea Shore* one of which celebrated Zimmerman's cottage as a 'romantic retreat, near Penzance'. This was Thomasin and Giddy's last day together before she returned to the Wedgwoods.[288]

In the late spring of 1800 Giddy's relationship with Thomasin came under pressure. Giddy was not without responsibility in the course of events. When Thomasin returned to the Wedgwoods at the end of March Giddy wrote to Jos asking for Thomasin to be treated with greater consideration and included 'constantly' in the family's evening parties.[289] Giddy wanted Thomasin to be happy but he had overstepped the mark with Jos who delayed replying and then said that he thought it might be best for his family if

Thomasin left; Jos then acquiesced when Giddy asked him not to act immediately.[290] Jos had probably achieved what he wanted in that he then did not need to make any change to domestic arrangements that suited his family; the governess would continue to keep the children occupied during his mother's dinner parties.

Giddy's request had coincided with the Wedgwood family stresses caused by the illness and death of Bessy's sister Olivia Allen and the inconvenience of needing to replace the roof at Gunville; Thomasin made light of the latter in her letters to Giddy. During the summer Thomasin, Jos, and the children coexisted harmoniously in the cottage at Christchurch, and Jos wrote to Bessy in Wales that Thomasin 'does exceedingly well in her situation'. Jos had kept himself some room for manoeuvre but Giddy was keeping a troubling secret from Thomasin which weighed on his mind; Jos' response to his request had left Giddy with unfair doubts about Thomasin's conduct at the Wedgwoods and whether the appointment he had recommended had been right.

In June 1800 Thomasin's mood lifted as she settled into the coastal cottage at Christchurch, went 'botanizing', and took seaside walks with the children. Writing to Giddy on 23 June Thomasin explained how she avoided being low spirited noting that 'it is only by shutting my eyes to these dark spots and opening them to the sun that I can think existence tolerable'. Thomasin urged Giddy, who was probably a deist, to become a Christian 'Even if it were a dream'. This letter crossed in the post with one written the same day by Giddy in which he confided that he was feeling unwell and feared he might have consumption; he was bled and stopped eating meat.

In Cornwall on 1 July Giddy accompanied Thomasin's father to breath 'Dr Davy's air' in John Edwards' laboratory at Hayle; it is possible that Giddy let Alexander Dennis know his misgivings about Thomasin and what Jos had said three months previously. Two days later Giddy wrote to Thomasin to say that he was feeling better; yet he seemed anxious about the future, burdened and dispirited, noting sardonically in reply to her nostrums of sunshine and faith

> Life is found scarcely supportable without the aid of Hope, apply therefore to some Fortuneteller, and obtain from him in exchange for a large fee some brilliant promise ... Who would not prefer such a state as this, to dry investigation of truth, or the possession of knowledge.[291]

For advice about his chest complaint Giddy turned to Beddoes in August, riding to Bristol along the breezy Atlantic coast through Cornwall, Devon, and Somerset. Thomasin must have noticed a shift in Giddy's feelings towards her but she did not say so, possibly attributing his mood to his health concerns; Giddy was later dubbed 'crotchetty' when he was an MP.[292] After staying with the Beddoes on this occasion Giddy entered into a correspondence with Anna who was attracted to her husband's friend.[293]

In September Bessy returned to Dorset and the Wedgwood family moved into Gunville. In *Sophia St Clare* Valmont breaks the news to Sophia that Lusignan will obey his father and marry an aristocratic woman. Giddy's letters to Jos had revealed the relationship between his circumstances living in his parental home and his attitude towards marriage; Jos or Bessy might have mentioned to Thomasin that Giddy had told Jos he had no immediate intention to marry because they recognised that Giddy had not entered into any formal engagement, they were aware of Thomasin's feelings for him, and thought that she should know.[294]

In 1798 when she first started working for the Wedgwoods Thomasin commented to Giddy that when Bessy was away books were her only companion; that quite suited

Thomasin because at times there was friction or unspoken tension between herself and Bessy, as well as with Jos' mother. As reported in her letters Thomasin's mood was most carefree with male company, the children, walks she enjoyed, and time to read. On 25 September Giddy wrote to ask how Thomasin was after his sister received a letter in which Thomasin said she was unwell. Thomasin wrote on 9 October to tell Giddy she had a 'nervous complaint with slight fever', 'a violent oppression on the breast with difficulty of breathing', had lost her appetite, and that her spirits could be 'roused from the deepest melancholy only by hysterics and tears'. Thomasin told Giddy she wanted to come home to Cornwall; and on 6 November Giddy wrote to let Jos know.[295]

By 12 November Thomasin was at Trembath and Giddy called to see her. Thomasin and Giddy each had feelings for the other but in their letters they often communicated obliquely through classical allusions, Thomasin's playful jibes, and gossip about the love affairs and wedding plans of others. If Thomasin had wanted to be with Giddy they were once again living a few miles from each other, but after she returned there was a hiatus in their regular meetings or letters. When Giddy arrived back at Tredrea after seeing Thomasin on 12 November he noted that his mother was 'very bad'; during the later years of Catherine Giddy's life the family organised their activities so that she always had her husband, son, or daughter at home with her.[296]

Thomasin was 30 years old; her other friends and contemporaries in Cornwall were marrying and starting families. After leaving the Wedgwoods Thomasin may have missed the constant presence of Jos and Bessy's children. If Thomasin wanted to write, she had previously been urged to write for publication, and also had financial support from her family. If Thomasin wanted to be employed she might have found a new job as a schoolteacher or governess. Her own disregard for shopkeeping, possibly echoing Giddy, reduced her other options. Thomasin had friends in Cornwall including Charles Valentine le Grice who discussed classical and other literature with her and may have commented on her writing. Their friendship did not end with le Grice's marriage and he later visited Thomasin with his young son.

Thomasin had previously socialised with Giddy's sister Philippa, and with Josepha. The latter friendship was largely discontinued after Josepha's marriage. Josepha's father Reverend Malachy Hitchins was said 'to be cruel cast down with the unhappy marriage of his only daughter' and Josepha's husband William Millet was described as 'a hard man, sure enough'.[297] The Hitchins family estrangement and tensions caused by Josepha's choice of husband did not diminish after she moved to Liskeard by 1805 with her husband and children before the family later returned to live at Marazion.[298] Thomasin was occasionally in contact with Philippa whose availability like Giddy's was affected by the demands of their parents, and later by Philippa's marriage and move to London. Thomasin developed new female friendships with a Miss Tregellas of St Agnes; and a few years later with a Miss Macdonald who moved to Penzance on doctors' advice for the winter of 1806-7 and then stayed for a second year.

After returning to Trembath in November 1800 Thomasin initially felt better and then in January 1801 told Giddy that her complaint had 'returned' and was worse than when she was at Gunville. Although they were now living within a few miles of each other Giddy proposed resuming their correspondence, which Thomasin welcomed because she said she could communicate with him 'with the freedom one uses to a Brother and the confidence as to a Father'.[299] Giddy wrote to her regularly, and began calling again at Trembath from early March. Thomasin then stayed at Tredrea for four days 20-23 May 1801. In Thomasin's novel Sophia realises she loves Lusignan because of the jealousy she feels when she sees him talking to another woman in a box at the theatre. The correspondence that Anna Beddoes had started with Giddy was continuing and it is possible that Thomasin became aware of this when she was staying at Tredrea.

Thomasin's letters to Giddy do not say how long or continuously she had symptoms, what these were, whether she received any diagnosis, and the extent to which she was prescribed medicines or other physical treatments. In the autumn Giddy took Thomasin a preparation of bark which had helped his mother, Thomasin found it beneficial and asked for more. By November 1801 Thomasin could look back on

> The experience of the last twelve months ... I believe there are few evils which a mind able to command itself, and accustomed to exert it's powers, may not support with patience, but ill health when it affects the spirits preys upon the mind as well as the body and reduces both to the same languid state.[300]

In December Thomasin went to stay with Miss Tregellas at St Agnes for a month. She talked with Miss Tregellas about the gothic; if Thomasin visited Lanherne before writing *Sophia St Clare* it may have been during one of her visits to Miss Tregellas. Giddy and Thomasin both had further bouts of ill health in the summer of 1802, when Thomasin had leeches applied to her temples for an inflamed eye.

In July 1801 Anna had written to Giddy 'I would infinitely rather be mistress to the man I love than wife, but since this is contrary to all custom, I must be contented with being wife in the usual way'. Faced with direct offers from Anna to be his mistress Giddy reminded her that geometrically 'two parallel straight lines can never meet'.[301] This principle of calculated separation applied to his friendships at that time with the two women both of whom he frustrated in their wish for an amorous relationship with him. Thomasin and Anna wrote poetry to Giddy who kept many of their letters and verses.

In March 1803 Giddy's mother died. It was Giddy's first experience of a close family bereavement and for a time he withdrew from his friends while continuing his other obligations. Giddy made a scrap book of memorabilia related to his mother which he kept throughout his life.[302] Thomasin's health was improved and she might have called on or written to Giddy or Philippa in the spring and summer of 1803 but she did not. Thomasin might have established a closer relationship with Giddy if she had taken the initiative to help him at that time. Instead it was Giddy who made the first move to renew their meetings writing to Thomasin on 26 September while Anna was staying at Tredrea. Giddy invited Thomasin to stay at Tredrea for four days 5 – 8 November which she did.

In the autumn of 1803 Anna stormed Giddy's defences. Anna had been invited to Tredrea by Philippa, travelling with her young daughter and a maid. While she was there Anna spent time with Giddy riding pillion through the Cornish countryside and talking freely. When Anna, her maid, and 'little Anna' left Tredrea Giddy travelled with them as far as Exeter. Anna craved romantic attention. If the bereaved Giddy had been more than usually neglectful of his appearance, Anna would take him in hand; she wanted their frank conversations to continue by letter, writing

> Oh I wish I had you here: I would cut a long sheaf of your hair off, and crop the stubble on your hands quite close and then see if I could not rouse you from your provoking apathy ... whenever the sulky cloud passes, and you choose to be as bright as yourself or the Cornish moor, take a large sheet of paper imagine yourself mounted on the white mare and begin talking to me on the paper as if I were behind you

At the end of November Giddy went to stay with the Beddoes in Bristol and arrived to find his friend Thomas was away overnight on professional business. Anna cuddled up to Giddy on the sofa and they kissed. Anna later wrote that from that moment she 'slept no more'; Giddy noted discreetly in his diary 'The evening of this day rather remarkable'.[303] Anna was nothing if not persistent following Giddy to Oxford in 1804, independently choosing to holiday near Tredrea in the summer of 1805, and travelling to London to see him at Philippa's in 1806. When Humphry Davy worked with Thomas Beddoes Anna flirted with him; after being rejected by Giddy in 1804 and 1806 Anna sent poems at Christmas time to Davy in London.

Thomasin sometimes flattered Giddy's narcissistic self-perceptions. Giddy was probably not a reader of fiction but Thomasin was. Her letters to Giddy occasionally cast their circumstances as like those in a novel. In February 1805 Thomasin quoted to him an exchange from Richardson's *Sir Charles Grandison* in which Grandison said 'I think I have done a marvellous thing to make a young woman in love with a man of exalted merit' and Miss Byron replied 'I think you have done a marvellous thing to find a man of exalted merit for a young woman to be in love with'.[304] Anna also convinced herself in relation to Giddy that she had 'warmed a heart glowing with virtue'. Giddy's conduct with his friend's wife was not entirely above reproach, although Beddoes was sufficiently unconcerned or trusting to facilitate opportunities for Anna to spend time alone with Giddy, and to appoint him as a trustee of his will. Only after Giddy met his future wife Mary Ann Gilbert did he suggest that Thomasin might meet up with Anna while she was holidaying in Cornwall, to which Thomasin replied coolly 'I believe that she does not remember me with advantage'.[305]

Thomasin's relationship with Giddy advanced her reading, provided opportunities to meet other writers, and inspired and encouraged her to write. Thomasin may have been unwell, as well as unhappy, in the Autumn of 1800 but it was also convenient for Giddy to identify ill health as the reason for Thomasin's departure from Gunville, and then for the same reason to step back from developing their friendship disappointing her hope that they might grow closer and marry. Thomasin was not an heiress and she lacked the forthright sexual confidence of Anna Beddoes as a married woman. Thomasin's ill health drew Giddy's solicitous attention. This made it more difficult for Thomasin to develop an independent life, including earnings in other employment or as a working writer. It was when Giddy temporarily withdrew from their friendship following his mother's death that Thomasin started to write her novel.

In December 1803 Thomasin sensed that Giddy's feelings had changed. In the new year Thomasin asked Giddy to help her to find a publisher for the novel she was writing. During the time that she was writing Thomasin regularly saw Charles Valentine le Grice and his young son Day Perry; in 1804 Giddy was mostly in London after he was first elected as an MP for Helston in May. Thomasin initially told Giddy that the manuscript of the novel would be completed by January 1805, and she finished writing and editing by March. It was Giddy who negotiated the novel's publication with Joseph Johnson who agreed to pay 10 guineas plus 20 free copies, and a further 20 guineas if a second edition was published.

This new venture provided a reason for renewed frequent correspondence between Thomasin and Giddy. In her letters Thomasin wrote about matters which had previously captured and held Giddy's attention including her meeting in June 1804 with 'the philosophical shoe-maker' and Methodist Samuel Drew of St Austell whose *Essay on the immateriality and immortality of the human soul* (1802) was widely read. The fact that Thomasin had written a novel became known in Cornwall despite the book's anonymous publication and she wrote to Giddy about its local reception.[306]

The character of Lusignan reflected Thomasin's perception of Giddy, and Sophia was based partly on herself. The novel was partly a critique of her own credulity and delayed realisations. Thomasin may have wanted to place her relationship with Giddy on a new footing. As events unfolded in 1803-5 Thomasin confessed through the character of Sophia that she had 'felt the misery of cruel disappointment as I can feel it no more. The pretended friend may now deceive me, and move me but little'.[307] In the novel Thomasin described a patriarchal social order with willing acceptance. The plot turned on the misdeeds of the fictional female characters of a wicked stepmother and a vengeful wife, neither of whom had direct parallels in Thomasin's life, but both of whom exaggerated aspects of women she knew and disliked through the tropes of novels and folklore.

By 1804 Giddy rarely discussed matters which affected him deeply with Thomasin. He did not share any concerns he had about Philippa's choice of husband with Thomasin. In 1805 some of his briefer letters from London were hastily scribbled notes confirming the progress of Thomasin's book publication. Giddy ignored Thomasin's efforts to engage him in discussion of politics, not least his anxieties about his parliamentary career in 1806 when Christopher Hawkins transferred the Helston seat and Giddy was left unseated for several months before being elected for Bodmin. Giddy did not discuss his friendships with Anna Beddoes or Mary Ann Gilbert with Thomasin.

In January 1805 Giddy visited the Wedgwoods at Gunville. Later Giddy gave a copy of Thomasin's anonymously published novel to Bessy who immediately guessed who had written it and said she would get a copy for Kitty Mackintosh. After returning to Cornwall

Thomasin initially does not appear to have remained in touch with the Wedgwoods, but

following the publication of her novel their contact was renewed. In December 1806

Thomasin was considering visiting the Wedgwoods in Staffordshire, where Jos and Bessy

now lived with their family at Maer Hall; she particularly wanted to see their son Joe

while he was home from school.[308]

In the new year of 1807 Thomasin entrusted Giddy with the task of finding a publisher

for her poems, some of which were addressed to him. When Joseph Johnson declined

the manuscript Thomasin was disappointed but sufficiently confident to write to Giddy

reminding him that she had received approbation from Coleridge and Wolcot. Thomasin

suggested Giddy ask Anna Letitia Barbauld for an opinion which he did; Barbauld

recommended Thomasin write another novel rather than publish her poetry given the

literary market at that time.[309]

Thomasin's family experienced commercial and professional setbacks which may have

led Giddy to further distance himself given that his political ambitions depended on

patronage. On 1 August 1804 'John Dennis and sons' woollen manufactory at Penzance,

which was of timber construction, burned down; none of the property had been

insured.[310] Three years later Thomasin asked Giddy to help her brother John obtain a

position as a naval surgeon after his partnership with John Bingham Borlase and William

Berryman was dissolved; this was followed a few days later by another letter in which

she reconsidered and retracted her request. Thomasin's first letter referred to the 'fraud'

of one partner and 'selfish cunning' of the other which may not have encouraged Giddy

to associate himself with the matter;[311] John Dennis then continued trading with William

152

Berryman for a further eighteen months before relocating to the West Indies. Thomasin's mother Catherine died in December 1807; as did her sister Elizabeth six weeks later.

The wedding of Davies Giddy to Mary Ann Gilbert in April 1808 took many friends and acquaintances of both singletons by surprise. Mary Ann Gilbert was the daughter of a Lewes grocer. She was educated and is remembered in the *Dictionary of National Biography* as an agronomist; she was also an amateur poet and talented illustrator whom Giddy helped to publish some of her artwork. They met in St James in April 1805, at the dinner party of Dr Fly an Anglican clergyman who, like Giddy, was a Fellow of the Royal Society. Giddy engaged Mary Ann in conversation after hearing her mention a visit to Fingal's cave, the geology of which suggested Scotland had previously been joined to Ireland; he then undertook to deliver a letter for Mary and her mother to a Mr and Mrs Pascoe in Penzance. In April 1808 Mary Frewen of Brickwall wrote that

> Miss Gilbert to the surprise of every one here was married yesterday morning to a Mr Davies Giddy of Cornwall, the Borough of Bodmin he's an MP for. His father came down with him & married them, her uncle came in his chariot to be father, Frewen & co bridesmaids. The bride & groom & his father after signing all the necessary parchments set off for her aunt's at Hastings in a new landaulet. The uncle returned home to Eastbourne to be ready to receive them in the course of a few days. They are to live in her house in town if it is not found too distant for him to attend the House of Commons. I wish her happy she seems so deserving but I am mistaken if she must not give up some serious part of her religion. The father studied to show by his responses made very loud at church on Sunday morning he was not orthodox & behaved very odd about staying to the Sacrament. He has no church preferment. Frewen says she thinks the first time Miss Gilbert saw them was at a dinner at Dr Fly's. I should hardly think it, the acquaintance is of 3 years standing. Old Giddy was telling of the length of time

his estate had been in the family from Harry the 7th & never incumbered with a mortgage but it is always so with Miss F, friends they are all swans.[312]

Giddy had succeeded in fulfilling his father's wish that he should marry an heiress; their first child was born fifteen months later. Mary Ann later inherited a fortune from her uncle the unmarried Lewes attorney Charles Gilbert.[313]

On 10 August 1808 Thomasin's brother John dissolved his Penzance medical partnership with William Berryman, and then departed for the West Indies.[314] In her first letter to Giddy since his marriage Thomasin wrote with frank foresight on 15 August 1808 that 'no time nor event can restore me to happiness'. In a further letter on 11 September Thomasin explained 'I had just parted with my Brother going to the West Indies. The past eight months have been marked by a succession of events either one of which would have been a sufficient trial for my fortitude'. The deaths of her mother and sister, Giddy's marriage, John Dennis' departure, and possibly physical illness 'a long series of most acute suffering has nearly destroyed in my mind the powers of action'. Thomasin packed up the books Giddy had loaned to her and sent them for collection at a nearby inn 'formerly Colenso's'. Giddy felt rebuffed by the lack of personal contact but replied anyway on 21 September 'the continuance of a Friendship as sincere as ever charmed my Heart is at your command and will so continue even though at this time it should not be accepted'. They remained in contact and in a later letter Thomasin included brief congratulations on the birth of his first child. With Giddy continuing his relationships on long-established parallel lines Thomasin never met Mary Ann Gilbert although Giddy made it plain that he kept no secrets from his wife.[315]

In the spring of 1809 Thomasin wrote to tell Giddy she had been ill for the previous four months and asked him to return the manuscript book of her poems; probably those which Giddy had shown in 1807 to Joseph Johnson and Anna Letitia Barbauld. Giddy did

not have the manuscript with him in London and promised to return it when he was next

at Tredrea which he soon did.[316] Thomasin's youngest brother Richard Dennis married

Patience Vinnicombe in March 1809. The newly weds occupied Trembath where

Thomasin died in late August the same year. Giddy was then in contact with Richard

Dennis who, at Giddy's request, agreed to return Giddy's letters to Thomasin to him; but

said the family wanted time to consider what to do with Thomasin's poems. These were

not published. Three decades later Giddy noted that 'Nothing of her poetry has been

given to the public; nor would it now be fair to print a few trifles'; an extant manuscript

of Thomasin Dennis' poems was listed in *Bibliotheca Cornubiensis* (1874) probably on

the basis of Giddy's report.[317] If the Dennis family eventually passed the manuscript on

to Giddy it is no longer part of his extensive papers now held in public archives and

which include verses by Anna Beddoes.

Thomasin's father Alexander Dennis was affected by the deaths of his wife Catherine and

two adult daughters Elizabeth and Thomasin, as well as the departure of his eldest adult

son John for the West Indies. The year after Thomasin died Alexander Dennis went on a

tour of England and Scotland. Alexander kept a journal with straightforward descriptive

summaries of where he went, what he did, and who he met. Alexander's journal of his

tour was later published by Thomas Vigurs of Penzance.[318] Alexander lived at Tolcarne

while Richard and Patience and their growing family continued to occupy Trembath.

Three of Richard Dennis' sons emigrated to Australia where the family have farmed at

Tarndwarncoort since 1840 and export hand-dyed wool.

Giddy was reactionary in the political opinions he voiced and voted for as a member of

Parliament. The book Beddoes dedicated to Giddy in 1793 described the right of children to education as 'imprescriptible';[319] as an MP Giddy opposed parish schools. Giddy, who changed his surname to Gilbert in 1817 to meet the requirements of Charles Gilbert's will, consistently opposed political reform; the 1832 Reform Act ended Gilbert's parliamentary career by abolishing the Bodmin borough seat he had held for 26 years.[320] Throughout his life Giddy retained most of Thomasin's letters to him and a copy of her novel; many years after Thomasin's death Gilbert had a Latin wall memorial to her installed in the church at St Levan.

The exaggerated extent to which Thomasin's learning was presented as extraordinary by Polwhele and Giddy said something about their personal expectations regarding girls' education and women in Georgian Cornwall; *The parochial history of Cornwall* included Giddy's evaluation of her novel.[321] In the 1920s Dr Joseph Hambley Rowe, then chairman of the Council of the Brontë Society, was one of the first to recall that Thomasin Dennis had written a novel, noting that he had been unable to find a copy to read. This was in the context of Hambley Rowe's efforts to identify historical individuals who became characters in Cornish folklore. Hambley Rowe was medically qualified and aware of the emerging science of hereditary characteristics. Partly because of Thomasin's renowned intellectual capabilities, Hambley Rowe suggested that another Georgian member of the Dennis family was the woman on whom the folklore character of 'The white witch or charmer of Zennor' had been based.[322]

'This magic country' the Brontës and Cornwall

Where do you feel at home? When Charlotte Brontë answered that question for Lucy Snowe, the protagonist of *Villette*, she described a room reminiscent of a mermaid's subterranean cave in a turbulent Cornish sea storm.

> My calm little room seemed somehow like a cave in the sea. There was no colour about it, except that white and pale green, suggestive of foam and deep water; the blanched cornice was adorned with shell-shaped ornaments, and there were white mouldings like dolphins in the ceiling-angles. Even that one touch of colour visible in the red satin pin-cushion bore affinity to coral; even that dark, shining glass might have mirrored a mermaid. When I closed my eyes, I heard a gale, subsiding at last, bearing upon the house-front like a settling swell upon a rock-base. I heard it drawn and withdrawn far, far off, like a tide retiring from a shore of the upper world - a world so high above that the rush of its largest waves, the dash of its fiercest breakers could sound down in this submarine home, only like murmurs and a lullaby.[323]

This imagery is striking from a writer whose family home was at Haworth in Yorkshire, and who was writing a novel set mostly in landlocked Belgium. Lucy recovered her health and well-being at the home of her godmother Mrs Bretton under the medical guidance of Mrs Bretton's son Dr John. Even the name 'Bretton' struck a chord of familiarity with Cornwall's seaborne cultural connections.

By the time she wrote *Villette* Charlotte Brontë was acquainted with the London physician Dr John Forbes whose first appointment after completing his MD had been in Cornwall at the Penzance dispensary in 1817-22; where Hester Piozzi described Forbes in

1820 as 'The Medical Man of the Place'.[324] Charlotte never visited Cornwall but the inner

landscape of her imagination drew on memories of her Cornish godmother and aunt

Elizabeth Branwell (1776-1842). Recollections of 'Aunt Branwell' referred to her room

upstairs at Haworth parsonage which she also used as a home schoolroom for the Brontë

sisters; she was sometimes described as being 'upstairs in her Room' while the children

occupied themselves with writing and other activities at the table downstairs.[325]

By all accounts when she was with others Elizabeth Branwell was a convivial companion

who engaged their attention.

> She talked a great deal of her younger days; the gayeties of her dear native
>
> town, Penzance, in Cornwall; the soft, warm climate, etc. The social life of her
>
> younger days she used to recall with regret; she gave one the idea that she had
>
> been a belle among her own home acquaintances. She took snuff out of a very
>
> pretty gold snuff-box, which she some times presented to you with a little laugh,
>
> as if she enjoyed the slight shock and astonishment visible in your countenance.
>
> In summer she spent part of the afternoon in reading aloud to Mr Brontë. In the
>
> winter evenings she must have enjoyed this; for she and Mr Brontë had often to
>
> finish their discussions on what she had read when we all met for tea. She would
>
> be very lively and intelligent, and tilt arguments against Mr Brontë without fear.[326]

Elizabeth Branwell refused to let changing fashion or etiquette get in the way of

continuing to enjoy her silk dresses, fancy boxes, snuff, social reminiscences, and

vigorous conversational exchanges at mealtimes. None of this conduct, recalled by

someone who stayed at Haworth parsonage and knew Elizabeth Branwell directly, was

characteristic of a Georgian Methodist.

For a century the Brontës' maternal family in Penzance was the focus of intermittent historical attention. The family origins of the Brontës' mother Maria Branwell (1782-1821) were first outlined shortly after the centenary of her death by the medically qualified Cornish antiquarian Joseph Hambley Rowe, then chairman of the Council of the Brontë Society.[327] In 1960 the writer and Bradford local historian Ivy Holgate was the first to seek connections between the Brontës' childhood compositions and the Branwell sisters' Cornish seaport origins; the influence of which Holgate thought had been superseded in the Brontë sisters' later writing by 'their own drab world' in Yorkshire.[328] Holgate's point in relation to the Brontës' juvenilia is well made. I want to show here that these influences continued to be present in their novels. In 2002 Margaret Newbold suggested that the Branwell family history in Cornwall included 'incidents' which had 'doubtless influenced the Brontë children and found their way into their novels'.[329] I think Newbold's intuition was sound.

The recent Brontë bicentenaries have been associated with more sustained attention to their maternal family origins and influences. Melissa Hardie's *Brontë territories* (2019) is a mine of information about families in Penzance and was the first to consider the Brontës' maternal grandmother Anne Carne (1744-1809).[330] Sharon Wright's biography of Maria Branwell made the stark point that the impact of their mother's death at the age of 38 'is plain to see in the Brontë novels, most glaringly in that their characters so often grow up motherless'.[331] Nick Holland's biography of Elizabeth Branwell suggested that 'stories told them by their Aunt Branwell' had a formative influence on the Brontë sisters' writing. Holland echoed Holgate in suggesting that, as well as sharing family memories, Elizabeth Branwell told Cornish folktales which he sees as having an enduring influence on surreal and supernatural elements in the Brontë sisters' writing.[332] This is explored further here.

Charlotte MacKenzie

Hambley Rowe's summary of the Brontës' maternal forbears did not consider connections between Cornish events or folklore and the sisters' writing. One of the first eight bards of Gorsedh Kernow in 1928 Hambley Rowe regarded William Bottrell, the Victorian narrator of Cornish folktales, as the 'posthumous founder' of the Old Cornwall movement. 'Brought up in an atmosphere of chimney-corner tale-telling' Bottrell was 'not the merely scientific recorder of facts of folk-lore' but the author of 'a type of narrative, half fact, half fiction' which recorded and imaginatively embellished historical individuals and occurrences. Hambley Rowe thought this approach was 'not without its interest and uses' disguising and recounting twilit truths through the entertainment of fireside storytelling.[333] It was an approach which lacked the candour and directness of Anne Brontë's preface to *The Tenant of Wildfell Hall* (1848) 'I wished to tell the truth', or the frank curiosity of Lucy Snowe's assertion in *Villette* (1853) that 'I always through my whole life liked to penetrate to the real truth; I like seeking the goddess in her temple, and handling the veil, and daring the dread glance ... To see and know the worst is to take from Fear her main advantage'.[334]

The article on Bottrell's folktales revealed Hambley Rowe's investigative and mystical traits alongside the pursuit of Cornish genealogies, and awareness of the emerging science of hereditary characteristics, which had been evident in his earlier discussion of the Branwells. Like the Brontës Hambley Rowe had family predecessors in west Cornwall. In his quest to historically identify several of Bottrell's folktale characters Hambley Rowe turned to Cornish parish records. He concluded that the real life prototypes of the pirate and the white witch or charmer of Zennor had been John Vingoe and Sarah Dennis who married at Sennen in 1743; noting the suggestion in Bottrell's folktale that the charmer's family had 'flighty ways, which every now and then (from grandfather to grandson in general) culminated in downright madness'.[335] Although the folklorist Robert Hunt sought to rediscover the earliest Cornish mythologies, other characters recalled in the Victorian printings of folktales by Bottrell and Hunt were based on historical individuals in Georgian Cornwall who became epic human legends.[336]

Throughout the second decade of his life Hambley Rowe lived on Mount Pleasant in Hayle. For Hambley Rowe, Bottrell's writing

> characterised the very spirit of all that we think of as "Old Cornwall". It is a narrow, winding lane of high moorstone hedges, topped with many an obscuring furze-bush and bramble, through which with a glance over every gap and an excursion over every stile, he leads us into this magic country … no-one who has once reached it has any doubt at all of its reality - it is "Home".

Bottrell's folktales evoked the 'intensely Cornish Cornwall' created by liminal experiences and narratives of landscape, history, and imagination.[337]

This was Brontë territory. After the deaths of the two eldest Brontë children, Elizabeth and Maria, the four remaining siblings were educated at home in 1825-31, with the girls' education organised by their aunt Elizabeth Branwell. She ensured that the household had a structured routine of organised learning, daily walks, and free time in between tea and bedtime. This was when the Brontë children began to create imaginary worlds and stories. At Roe Head school in 1831 Ellen Nussey recalled that at night

> Charlotte caused such a panic of terror by her thrilling relations of the wanderings of a somnambulist. She brought together all the horrors her imagination could create, from surging seas, raging breakers, towering castle walls, high precipices, invisible chasms and dangers.[338]

Strongly reminiscent of the ocean edge cliff buildings, crevassed coves, and sheer shaft mine drops of Cornwall.

The purpose here is also to take a fresh look at the historical evidence. Firstly to reveal the historical Branwells by removing cognitive biases and narrative leaps which lack evidence. Secondly to historically document that there were events, circumstances, people, places, and tales of Georgian Cornwall which were echoed in plots, incidents, experiences, and individual characters of Brontë novels, as surely as some featured in newspapers and magazines, or Victorian collections of Cornish folktales. Cornwall's topography, culture, society, ethos, maritime connections, and family experiences had a formative influence on the Branwell sisters and through them on the Brontës.

Central to this was what they learned as girls about women's lives and opportunities. The Brontës' grandmother Anne Carne was the role model for her daughters. Maria, Elizabeth, and Jane became young women in the last decades of the eighteenth century. In Penzance at that time the daughters of traders were mostly employed from their teenage years. The sisters received annuities from their father's will in 1808 which gave them each an unearned income of £50 a year;[339] they continued to be partly employed. The experiences of Maria and Elizabeth influenced the Brontë sisters most directly.

The Brontës' mother Maria left Penzance in the spring of 1812 after her parents died and the sisters moved out of the Branwell family home at 25 Chapel Street. Maria went to work with her aunt Jane Fennell at the Methodist Woodhouse Grove school near Bradford. A decision that may not have been easy to make but which led Maria to meet Patrick Brontë, marry, have a family, and create her own home at Haworth parsonage. In broad outline the protagonists of two of Maria's daughters' first novels *Agnes Grey*

(1847) and *The Professor* (1857) trod a broadly similar path working in education, marrying, and having children.[340]

Elizabeth Branwell was the most influential role model as a woman for Charlotte, Emily, and Anne Brontë. When Maria died Elizabeth stepped in to care for her Brontë nieces and nephew. In November 1821 Patrick Brontë told a friend that 'Miss Branwell' was 'behaving as an affectionate mother to my children'.[341] Two decades later Branwell Brontë sat with his dying aunt Elizabeth who 'has for twenty years been as my mother'.[342] In *Shirley* Caroline Helstone, whose surname derived from a Cornish place name, observed of the protagonist's governess and companion Agnes Pryor

> No matter that she perseveringly wore old-fashioned gowns; that her speech was formal, and her manner cool; that she had twenty little ways such as nobody else had – she was still such a stay, such a counsellor, so truthful, so kind in her way, that, in Caroline's idea, none once accustomed to her presence could easily afford to dispense with it.[343]

Agnes Pryor later reveals to Caroline that she is her birth mother.

Elizabeth recognised that work and an independent income were important for women. She contributed to the household income at Haworth parsonage, purchased periodicals which were shared by the Brontë family, paid travel and other costs of Charlotte and Emily's temporary residence in Brussels, and was willing to invest when the sisters wanted to establish a school. Finally, other than a japan box which was bequeathed to Branwell, Elizabeth's will divided her financial assets equally between four of her nieces: the Brontë sisters and Elizabeth (Eliza) Jane Kingston in Penzance who was named for her aunt and mother.[344] It was from their aunt Elizabeth that the Brontës learned about their mother's childhood home and family, and life in Georgian Cornwall.

Women worked. Georgian apprenticeship records, trade directories, and land tax books for Cornwall listed women traders including some who kept schools. At Penzance women traded as grocers, innkeepers, mantua makers, mercers, milliners, and other shopkeepers. These included the mercer Grace Dennis, the milliner Mary Gingell, the grocer Jane Penberthy, and shopkeeper Margaret Ward; the victualler Susanna Phillips and several women listed as innkeepers; and a payment from William Borlase to 'Molly Tregere at Penzance for wine & carriage'.[345] Henry Boase noted that Penzance in the 1770s had numerous 'smoking, drinking, and gaming clubs, of which there were some for all ranks, and almost all ages'. [346] In 1786 Penzance Borough resolved to try to reduce the number of alehouses by half to fourteen;[347] but they may not have succeeded in doing this. After John Stone died in 1793 his widow Elizabeth continued to manage the Ship and Castle coaching inn, including fortnightly assemblies in the Assembly Room, and dramatic performances in the 'stable theatre' above the horses' stalls. Elizabeth Stone later divided her estate equally between her five daughters.[348]

In many locations women predominated as early followers and members of Methodist societies. Lists of west Cornwall members in 1767 recorded that two out of three were women. One in three of whom were trading or employed in occupations ranging from shopkeeping or schoolteaching to mending fishing nets.[349] In 1799 when the Methodist itinerant preacher Thomas Longley moved from Redruth to Penzance he 'left [his teenage daughter Martha] at Mr Henry Pearce's as an Assistance in the shop'.[350] In the early 1800s the novelist and children's author Eliza Fenwick worked in a linen draper's shop on the market place in Penzance which also employed two 'shop women'.[351]

Female clubs and societies were established in Georgian Cornwall. Predominant among these were female friendly societies. In Truro in 1775 Josiah Wedgwood coincided with a women's procession to the annual meetings of two of these clubs 'who had associated for the same purpose that the men in this & other parts of the island do, to lay by a little bit of money whilst they are in health & can spare it, & receive it again in time of sickness'.[352] In Mount's bay there was a female friendly society at Ludgvan.[353]

Bookshops, circulating libraries, book clubs, and committees to provide town libraries proliferated in Georgian Cornwall responding to and building readers' demand. The Roseland book club, which held an annual dinner at the Queen's Head in Tregony, became known as the Powder Literary Society after it was usurped by women members. Out of a maximum of thirteen members the Society's steward Reverend Trist was the only man subscribing to the club which shared volumes of biography, history, literature, politics, and travel writing.[354] In the 1770s when Henry Boase commenced employment as a clerk in Penzance he was relieved to discover 'the only bookseller's shop in the town' owned by John Hewett; where William Borlase was also a customer.[355] The Penzance ladies' book club purchased and shared a range of titles with the requirement that each volume borrowed should be read and returned within three days.[356] By 1801 there were Lane's circulating libraries in eight Cornish towns distributing novels many of which were written by women and intended for women readers, including Thomas Vigurs' bookshop at the top of Chapel Street in Penzance.[357]

The Brontës' grandfather worked alongside women traders at Penzance. Of his daughters' commercial activities and employment in Penzance most is known about Margaret and Jane Branwell. Charles Fisher who married Margaret Branwell in 1792 was the son of a surgeon and Grace Treweeke whose father was a Penzance mayor; Fisher's

great aunt Mary Treweeke was later president of the Penzance ladies' book club. By 1797
Fisher had become sufficiently well-established as a printer and bookbinder in Penzance
to recruit an apprentice; [358] he died in January 1798. Land tax records listed Grace
Dennis as holding a joint lease with 'Mr Fisher' and then with Jane Branwell in 1799. [359]

This confirms that by then Jane had her own financial resources. If Jane had a subtenant
at Fisher's print shop premises they were not listed. This address would probably have
been the Fishers' home as well as shop and Margaret may have continued to live there,
and possibly Jane did too, if only to help her sister who died in March 1799. When Jane
later lived in America with her family it was printing and bookselling that her husband
John Kingston chose as his new profession in Baltimore. After returning to Penzance Jane
owned a shop on Causewayhead which was let to a jeweller by 1844. [360] As an adult
Jane's youngest daughter Eliza Jane Kingston, who had been born in America, traded at
Penzance where she had a bookshop and library, and was a lodging house keeper. In
1864 Eliza moved her bookshop and library to 3 East Terrace opposite the railway
station, well located for passengers leaving or waiting for trains with time to browse
rather than market place shoppers. By 1871 Eliza returned to South Parade where she
was described in the census as a 'librarian and tea dealer'. In December 1878 a local
newspaper reported the death of 'Miss Kingston, of Penzance, who used to keep a small
lending library in Parade Street and was somewhat eccentric'. [361] Possibly Eliza's library
had been assembled from the booksellers' stock of Charles Fisher or John Kingston, or
by her mother Jane, as well as any purchases that Eliza was able to make herself.

In Georgian Cornwall the families of farmers, traders, and some miners as well as gentry
learned to read and had access to publications tailored to meet consumer demand for
entertainment, information, self-education, and spiritual reflection. Book clubs

associated with a range of social, utilitarian, and faith groups were established. A gentlemen's newspaper reading room known as a 'newsroom' was established in Penzance from 1799. There were 35 subscribers to this 'newsroom' in 1806, mostly merchants or professional men including naval officers, who may have found it congenial and convenient for informal meetings or waiting between engagements in town.[362] The Penzance library opened its doors in 1818.

In the summer of 1820 Hester Piozzi took a house on Regents Terrace in Penzance for three months, writing happily on Friday 28 July

> ... nor is Penzance a Place like Weston super Mare, where when I asked for Books a Woman told me there were but Two ever seen in the whole Town – The Bible and Paradise Lost.

> We have here a public Library well furnished with volumes of Science: a Geological School where Lectures are read by Professors; and where I purpose to study with the Assistance of a Gentleman highly qualified, and of Doctor Forbes – The Medical Man of the Place, who meets me on Saturday next to Tea at the House of a highly-informed Lady – Mrs Hill: Great Grandaughter to Borlase ...

> Here are no Machines – or Appearance of Convenience for Bathing, but I am a good Waterspaniel, and shall be happy to plunge into this blue Sea tomorrow. Never was Sea so beautiful, so calm – Vessels going constantly to Wales – to Scotland, to London – *everywhere*.[363]

When Britain was a maritime kingdom Cornwall was not at the periphery. Cornish merchants travelled or sent agents to conduct their business in overseas ports, and some emigrants settled in Cornwall. These European settlers included the Jewish communities established in Georgian Falmouth and Penzance. Fisheries and trade with Europe comprised the majority of Mount's bay shipping. Returning home to Mount's bay in September 1776 the Methodist itinerant preacher Peter Jaco, whose first employment had been as a Newlyn fisherman, noted with satisfaction 'at this moment I can see nearly twenty sail of ships, and upwards of a hundred large fishing-boats'.[364] Ships carrying barrels of fish from Mount's bay to southern Europe mostly returned with Iberian produce including wine and spirits.

In Mount's bay smuggling led and organised by merchants was common from the activities of the Tremenheere brothers in the 1680s to those of John and James Dunkin a century later. Jacques Cambry's travel writings described trade at Roscoff in France in 1763–89 as mainly comprised of British smugglers. Products traded through Roscoff included tea brought from China to Lorient, wine, eau-de-vie, salt, flax, coal, and wood. René Yves Foucaud who died in 1776 left a manuscript account of his involvement in smuggling from Roscoff to Cornwall and Wales where he utilised local distribution networks and employed two agents; Foucaud was one of three eighteenth century merchants and shipowners at Lorient estimated to have become French millionaires.[365] A review of shipping records for Roscoff in 1783–7 found boats making regular trips 'from a multitude of small ports on the coast of Cornwall' including 87 recorded trips from Mount's bay and 91 from Coverack.[366] A century later this trade remained sufficiently clear in folk memory for William Bottrell to recall tales of eighteenth century tin streamers downing tools for several weeks in the summer to join a 'Ludgvan crew' and complete 'three or four' return trips 'over to Roscoff, in Brittany, for brandy, silk handkerchiefs, lace, and other things.'[367] Smuggled or not the silk, fancy boxes, and snuff Elizabeth Branwell acquired a taste for in Penzance were transported to her by sea.

In the 1770s merchants including John Copinger supplied tea imported to France at Lorient to British smugglers calling at Roscoff, undercutting imports of the British East India Company. These trading connections were sufficiently strong for Copinger to move to live in Cornwall from the early 1770s and for British merchants at Roscoff like James Maculloch to sit out the American revolutionary and French wars living in Penzance. The reduction of duties on tea in 1783 had some impact but salt, silk, spirits, and Russian imports continued to be smuggled in Mount's bay. When Henry Boase of Penzance wanted to travel to Britanny in 1785 he found he 'could pass over by one of our Mount's bay boats for nothing' landing at Roscoff; and in April 1791 when the smuggler Henry Carter sailed in an open boat from Prussia Cove in Mount's bay to Roscoff he travelled 'in company with a merchant who had business there'.[368]

There was coastal trade with British ports including transportation of salt for Cornwall's fish processing industry. The Cornish tin and copper trade and mining requirements generated regular sailings between Cornwall and London, Bristol, and south Wales. Tin ships sailed regularly between Penzance and London returning with cargoes which included plantations produce. When Maria Branwell was planning her wedding in December 1812, and preparing to move into her first home with Patrick Brontë, she asked for her things to be sent by sea from Penzance; they were lost when the *Trader* ran onshore near Ilfracombe.[369]

Mines drew commercial and scientific visitors to Cornwall. During the French revolutionary and Napoleonic wars naval shipping increased in Cornish ports. The wars and blockades at sea made it more difficult for British patients to travel to warmer climates, and doctors instead recommended wintering in Penzance.

Charlotte MacKenzie

There was transatlantic trade from Cornish ports including occasional sailings between Penzance and the Americas. The packet service for the West Indies sailed routinely from Falmouth carrying passengers as well as mail. Three generations of West Indian planters lived at Mount's bay where John Price was Mayor of Penzance, and Sheriff of Cornwall in 1774. The Price family had a house on Chapel Street and at different times occupied the substantial out of town properties of Chywoone, Trevaylor, Kenegie, and Trengwainton.[370] In 1792-5 Rose Price lived in Jamaica on his family's plantations.[371]

By the late eighteenth century an estimated 3 per cent of mariners on British ships were of African origin or descent, and other individuals of African descent lived in or visited Cornwall. To place that percentage in a comparative perspective Georgian Cornwall has been perceived as strongly influenced by Methodism; in 1791 just under 3 per cent of Cornish residents were members of Methodist societies.[372] Cornwall's maritime communities included black mariners and their families.[373] In these communities it may have been as common to meet a black mariner as a Methodist society member.

In Cornwall in the late 1780s merchants and professionals were at the forefront of the campaign to abolish the slave trade which mobilised widespread participation including Methodist and Quaker congregations. The Abolition Society list published in 1787 did not include any Penzance subscribers. Quakers were well represented in this list and these included five Cornish women who were traders in Falmouth.[374] In 1791 the Penzance ladies' book club purchased Olaudah Equiano's autobiographical account of his experiences as an enslaved African which persuaded many readers to support abolition.[375] By 1792 a newspaper reported that 12,000 people in Cornwall were supporting the boycott of West Indian sugar.[376] It is likely that by then this included the Methodist and Quaker congregations in Penzance.

In 1789 at Penzance Rose Price fathered a daughter outside of marriage with Eliza Robins; their daughter Elizabeth Robins was christened at Madron in January 1790.[377] In Jamaica Rose Price manumitted Lizette Naish a 13 year old girl described as a 'quadroon' with whom he had two children. Price later arranged for their son and daughter to be educated in Britain where Elizabeth married Reverend Alexander Lochore of Dumbarton in Scotland and John Price trained as an engineer before returning to live and work in Jamaica. After returning to Britain Rose Price married a woman of Irish descent named Elizabeth Lambart; they had fourteen children. The Prices lived in Mount's bay where Rose Price was a magistrate, sheriff of Cornwall in 1814, and active participant in educational and cultural organisations including being president of the Penzance library and the Penzance Society for the Promotion of Christian Knowledge. He was a vocal opponent of the abolition of slavery in the 1830s. Sir Rose Price's will, made and witnessed in Penzance, included annuities for Lizette Naish and Elizabeth Lochore.[378]

The men and women who were traders in Penzance were not without literary interests and connections which flourished during the French revolutionary and Napoleonic wars. There were published authors closely associated with Mount's bay families including the women writers Anne Batten Cristall, Eliza Fenwick, and Thomasin Dennis. Eliza described John Vigurs, the tallow chandler brother of the Penzance bookseller Thomas Vigurs, as 'a tall pleasing young man who reads much, draws well from Nature, & writes agreeable verses'.[379] In 1811 Reverend Charles Valentine le Grice, a former school fellow of Charles Lamb and Samuel Taylor Coleridge, boasted of Penzance's gentility and finery

Our ball-room too has few compeers;

See, see, those blazing chandeliers!

What music! ravishing the spheres!

And ah! What pretty little houris

Whose charms are more than ample dowries,

Lightly thread the mazy dance!

Say, say, ye Gods, is this Penzance?[380]

In the following winter the sinking of *HMS St George* off the coast of Denmark with the loss of almost 700 men prompted the St Ives attorney and poet Fortescue Hitchins to write and publish *The tears of Cornubia*. In which he criticised the jollifications and seeming indifference of some local residents to this disaster after two decades of largely uninterrupted war

Can you with smile complacent, gaily join

In sports where mirth and melody combine,

Threading the mazy dance; or more sedate,

Watching the ratling Die's uncertain fate,

As if your lives knew no superior woe

Than rested on the issue of a *throw?*[381]

In 1815 the Independent minister Joseph Batten, who was Anne Batten Cristall's uncle, penned an appreciation of Penzance in verse in which he recognised that Cornish women as well as men were educated

GEOLOGY too, 'mong all ranks, the trade is,

Beaux are turn'd Chemists, and so are the Ladies

The new terms of Science they learnedly quote,

172

Sing "Oxygen, Hydrogen, Gas, and Azote."[382]

These verses by Fortescue Hitchins and Joseph Batten were both printed by Thomas Vigurs, whose bookshop was known as a convivial Penzance centre for gossip, and who continued trading until 1838.[383]

In writing about the books on the shelves at Haworth parsonage Elizabeth Gaskell focused on the Branwell sisters' purchases and quoted from *Shirley*

> Up and down the house were to be found many standard works of a solid kind. Sir Walter Scott's writings, Wordsworth's and Southey's poems were among the lighter literature; while, as having a character of their own – earnest, wild, and occasionally fanatical – may be named some of the books which came from the Branwell side of the family – from the Cornish followers of the saintly John Wesley – and which are touched on in the account of the works to which Caroline Helstone had access in "Shirley" – "Some venerable Lady's Magazines, that had once performed a voyage with their owner, and undergone a storm" – (possibly part of the relics of Mrs Brontë's possessions, contained in the ship wrecked on the coast of Cornwall) – "and whose pages were stained with salt water; some mad Methodist Magazines full of miracles and apparitions, and preternatural warnings, ominous dreams, and frenzied fanaticisms; and the equally mad letters of Mrs. Elizabeth Rowe from the Dead to the Living".

As Mrs Gaskell might have continued her quotation 'From these faded flowers Caroline had in her childhood extracted the honey'. [384] Sea storms, shipwrecks, supernatural appearances, and the preferred reading of women or Methodists, all played a part. In December 1840 Charlotte Brontë wrote in a draft letter to Hartley Coleridge

> I am sorry I did not exist fifty or sixty years ago when the lady's magazine was

flourishing like a green bay tree – in that case I make no doubt my aspirations

after literary fame would have met with due encouragement ... - You see Sir I

have read the lady's Magazine and know something of its contents.[385]

Elizabeth Rowe's *Friendship in death, in twenty letters from the dead to the living* (1728)

was a best seller written by a woman which went through many editions and continued

in print until the mid nineteenth century.

Methodists in Georgian Penzance accepted appearances in dreams might be part of

individual spiritual epiphanies, as when Thomas Longley wrote of his sick daughter

Martha, to whom John Fennell had appeared in a dream, that 'We [Longley, his wife, and

Mr Fennell] all told her there might be something in Dreams and hoped it portended

something good towards her'.[386] Of the two Branwell sisters at Haworth it was Maria who

was plainest in her faith and wrote an article on 'The advantages of poverty in religious

concerns' which she probably sent to Patrick Brontë at Hartshead in 1812.[387] Elizabeth

purchased and enjoyed reading periodicals which she shared with the Brontë family

including the sea sprayed copies of the *Lady's Magazine*, as well as *Blackwood's* and

Fraser's magazine.[388]

Members of the Carne and Branwell families traded in early Georgian Penzance. The

Brontës' great grandfather John Carne described himself as a 'silversmith' in the

1740s;[389] his father Henry and elder brother William were shoemakers. Penzance traders

favoured the retail premises clustered near the market place. It is easy to imagine that

in the late 1760s the silversmith's daughter Anne Carne and the young Thomas Branwell

may have caught each other's eye as their families went about their business near the

market place. The Branwells traded as builders, butchers, and victuallers. Some

members of the family were later shipowners or mariners including at least one sea captain and several naval officers. The Brontës' maternal grandfather Thomas Branwell was the second son of the builder Richard Branwell and his wife Margaret John.

The experiences of the Carne and Branwell families shaped the expectations and aspirations of Maria, Elizabeth, Jane, and Charlotte Branwell. Their mother Anne Carne had the opportunity to know both her grandmothers, Frances Carveth and Eleanor Colenso, and to learn and pass on the back stories of both of her parents. Both Anne Carne's grandmothers left written records which confirmed that they were party to the financial and legal decision making of their families who had property and trading assets which made this necessary. Anne Carne's paternal grandmother Eleanor Colenso lived to be 90, dying in the year that her granddaughter married Thomas Branwell. Eleanor wrote a large letter 'E' as her mark.[390]

Anne Carne's mother Anne Reynolds (1720-75) was the granddaughter of a controversial former mayor of Penzance John Carveth and his second wife born Anne Darell (1667-1729) of Trewornan in St Minver. John Carveth was described by a contemporary as 'a very froward and litigious man'. He was an attorney with Penzance and other property and commercial investments including the Chyandour blowing house in Gulval, who later leased and lived at Nancealverne. Both Carveth's marriages were to widows who had inherited property. The first of these in 1687 was to Mary Tremenheere (d 1695) whose family were suspected of smuggling on a large scale in Mount's bay.

Following his second marriage John Carveth displayed obdurate tenacity in Penzance Borough affairs in the early 1700s. He refused to transfer the mayoralty to his successor following a disputed election, and locked the vicar out of St Mary's chapel of ease in

Penzance after a dispute over whether the parish or the borough appointed the curate.[391]

A defendant in numerous civil court cases John Carveth died intestate in 1730 leaving a

legacy of property disputes the last of which, between his grandson Peter Carveth and

John Borlase of Pendeen, went to the chancery court in 1739.[392]

When Anne Carne's parents Anne Reynolds and John Carne (b 1717) married in October

1740, their wedding licence was witnessed by Lydia Borlase. The willingness of John

Borlase's granddaughter Lydia to witness the wedding of her friend Anne Reynolds, who

was Peter Carveth's cousin, shows that the women were ready to put their families'

dispute behind them. Lydia was the eldest daughter of the local vicar Walter Borlase, an

MP's son and Oxford university educated cleric who qualified as a lawyer before he was

ordained, who was later a magistrate and mayor of Penzance prominent in civic as well

as parish matters. In 1750 John Carveth's probate was finally administrated by his

daughter Frances, a widow who had remarried to a tinner James Tocker in the year that

her granddaughter Anne Carne was born.[393]

As adults Maria, Elizabeth, and Jane Branwell would all have remembered their father's

parents who died in the early 1790s; but not their mother's parents. They had cousins,

aunts, and uncles living in Mount's bay. Their aunt Eleanor Carne, named for her

grandmother, married James Downing of Paul in 1781; her children were immediate

contemporaries as well as cousins of Maria and Charlotte Branwell, and Eleanor named

one of her younger daughters Ann Carne Downing for her mother and sister.

The Brontës' grandfather Thomas Branwell traded and prospered in Georgian Penzance.

Ten years after Anne Carne married Thomas Branwell he described himself as an 'innkeeper' when he insured his inn on the market place in Penzance for £500 in 1778; these premises were identified as the 'Golden Lion Inn' in Branwell's will written 30 years later.[394] In December the same year Customs and Excise officers called to inspect Thomas Branwell's premises. The official correspondence about this confirmed that the inn was his 'dwelling' and family home;[395] where at that time Thomas and Anne would have been living with six children including nine months old Thomas. In the three years that followed Anne had two further pregnancies and their three youngest children died in infancy; perhaps prompting their decision to move to a new home which was separate from Thomas' retail premises.

Customs and excise officers made routine checks on traders' premises and were sometimes successful in bringing prosecutions. Excise cases were common with hearings held routinely in the meeting rooms of Penzance inns.[396] The correspondence in December 1778 arose from the fact that Thomas Branwell had refused officers' entry to his house. No prosecution was brought after senior officials in London decided that there had been lapses in the local officers' administrative organisation.[397]

In the markets in which Thomas Branwell operated it is difficult to imagine that he would have been as successful as he was if he had not accepted and participated in the exchange of smuggled goods. The Branwell family's commercial conduct was generally characterised by financial calculation and tolerance as they even handedly assisted the rabbi Abraham Hart (d 1784) in finding premises for the Penzance synagogue in the 1760s; the Methodist William Carne to lease premises to accommodate itinerant preachers in Penzance; and the Quaker shopkeeper Grace Dennis to let her large retail premises near the market.

Charlotte MacKenzie

Women predominated in the Methodist society lists in 1767 which indicated when members were minors and participating with parental consent. As no age or confirmation of parental consent was given for the Jane Branwell listed at Penzance it is most likely that this was Jane Branwell (1740-1804) the adult daughter of Sampson and Joan Branwell, not aunt Jane (b 1753) who was aged 14 in 1767.[398] Nonetheless the marriages of Thomas' sisters Elizabeth Branwell to the Methodist shopkeeper John Keam in 1788, and Jane Branwell to the Methodist schoolmaster John Fennell in 1790, confirmed these two women's later associations with Methodism.

Thomas Branwell participated in ventures with other Penzance traders including members of his family not all of which were equally successful. These included a construction contract to extend the quay at Penzance in the 1780s when part of the payment was withheld by the Borough while some of the works were redone.[399] In the 1780s Thomas Branwell was able to extend his trading activities as a merchant and victualler, and he acquired shares in ships. In 1785 Branwell insured his premises for £800.[400] Thomas' eldest brother Richard Branwell later occupied and kept the Golden Lion while Thomas and Anne lived with their family at 25 Chapel Street. In the evenings the Branwell children may have watched people riding pillion and walking to and from the assemblies and theatre performances at the Ship and Castle, and later attended these themselves.

Branwell was a shipowner at a time when ships were the only transportation available to retailers. The shared ownership of ships meant that individual owners could not prevent their fellows completing voyages to which they objected. This was evident in Cornwall in the 1770s when the Quaker surgeon Joseph Fox of Falmouth objected to a trading ship in which he had shares being issued with letters of marque as a privateer. Fox felt so

178

strongly about this that he sent one of his sons to France to find and reimburse the owners of French ships captured by the privateer which had continued to sail with letters of marque despite Fox's anti-war objections. In 1777-82 Thomas Branwell did not own shares in any of the Mount's bay privateers; Branwell was not a Quaker so this suggests that he may have been a risk averse investor or lacked capital due to his family and other commitments at that time. Some Penzance merchants including John and James Dunkin and Richard Oxnam invested in Mount's bay privateers which were relatively successful in capturing prizes, and these merchants then became Penzance's most substantial shipowners for a time. In 1791 two ships used by smugglers who fired on a revenue boat off Tresco, the *Friendship* brigantine and the *Liberty* sloop, were owned by the merchants John and James Dunkin with whom Thomas Branwell owned another ship named the *Penzance*.[401]

In the following year one of the ships in which Thomas Branwell had shares completed a transatlantic voyage, which required substantial financial outlay. The *Nancy and Betsey*'s owners obtained an Admiralty pass for Jamaica.[402] On 5 June 1792 *Lloyd's List* reported the *Nancy and Betsey* had completed its homeward journey to Penzance after sailing from North Carolina; it was not unusual for merchant ships completing transatlantic voyages to call at ports in the West Indies and America to trade or service their ship. Port records in Jamaica are not extant for that year but it is likely that the ship's trade was similar to that of the *Nancy* brigantine in 1787 which carried 642 barrels of pilchards and 5 tons of potatoes from Penzance to Kingston, Jamaica, returning with a cargo of sugar, rum, tamarinds, mahogany, and 'old copper'.[403] Trade in fish, sugar, rum, and timber was of commercial interest to most of the *Nancy and Betsy*'s owners. In addition to Thomas Branwell the brigantine was owned by the fish merchant and cooper Thomas Love; the innkeeper John Stone; the shopkeeper Lazarus Hart; and William Woolcock possibly a relation of Thomas Branwell's brother in law Richard Woolcock.[404]

Charlotte MacKenzie

In 1793 the *Nancy and Betsey* was lost at sea near Lundy island after leaving St Ives for Swansea. The brigantine's captain Robert Charlton, who had completed the transatlantic voyage sailing the same vessel, was one of those who drowned. As the French revolutionary wars unfolded Branwell did not invest in privateers although in 1795 he purchased shares in a chasse marée named the *Liberty*; the other owners were the fish merchant Thomas Love and the grocer Barnaby Lloyd. This was not the same vessel as the *Liberty* sloop which had been impounded by Customs officers at Penzance in September 1791 following the shooting off Tresco.

Thomas Branwell increasingly prioritised investments in property which were least vulnerable to wartime and other risks. In 1789 Branwell, who was later a member of the corporation, had leased land known as Todman Gear to Penzance Borough on which a school was provided.[405] By 1790 Branwell was a freeholder of land in St Just which qualified him as an elector of the MPs for Cornwall in the same year; he voted for Sir William Lemon and Francis Gregor who were politically independent men with a reputation for advocating Cornwall's trading and commercial interests.[406] Branwell's joint ownership of the *Penzance* with the Dunkins, whose finances stalled and foundered after James Dunkin went on the run in 1791; the abolitionist boycott of West Indies' produce; and the loss of the *Nancy and Betsey* in 1793 may have decided the future direction of Thomas Branwell's investments. Thomas Branwell may have received property from his father the builder Richard Branwell who died in 1792. By the late 1790s Thomas Branwell was a substantial property owner listed in Penzance land records as freeholder of six houses leased to tenants and the occupier of other premises.[407]

In the closing decade of the eighteenth century there were eight Branwell family weddings of the next generation. Three of these were of Maria and Elizabeth's brother

Benjamin Carne Branwell (1799), and sisters Margaret (1792) and Jane (1800). Five of uncle Richard's children married in the 1790s in weddings which were all witnessed by Honor and Richard Branwell or some of their adult children: Catherine (1794), Honor (1797), Robert Matthews (1797), Thomasine (1797), and Richard (1799). Maria, Elizabeth, and Jane would have known that their eldest cousin Richard Branwell (1765-1845), a Penzance innkeeper, had been born outside of marriage to their uncle Richard and Catherine Veale and christened 'Richard Branwell'.

In the miniature portraits of the Branwell family Thomas and Anne appear to be a slightly incongruous couple. A plainly dressed woman, with a soft dark shawl around her shoulders, who looks as though her thoughts are elsewhere. And a dapper man about town with powdered hair and a top hat, gazing directly at the viewer. Maria was visibly younger than her sisters. There were strong similarities between Jane and her mother. Elizabeth in her early twenties looked like her father's daughter with a ribbon in her hair and a corsage pinned on her chest; she was a bridesmaid at both her brother and her sister's weddings around the time that these portraits were drawn.[408]

In the 1790s Elizabeth would have been more aware of family and other matters than Maria who was seven years' younger. Following winter shortages letters were circulated in six west Cornwall parishes in March 1795 urging people to prevent grain being shipped out of Penzance. Crowds containing hundreds of people drawn mainly from the mining districts around St Just assembled in Penzance on 10 and 11 March and were dispersed.[409] Maria and Elizabeth would both have been affected in October 1803 when tragedy struck at the Chapel Street home of Lemon Hart, the son of the ship and shop owner Lazarus Hart, and grandson of the Penzance rabbi Abraham Hart. Lemon's wife Letitia Hart received severe burns after a candle set her dress alight; Letitia was

pregnant and was delivered of a daughter who lived. Letitia died a few days later of the
fatal burns she had received in the fire.[410] Both sisters would also have known of the
destruction by fire of the Dennis family's woollen mill at Penzance.[411]

In 1804 when Grace Dennis retired as a draper and grocer after more than twenty years
Thomas Branwell was the commercial agent for enquiries from retailers interested in her
large shop premises.[412] After Thomas' son Benjamin married Mary Batten the new
partnership of Branwell, Batten and Branwell advertised to recruit a brewer in 1804. It
was in connection with development of this enterprise that Thomas Branwell leased the
Penzance shop premises formerly occupied by Thomas James Fenwick from Thomasin's
father Alexander Dennis in December 1807.[413]

A few months later Branwell's will itemised six dwelling houses let to others, and the
Golden Lion Inn on the market place occupied by his brother Richard Branwell; plus
freehold cellars and premises near Penzance Quay occupied by Branwell himself and
John Badcock. It was intended that these properties and related land would generate the
£250 annual income needed to pay £50 annuities to his wife and each of his four
daughters, while his son Benjamin Carne Branwell was his executor and inherited the
remainder. His total estate was valued at under £3500.[414] When Thomas Branwell wrote
his will only one of his daughters was married; the fact that he stipulated Jane
Kingston's annuity should be free of her husband's control was common in Cornish will
bequests to adult daughters at the time.

Despite or because of this extensive property portfolio it was Richard rather than
Thomas who owned the majority share of the Branwell family home at 25 Chapel Street.

Therefore Thomas also left Anne a 'Leasehold Dwelling House with the Garden and appurtenances' on Causewayhead which was tenanted by a butcher named Michael Rowe. If this was the Causewayhead property which was later owned and let to a jeweller by Jane Kingston it is possible that it had been Anne's childhood home, and John Carne's premises as a silversmith, and that this is what lay behind Thomas Branwell's decision to leave the property to Anne Carne as a family dwelling, place of employment, or source of additional income.[415] In the event, with Richard's agreement, Anne lived at 25 Chapel Street with her daughters until her death in December 1809.

The lives of three men of the Branwell family changed course because of suspicions of wrong-doing and related proceedings. The most grave of these was in September 1791 when the mariner Captain George Bramwell was named in notices of wanted men following the confrontation between smugglers and Customs officers off Tresco in the Isles of Scilly. This incident left two revenuemen dead and others wounded. After the notices were published George Bramwell does not appear to have returned to Cornwall, and he died as a French prisoner of war in February 1795. George Bramwell was a widower with a teenage daughter Elizabeth, the same name and age as the Brontes' aunt. Despite being left to fend for herself at Penzance in these difficult circumstances Elizabeth Bramwell later married Thomas Duncan of Paul and had a family including a daughter named Grace Poole Duncan.

Richard and Honor's daughter Thomasine was married to William Argall, a mariner who had been a midshipman in the Navy. William and Thomasine had two sons Philip (b 1798) and William (b 1800). During the brief interlude in the Napoleonic wars in 1802-3 William Argall was in Portsmouth. While there Argall hired a horse and chaise in which he was seen driving with an unidentified woman and a little girl. Argall drove them all to

Charlotte MacKenzie

London where he sold the horse and chaise separately. He may have been an impulsive man, or thought that the risk of prosecution was minimal because it would be difficult for the owner to discover what had happened, find Argall, and bring a private prosecution as the law required at that time.

After Argall failed to return the rented vehicle the owner travelled to London where he found and retrieved his horse and chaise. By chance the owner saw Argall walking on the Strand. Argall was unable to avoid a confrontation in which he offered the aggrieved owner £100 to drop the matter. The owner declined and had Argall apprehended. Argall was then held in custody at Newgate and pleaded guilty in court. The judge recommended clemency to commute the death penalty to seven years' transportation. In April 1804 Argall's name appeared on a long list of reprieves granted by the King which permitted convicted prisoners to join the Army. Britain had returned to war with France.

It is unclear whether or when Argall was informed of this decision. Held on the prison ship *Captivity* Argall wrote offering to rejoin the Royal Navy if he was pardoned. This letter was circulated in Cornwall and supported by numerous signatories who knew Argall's character, and a separate letter was sent by Cornish magistrates and others making representations on his behalf. The judge was asked for his opinion and replied confirming that clemency had already been extended to Argall through his court recommendation that the death penalty be commuted to transportation. In 1804-6, like many other prisoners sentenced to transportation, Argall endured a long and uncertain wait offshore onboard the prison hulk. In March 1806 Argall was one of a group of prisoners who left the *Captivity* to join the Army. Five years later, when Thomasine's father Richard Branwell made his will, Argall's whereabouts were no longer known to his family, who feared that he was dead.[416] Thomasine continued to live at Penzance with her sons where censuses recorded that she lived with, or visited and stayed with, other members of her family.

John Kingston travelled as a missionary in the West Indies and America before marrying Maria and Elizabeth's sister Jane Branwell in 1800. Kingston returned to America with his family after being expelled as a Methodist minister in July 1807. The Methodist Conference acted following allegations of financial dishonesty and rumours of 'improper behaviour' with 'two young men' in a case which had similarities with others where the disapproved of conduct was sexual. Kingston offered an explanation to the hearing in Birmingham for the shortfall in the Shrewsbury book fund of £19 7s 4d but was immediately suspended, and expelled four weeks later by the Methodist Conference in Liverpool. The amount that Kingston was said to have misappropriated was quickly talked up by his successor at Shrewsbury George Lowe who wrote to Mary Fletcher of Madeley that Kingston 'I believe has taken upwards of £100 of book money'.[417] The arrival of 'Revd Mr John Kingston and family' on the *George* from Liverpool in September 1807 was noted in the Port of Baltimore shipping report.[418]

The Brontës may never have met their aunt Jane (1773-1855). Historical records show that in the 1790s Jane Branwell witnessed the weddings of her sister Margaret, cousin Catherine, and orphaned friend Mary Michell; and briefly leased Charles Fisher's former print shop in Penzance.[419] Jane was aged 27 when she married John Kingston, moving with him to St Austell, Truro, Launceston, Nottingham, Shrewsbury, and ultimately America. In March 1808 Thomas Branwell's will identified his daughter Jane as resident in Baltimore.[420] The Kingstons youngest child Eliza Jane Kingston was born in Baltimore. Jane later returned to Penzance with her youngest daughter where they were recorded living together in censuses from 1841. Contemporaneous and extant historical evidence of Jane Kingston is lacking or inaccessible for 1809-40.[421]

This contrasts with a relative abundance of contemporaneous information related to John Kingston's commercial activities as a printer and retailer, and newspaper obituaries in 1824. Kingston was a bookseller and printer in Baltimore where he naturalised as a United States citizen in 1814. Like many booksellers Kingston was an agent for some patent medicines, and by 1816 was presenting his shop as a 'dry goods store' which carried a stock of books.[422] He may have sold his Baltimore print works. In May 1819 a Sheriff's sale of printing presses and other items in Baltimore was at the suit of John Kingston for rent unpaid by a Tobias Watkins, who may have purchased Kingston's old press.[423] Kingston was listed in directories for Baltimore up to and including 1819 and later moved to New York, once again establishing himself as a bookseller.

Jane was aged 35 when Eliza Jane Kingston was born and might have had further children if she had been living with her husband. One commonly accepted possibility is that Jane returned to 25 Chapel Street after her father died, because she had an annuity of £50 for her own use, and with time to see and care for her mother who died in December 1809.[424] When Anne Carne was widowed three of her daughters Elizabeth, Maria, and Charlotte were living with her at 25 Chapel Street. It would have been unusual for a mother of five children to return home to her parental home in these circumstances; and if Jane did so she might then have returned to America. Jane's annuity provided her with the means to leave her husband if she was not happy in their marriage. Whatever the circumstances and reasons for discontent, leaving a husband and children were both unusual at the time.

As was standard, the naturalisation process in which John Kingston swore an oath transferring allegiance from Britain to the United States made no mention of his wife or children. In later records Elizabeth Jane Kingston identified herself as a 'British Subject' born in America. It is possible that Jane was not comfortable with changing citizenship and left her husband, who commenced his application in 1811. John Kingston completed his naturalisation after 7 years rather than the minimum requirement of 5 years, which may suggest that he delayed his initial notice of application for some reason.

Jane may have returned from America to Penzance with her teenage daughter Eliza after her husband died. The Kingstons' older children continued to live in the US at that time, where the eldest son Thomas Branwell Kingston (1801-59) administrated his father's probate at New York in 1824.[425] Thomas Branwell Kingston later moved to London where he married in 1836 and had a family. When Elizabeth Branwell made her will in April 1833 she included £25 'advanced to my sister Kingston' 'in lieu of her share of the proceeds' of sale other items, which she had deposited in Bolitho's bank at Chyandour near Penzance. Jane and Eliza Jane Kingston were listed at Penzance in censuses from 1841 and 'Mrs Kingston' owned the freehold of a shop on Causewayhead by 1844.[426]

Elizabeth Branwell was deceased and her sister Charlotte Branwell may have surrendered any claim she had to a share of her mother's property on Causewayhead. It has been suggested that the 'Causewayhead' property left by Thomas to his widow Anne was on St Clare Street, and that Jane Kingston established a separate home for herself and her daughter at 10 Morrab Place.[427] These were later residential addresses of Jane and Eliza Jane Kingston in Penzance recorded in the censuses, a letter from Charlotte Brontë, directories and advertisements. These place the Kingstons at Windsor Terrace (off Chapel St Clare) in 1841; at 17 St Clare Street in 1846; and at Cornwall Terrace in

Charlotte MacKenzie

1851. And Eliza Jane Kingston following her mother's death at Morrab Place in 1856 and 1861; at 3 East Terrace in 1864;[428] and in South Parade in 1871. These Penzance street names remain current and did not replace each other over time.

Eliza Jane Kingston's move into 10 Morrab Place followed the relocation from Morrab Place to Clarence Street of some of her Penzance cousins, the three Branwell sisters who received annuities from Miss Stone's will in 1855, the same year that Jane Kingston died. Eliza Jane Kingston then operated a lodging house at 10 Morrab Place, probably because she needed to replace the lost household income when Jane Kingston's annuity was no longer paid. Showing something of her mother's resourceful independence in October 1864 Eliza Jane Kingston advertised that she had moved her bookshop and library to '3, East Terrace, opposite the railway station'; in the same year Joseph Hall was listed in a Penzance directory as the next occupant of 10 Morrab Place.[429] Seven years later the census placed Eliza Jane Kingston at South Parade where she continued her library and was also a 'tea dealer'. In September 1878 Eliza Jane Kingston was admitted to 'the House' or workhouse 'her mind seemed far gone; she was not troublesome at all, but restless' and died there two months later.[430]

The Brontës learned about their aunt Jane's circumstances and their American cousins from their aunt Elizabeth. Charlotte Brontë was in contact with her family in Cornwall after her aunt Elizabeth's death and corresponded with her cousin Eliza Jane Kingston who was living with her mother in Penzance. Perhaps aware that the Kingstons might not be able to travel, Charlotte Brontë invited her aunt and uncle Charlotte and Joseph Branwell to her wedding in 1854.[431] Jane Kingston had an independent life in Penzance, where she may have read her Yorkshire nieces' novels and poetry, including Anne Brontë's second novel about the robustly independent thought and action of a Georgian woman who left an unhappy marriage. While the circumstances of Jane and her cousin Thomasine were different, neither was alone in raising children as single mothers in Penzance at a time when seafaring and war frequently separated Cornish families, and mining and disease were also common causes of premature death.

In February 1811 Thomasine's father Richard Branwell described the house he owned in Chapel Street, which he intended to bequeath to his son Lieutenant Thomas Branwell, as formerly occupied by his brother Thomas' widow and now occupied by her daughters.[432] The sisters had left 25 Chapel Street within a year, possibly moving to the Causewayhead property bequeathed to Anne Carne or using their annuities to rent another address. In September 1811 Richard's wife Honor Branwell died. Two months later Richard and Honor's son Lieutenant Thomas Branwell RN drowned at sea in the wreck of the *HMS St George* which was commemorated in Fortescue Hitchin's poem *The tears of Cornubia* (1812). Richard Branwell was unwell and said to have 'been confined to his bed for many years' when

> On Christmas Day, so unfortunate to that ship [the *HMS St George*], and nearly about the time when she perished, the old gentleman called for his daughters, and informed them that he had seen his son Thomas, very wet, with his hair and clothes covered with sand, and he supposed that he had, in landing, fallen on the beach. He therefore desired them to get some refreshment, whilst their brother was shifting his clothes. The young ladies endeavoured, but in vain, to persuade their father that he had not yet returned, though the ship was expected home daily.[433]

In the new year following this 'supernatural appearance' Lieutenant Thomas Branwell's father received news of his son's death, and he died himself a few months later. Richard Branwell updated his will in January 1812 which confirmed that his nieces had by then vacated their Chapel Street home.[434] The amended will bequeathed the Chapel Street house to Richard's middle son and executor Robert Matthews Branwell who lived in it with his family; Robert's second wife and widow Jane Vivian was resident at 25 Chapel Street when the 1844 tithe map and book were compiled, and listed there with their children in the censuses of 1841 and 1851.[435]

For whatever reason Richard and Honor's first son together, also named Richard Branwell (1772-1815), was not settled or successful in life. He never married, responded ungraciously to at least one of two paternity suits in Cornwall, and then relocated to Somerset where he was employed as a bank clerk. In 1812 he had no option but to accept that his father had chosen to bequeath all of his commercial assets at Penzance to one of his younger sons, Robert Matthews Branwell, whom he also named as his executor.[436] Three years later the younger Richard Branwell died.[437] Their youngest son Joseph married in December 1812 to his cousin Charlotte Branwell.

Unfortunately information appears to be lacking about occupations of Elizabeth Branwell in 1790–1821 (except for 1815-16 when she was living with her sister Maria's family in Yorkshire); nor is this information known for Maria Branwell in 1797-1812. The two daughters who had been living at home and nursing their sick father Richard Branwell were probably the 'Miss Branwells' who a few years later kept an infant school in Penzance. Grace Boase attended this school in 1816-17 before becoming a pupil at 'Miss Stone's' when she was 8 years old. Grace Boase remembered her infant school teacher by the informal name 'Peggy' rather than Margaret Branwell; and the sister she spent less time with, who managed the school kitchen, as 'Mary' rather than Eliza Branwell.[438]

One of the five daughters who had inherited Elizabeth Stone's estate later bequeathed £1500 which enabled the Penzance Dispensary to move to new premises on Chapel Street.[439] Miss Stone probably did not approve of Elizabeth Branwell's decision to make bequests to the Brontës and Eliza Jane Kingston, but not to her other nieces and nephew in Penzance. Miss Stone bequeathed annuities to three of Elizabeth's other nieces who also kept a school in Penzance, each of which was supported by a £150 investment.[440]

Four of the seven novels written by the Brontës were set in the Georgian period. *Wuthering Heights* (1847) in the three last decades of the eighteenth century; *Jane Eyre* (1847) in the first two decades of the nineteenth century; *Shirley* (1849) before the end of the Napoleonic wars; and *The Tenant of Wildfell Hall* (1848) in the 1820s.[441] While they might not have conceptualised these as historical novels all three sisters chose to write about times which were outside their direct experience as adults. In doing so they drew partly on what they had learned from their aunt Elizabeth about Georgian Cornwall and their Cornish family.

After being snowed in at *Wuthering Heights* Mr Lockwood complains to Heathcliff that it is 'swarming with ghosts and goblins' and that Catherine 'must have been a changeling'. If aunt Elizabeth told Cornish folktales to her nieces and nephew, as well as family stories, it is likely that these would have included some of the many stories of children and fairies being exchanged, and often returned.[442] The 'poor, fatherless child' Heathcliff, neither of whose parents was identified in the novel, might have been a child outside marriage of Mr Earnshaw. Heathcliff's arrival is objected to by Mrs Earnshaw, and his presence disrupts the relationships of Hindley and Catherine Earnshaw with their father.

This core element of the plot of *Wuthering Heights* echoed one family circumstance of Elizabeth's uncle Richard whose eldest child was born outside of marriage to Catherine Veale, accepted by his father, and familiar with his half-siblings. Richard Branwell's two eldest sons were both christened with their father's name; his eldest daughter with his wife Honor Matthews was named Catherine, which was not a Branwell or Mathews family name. Catherine Veale's son Richard Branwell (1765-1845) later prospered, as surely as Honor Matthews' son Richard Branwell (1772-1815) foundered.[443]

Wuthering Heights, *Jane Eyre*, and *Villette* all included supernatural elements. It was Elizabeth's uncle Richard Branwell who was reported to have personally experienced a 'supernatural appearance' in December 1811 when another of his sons Lieutenant Thomas Branwell RN drowned in the wreck of the *HMS St George*.[444] Uncle Richard's experience was an appearance of a longed for loved one who was lost, whether or not anyone chose to regard it as a passing haunting of the living by the dead. The dream in which 'Mr Fennell' appeared to Martha Longley would probably have been known to Maria and Elizabeth Branwell; Martha told her dream to their uncle John Fennell before she died. And Martha's father Thomas Longley was a Methodist and close friend of the family who had witnessed the wedding of John Kingston to Jane Branwell.[445]

These reports confirmed that there was discussion and tolerance of liminal experiences, dreams, and the supernatural in Georgian Penzance. Within the Branwell family. Among Methodists. By those who enjoyed hearing and telling Cornish folktales. And among those who were persuaded by the scientific potential of materialism to explain subjective mental experiences after reading Darwin's *Zoonomia* or *The temple of nature* (1803)

So in dread dream amid the silent night

Grim spectre forms the shuddering sense affright;

Or Beauty's idol image, as it moves,

Charms the closed eye with graces, smiles, and loves;

Each passing form the pausing heart delights,

And young SENSATION every nerve excites...[446]

The Brontës inclusion of supernatural and liminal experiences in their novels was probably based on similar story-telling, reading, and lively conversational exchanges at home in Haworth parsonage although Anne chose not to include these in her novels.

Charlotte Brontë must have been directly aware of Chartism, but her understanding of Georgian economic conflicts and industry was probably informed by her aunt Elizabeth's memories of food riots to prevent grain being shipped out of Penzance in 1795, and the destruction by fire in 1804 of John Dennis' uninsured woollen mill. The Brontës lacked direct knowledge of their Cornish grandfather's trade as a shipowner and merchant including the transatlantic voyage of the *Nancy and Betsey*. Nonetheless merchants, maritime trade, wartime disruption, and disasters at sea featured in *Agnes Grey, Jane Eyre, Shirley,* and *Villette*. Agnes' father Richard Grey loses money as a result of a shipwreck in which a merchant drowns. In *Shirley* the disruption of trade with America during the Napoleonic wars reduces the profitability of Robert Moore's mill. It was Robert Matthews Branwell (1775-1833) who inherited his father's commercial assets and 25 Chapel Street, and who started the consolidation of the family's fortunes which made the Branwells pre-eminent in Victorian Penzance; although it was Thomas not Richard Branwell whose 'vessel which contained our fortune had been wrecked' on the way to Swansea in 1793. Agnes Grey's resilient response may have echoed aunt Elizabeth's to her father's loss 'with the elasticity of youth, I soon recovered the shock'.[447]

Charlotte MacKenzie

Charlotte Brontë had no direct knowledge of the West Indies. Nonetheless in *Villette* the progress of Lucy Snowe's relationship with M. Paul Emanuel is interrupted when he is sent to Guadaloupe for three years to manage his family's plantations and drowns in a shipwreck on his homeward voyage. M. Emanuel's absence for three years paralleled the time Rose Price was resident in Jamaica in the early 1790s. Rose Price's relationship and children with Lisette Naish before he returned to Penzance has echoes in *Jane Eyre* in the discovery of Mr Rochester's wife from the West Indies, and the descriptions of Bertha Mason which have been read as meaning she may have been partly of African descent. Rose Price's Jamaican children, his child outside of marriage in Penzance, and the varied circumstances in which three children were fathered outside of marriage by two of the Richard Branwells, may all have informed Charlotte Brontë's construction of ambiguities around the paternity of Mr Rochester's adopted daughter Adèle. The death of Bertha Mason, and injuries that Rochester sustains in the fire she started, echoed the tragic accident at home on Chapel Street in Penzance in which Letitia Hart was fatally injured.

Last but not least *The Tenant of Wildfell Hall* may have drawn on what Anne Brontë knew about her aunt Jane's character and experiences. The protagonist Helen Lawrence is independent and resourceful, and leaves an unhappy marriage in which her husband has been unfaithful and violent, taking her only child with her. After leaving her husband Helen rents a property found with the assistance of her brother and earns her living as an artist, painting landscapes for a popular retail market. She presents herself to her new neighbours as a widow named 'Mrs Graham', and keeps her true situation private. After Helen's whereabouts are discovered by her now seriously ill husband she cares for him until he dies. In writing about the Cornish associations of Anne, Emily, and Charlotte Brontë 'I wished to tell the truth' about their relations, and life in Georgian Penzance, rather than be the author of 'a type of narrative, half fact, half fiction' which imaginatively embellishes historical individuals and occurrences.[448]

194

'Liberality of communication'? Charlotte Champion Pascoe

In her 20s and early 30s Charlotte Champion Willyams (1782-1874) was part of family and social circles in Truro which included four women who later published novels or verses. The youngest and most prolific of these was Emma Caroline Michell, a Cornish Admiral's daughter born at Lisbon, who many years later when aged in her 60s and 70s wrote and published thirteen sensation novels which were mostly set in Cornwall; initially using the pseudonym 'C. Sylvester' and later in her own married name Lady Wood. Emma's sister Maria reported that in 1866 'the publisher autocratically prefixed the real names' to a second edition of *Ephemera*, verses which Emma had published jointly with one of her daughters Anna Caroline Steele who was also a Victorian writer; *Ephemera* had originally been published using the pseudonyms Helen and Gabrielle Carr.[449] Another daughter Emma Barrett-Lennard was a writer and composer who set songs to music.

Charlotte and her sister Jane Louisa Willyams (1786-1878) wrote a novel together which was published in 1818.[450] Louisa was nearest in age to Emma's elder sister Anna Maria Michell (1791-1889) who also printed and circulated verses in 1838. Nonetheless it was Charlotte with whom Maria established a lifelong friendship and correspondence which partly discussed these four women's writing. Maria and Charlotte both married in 1815, and five years later Emma married her brother in law Reverend Sir John Page Wood. The Willyams and Wood families included active participants in Liberal politics who were MPs.

Charlotte MacKenzie

Charlotte was born into a family which had experienced many of the transformative influences on Georgian Cornwall. Her father James Willyams was a banker and partner of the Miners' bank started in Cornwall and London in the 1770s by his relation the Cornish mines magnate and MP William Lemon.[451] Charlotte's mother Anne's family were part of the Quaker merchant community in Bristol. Charlotte's maternal grandparents were Anne Bridges, whose father was a distiller, and William Champion an innovative metallurgist; Champion was declared bankrupt in 1769 finally obtaining his certificate 12 years later.[452]

James and Anne Willyams raised their children in Cornwall where they occupied town centre premises in Truro intended for commercial as well as residential use, described as a 'Modern and Commodious Dwelling House, Offices and yards extending down to the river'.[453] As well as managing the Truro operations of the Miners' bank James was the agent for Carnanton and probably knew by the early 1790s that his childless and widowed cousin John Oliver Willyams intended to bequeath the estate to him, which James inherited in 1809.

Of the ten children born to James and Anne Willyams two died in infancy. Their children were christened in the Anglican church which was later of some importance to at least three of their daughters; as adults Charlotte and Sarah were both Cornish vicars' wives, and Louisa wrote and published pamphlets in support of providing aid to Protestants living in some Catholic countries. James was a captain in the militia; his eldest son James Bridges also joined the militia and his younger son John was in the Royal Navy. When Charlotte was aged 12 her eldest brother James Bridges Willyams married Sarah Mendez da Costa whose paternal family were Portuguese Jews trading with the West

Indies. Sarah Bridges Willyams was later a correspondent and substantial financial benefactor of Disraeli.

Born in 1782 Charlotte was probably named for Charlotte Townsend who was married to John Oliver Willyams. Charlotte Townsend was the daughter of the London merchant and MP Chauncy Townsend and Bridget Phipps who was of Eurafrican descent and lived in Africa until she was 10 years old. The naval surgeon John Atkins noted that Charlotte Townsend's maternal grandmother Caterina, a merchant at Cape Coast, had refused to travel to England with her husband James Phipps, an employee of the Royal African Company

> she still conforming to the Dress of her Country, being always barefoot and *fetished* with Chains and Gobbets of Gold, at her Ancles, her Wrists, and her Hair; to alter which in *England*, she thinks would sit awkward, and together with her ignorance how to comport herself with new and strange Conversation.[454]

Caterina and James Phipps nonetheless sent their daughters to school in London.

Atkins' description exoticised Caterina but the anticipated cross-cultural tensions echoed unwelcoming English reactions to members of the Phipps family. In 1715 James Phipps' brother diminishingly referred to two of his nieces, who had arrived in London, as 'some issue of yours'; Bridget and Susan Phipps' schoolmistress complained that the two girls had been 'very carelessly delt with' before coming to school. In 1721 James Phipps' cousin Seth Grosvenor, a London based employee of the Royal African Company who had previously been at Cape Coast, advised that if Caterina travelled to England 'She would be slighted'.[455] Three of James and Caterina Phipps' daughters married in England including Bridget to Chauncy Townsend.

Charlotte MacKenzie

In the next generation in addition to Charlotte Townsend's marriage to John Oliver Willyams three of her siblings married into Cornish families. Her widowed sister Judith Wordsworth married Thomas Haweis, Willyams' cousin, who encouraged the former slave ship captain John Newton to be ordained. Newton later became a prominent proponent for abolition. Another sister Sarah Townsend married Thomas Biddulph the vicar of Padstow. The sisters' brother Joseph Townsend, a vicar who visited Cornwall to pursue his avocation as a geologist, married Joyce Nankivell of St Agnes. While the Townsend sisters' eldest brother James Townsend was the MP for West Looe in 1767-74, Lord Mayor of London, and a political reformer; and another sister was married to a solicitor employed by the East India Company.[456]

James and Anne Willyams both enjoyed reading and the arts; Anne's brother William Bridges Champion bequeathed her his library of books in 1771.[457] As parents they provided their five girls and three boys with an education which encouraged them to be active cultural and social participants. As late as 1841 Charlotte's friend Maria asked her 'Do you remember your dear father questioning whether you and I could "play at verses" all the way from Cornwall to London?'.[458] Three of the Willyams children were later published authors. The eldest son James Bridges was educated at boarding school in Bideford before going to Cambridge; the youngest son Humphry, who later inherited Carnanton, followed his father as a Truro banker, acquired a substantial collection of European art, and was an active political reformer and Liberal MP. The elder James wrote to his daughter Louisa when she was at school about occasional concerts in Truro; his personal bequests to her included his grand piano, music box, and books of music. A portrait of Charlotte Champion Pascoe showed her holding a sheet of music.

We know from James' letters that Louisa was a boarder at the Lees' school in Bath. The extant letters from James to Louisa at school dated from April 1801 and February 1802 when she was aged 15. By then Charlotte was aged 19 and was probably the 'Miss Chatty' referred to by her father who had urged him to write to her and then not replied; in April 1801 'Miss Chatty' was staying with her sister in law Sarah Bridges Willyams at Dawlish in Devon while Sarah's husband was away on duty with the Cornwall militia.[459] It is likely that James and Anne Willyams educated all of their children at least partly in schools, and that Charlotte may also have been a former pupil of the Lees' school.

There were four Lee sisters Sophia, Charlotte, Harriet, and Anne. Sophia and Harriet were writers. Charlotte Lee had taught at the school of 'Miss Rosco' on Royal Crescent, and briefly operated her own school 'above Mr Derham's, Fountain Buildings' from July to December 1780. The finance for the new school came from the proceeds of Sophia's successful first play a comedy *The chapter of accidents* in the summer of 1780. 'Miss Lee in partnership with Miss Charlotte Lee (late from Miss Rosco's) & their two younger sisters' all worked at the school which opened in January 1781 at '9 Vineyards' opposite the Paragon Buildings; later moving to the larger Belvedere House as the school expanded. Charlotte Lee married and moved to Bristol in 1793 but the three other sisters continued their school in Bath for another decade.

The educators had not necessarily received a sound education themselves, as their actor parents John and Anna moved between theatres in Bath, London, Manchester, Dublin, and Edinburgh in the 1740s-70s occasionally completing seasons in separate locations; John Lee spent some years working as a theatre manager including in Bath at the Theatre Royal in 1768-71. The Lee children were probably mostly home educated given that boarding schools might have over-stretched the insecure employment and fluctuating finances which took their father to debtors' prison on two occasions. After being declared bankrupt in Edinburgh in 1756 John Lee received his certificate in 1760.

Aged 20 when her mother died Sophia and her eldest sister Charlotte no doubt assumed much of the responsibility for their three younger siblings Harriet (aged 11), George Augustus, and Anne. After the death of Anna Sophia in September 1770 John Lee may have swiftly moved on; by November 1771 the former Mrs Jeffries, who since 1767 had been appearing in London at Drury Lane and the Haymarket, was identified as 'Mrs Lee' on playlists at Crow Street, Dublin where 'Mr Lee' later attended a performance for her benefit. By 1772 John Lee was once again in financial difficulties and may have been confined to the King's Bench prison for two years; he gained his release by declaring himself insolvent in 1774, and returned to acting. At this stage of his career John Lee had the opportunity to play major Shakesperean roles including Richard III and King Lear, with his daughter Harriet playing Cordelia.

The Lee sisters learned from their experience of the theatre and their father's precarious finances; operating their school with strong commercial sense and fashionable appeal. The Lees' school was initially marketed in newspaper advertisements, and through Harriet's private tutoring of girls in Bath 'in reading and grammar at their own houses'.[460] The kudos of Sophia and Harriet's theatrical and literary productions, publications, and connections consolidated the school's fashionable reputation. Weekly public dances had been a feature of Miss Rosco's school; once every three years pupils from Belvedere gave a dance performance at the Assembly rooms which attracted Bath's most socially prestigious, and on occasions royal, clientele. The sisters were visible outside as well as inside the school, present at public events including church attendance. In 1795 Sophia Lee subscribed to James Marshall's circulating library in Bath whose books were mostly non-fiction, and 80 per cent of whose subscribers were men. A rounded education required attention to academic learning as well as social accomplishments.

The Lee sisters were not directly involved in teaching and it is unclear how the responsibilities for organisation of the school administration and teaching were divided and shared between them. They employed a master 'Mr Perks' who taught writing and arithmetic, as well as a succession of 'Mam'selles' to teach French; with other regular lessons from dancing, drawing, and music masters who had established reputations in Bath. The sisters provided continuity as teachers came and went; they were present at meal times and established influential relationships with the school's pupils as authority figures, mentors, and role models. When 17 year old Susan Mein left Belvedere she was 'much grieved at leaving the Misses Lee. I shed tears at parting from them, all formality over now, and I kissed them and hung round their necks, I was so sorry'.[461]

Girls boarding at Belvedere often spent Sundays and holidays such as Christmas with nearby family and friends. These social connections helped to ensure that parents could gather reliable impressions of the school when they were planning their daughters' education. Dr Mein asked Mrs Gambier a naval widow living in Bath to recommend a school before placing Susan at Belvedere House. One of James Willyams' letters to Louisa noted the plans of her elder married sister Eliza Bridgeman O'Bryan to be in Bath, and his wife also had family in Bristol.

Women who ran schools successfully were relatively independent. With four sisters jointly running their school Sophia and Harriet Lee continued writing for publication. Sophia and Harriet's novels and plays, often assumed to contain autobiographical elements, included strong female characters. During the quarter century that the Lee sisters had their school Sophia published a novel, a ballad in verse, and a play which was a tragedy. *The Recess* (1783-5) is an historical novel based on the conflict between Elizabeth I and Mary Queen of Scots as it was discovered, revealed, and rekindled by the

Charlotte MacKenzie

imaginary twin daughters of Mary and the Duke of Norfolk. It included an account of a slave uprising in Jamaica which enabled Sophia Lee to include a strong female voice opposing slavery. Sophia's next publication was the verse ballad *A Hermit's tale* (1787). Her tragedy *Almeyda Queen of Granada* (1796) portrayed an invented female lead character of African descent who loves Alonzo, the prince of Castile, and seeks to evade an arranged marriage with the Moors' General Orasmyn; despite having Sarah Siddons in the lead role the play was not a success and closed after a few days. In the late 1790s Sophia contributed to the *Canterbury tales* (1797-99) started by her sister Harriet. In the year after the Lee sisters sold their school Sophia published a six volume novel which she had written earlier *The life of a lover* (1804). Her last stage comedy *The Assignation* (1807) closed and was not published after allegations that it contained a libel.

The influence of Sophia as a role model for women writers can be seen in the literary career of Jane Louisa Willyams, and to a lesser extent of Charlotte. The sisters' first novel *Coquetry* (1818) was written jointly. Several of Louisa's later publications emulated the historical fiction of Sophia's most successful novel *The Recess*. In the 1820s-40s Louisa probably also read the historical novels of Anna Eliza Bray several of which included accounts of the persecution of Protestants by Catholics. *The Protestant* (1828) was set in the time of Queen Mary I; Bray's fictional correspondence in *Trelawny of Trelawne* (1837) was at the time believed to have been transcribed from extant letters.[462] In 1840 Charlotte wrote to Maria 'My present companion is also brimful of glowing pictures and romantic legends ... It is Louisa, fresh from Italy, and who spent months of last summer in the Chateau de Chillon...'. Louisa later drew on the information gathered during her travels to write *Chillon* (1845) which blended history, folk memory, and fiction to tell the story of religious conflicts in sixteenth century France.

Some of Louisa's writing was more direct polemic which reflected the growing advocacy and support of liberal social and political values by the Willyams family of Carnanton. She anonymously published *The reason rendered* (1848) appealing for aid for Protestants in Madeira and Vaud; her *Short history of the Waldensian church in the valley of the Piedmont* (1854) was accompanied by a fundraising appeal for an orphan asylum and industrial school in the region. In *The tower of the hawk* (1871) Louisa resumed a partly fictional approach and applied it to Hapsburg history.

Charlotte and Louisa's mother died and was buried at Truro in 1805. If Charlotte was 'Miss Chatty' it is possible that she continued to occasionally stay at her brother's home. Maria referred in one of her letters to first meeting Charlotte in Truro; it may have been Sarah Bridges Willyams who made the initial introductions between Charlotte and Maria when the Michell family returned from Lisbon where Sarah's parental family lived. In 1809 the elder James Willyams moved into Carnanton with his four unmarried children.

Charlotte valued and consciously curated Cornish identity. Charlotte first wrote to Walter Scott in 1811 who replied thanking her for her 'transcript of the very curious Cornish legend concerning the fairies'. Scott observed that this legend was similar to those found in the highlands and in mediaeval Germany, leaving open the question of whether 'the same subjects are apt to occur' 'in remote countries' or shared a common ancient origin. Scott also knew of the seventeenth century Cornish reports of Anne Jefferies and the fairies; stressing his regard for the historical support in the same century for the royalist cause, even if Cornwall were ever to be 'divested' of associations with Arthurian legends and fairies. In the same letter Scott commented that 'Cornwall has been long celebrated as a land of fancy and romance'.[463] This was half a century before Robert Hunt and

Charlotte MacKenzie

William Bottrell came forward with the intention of recording a culture which they perceived as endangered, and published their collections of Cornish folktales.

The transition to living at Carnanton may be one reason why the epistolary novel that Charlotte and Louisa wrote together some years later revolved around the experience and decisions of a single woman after she inherited a large country house near the sea. Exactly when the novel was written, and how Charlotte and Louisa collaborated in writing it is unclear. The weddings of James' youngest daughter Sarah to Reverend Thomas Grylls in January 1815, and of Charlotte to Reverend Thomas Pascoe nine months later, left 29 year old Louisa as the only sister who was not married, and living at Carnanton with her widowed 78 year old father and 23 year old brother Humphry. By the spring of 1817 Charlotte consulted Walter Scott about the publication of *Coquetry*.

The novel included elements which were separately present in the later individual writing of Charlotte and Louisa. These were probably continuing interests and personality traits which each of the sisters brought to their collaboration. Like *Sophia St Clare* Louisa and Charlotte's novel was set partly in a residential community of women, and one which was initially advertised as the establishment of a Protestant convent in the former 'Trevylyan abbey'; Carnanton is near Lanherne where Charlotte later said she used to visit 'the nunnery'.[464] The influence of the Lees' school can be seen as the novel is about women collaborating to create an all female community within which their independence, creativity, and in the case of the novel their faith and spirituality, become more viable or flourish. The relationships between women in Charlotte and Louisa's novel were not characterised by the tropes Thomasin Dennis drew on to develop malevolent female characters in *Sophia St Clare*.

As its title suggested *Coquetry* was light in tone. It was largely optimistic. A coastal shipwreck of the 'Gad-fly sloop of war, bound for Portugal' brings men and women rushing to the beach as rescuers. The officers, passengers, and crew are saved. The shipwreck brings a group of eligible men into the neighbourhood who require temporary lodgings and are mostly accommodated in the large country house which had briefly been an all female community. The interactions and relationships between individual male and female characters unfold through three volumes of reported conversations and letters and the novel ends with several weddings. The acute social observations of people, humour, and use of the coastal location in the plot of *Coquetry* may have originated from Charlotte.

When Charlotte asked Scott's advice as an author he initially wrote to her without great encouragement in February 1817 that 'A novel is that sort of thing which should be very clever or not at all and notwithstanding the name of *novel* they are in great measure copied from each other.' Nonetheless Scott forwarded the manuscript to his publisher Alexander Constable in Edinburgh who published *Coquetry* anonymously in 1818. When Scott read the novel manuscript himself in June 1817 he warmly expressed his 'high sense of its merit' and subsequently acted as an intermediary to facilitate publication and payments to the sisters.[465]

Although Charlotte's only relationship with Walter Scott was through their occasional letters in one respect their correspondence over eleven years followed the pattern of that between Davies Giddy and Thomasin Dennis. They initially exchanged cultural and literary observations, and identified shared interests. In 1814 Scott wrote that he had read Polwhele's 'Local Attachment', who he thought 'does so much honour to his native country' of Cornwall; and more conversationally that ten or twelve years earlier when fishing on the river Tweed he had met two medical students from Cornwall who were studying at Edinburgh.[466] Scott appeared unsurprised and was receptive when Charlotte approached him for advice on publication. Scott provided straightforward assistance with publication and payment issues, but their friendship and exchange of ideas was not developed further and he allowed their correspondence to draw to a close when these matters had been dealt with.

It was at this point that Charlotte wrote to rekindle her friendship with Maria and their correspondence then continued for over half a century. After marrying Maria moved to London with her husband Benjamin Wood, then lived at Buckland in Kent, later acquiring Eltham Lodge near London. Maria wrote to Charlotte about her love for her husband, and also from Buckland about how little she saw of Benjamin who often stayed over in London. A poem by Anna Maria Wood published, alongside one by the London attorney Barry Cornwall, in the Philadelphian magazine *Godey's Lady's Book* in 1832 hinted at fears of infidelity and voiced unhappiness at being neglected by a partner who frequently arrived home late

Expectation

When at the midnight hour I speak

Thy welcome home, with playful smile,

If bloom be brightening o'er my cheek,

And gladness light mine eyes the while -

Thou'rt pleased, nor dost thou seek to know

If festive hours with others spent,

Have kindled on my cheek the glow,

And lustre to mine eyes have lent.

But when my vigil lone I keep,

And, through the hours that linger drear,

While reigns around me tranquil sleep,

Intensely watch thy steps to hear,

Till wayward doubt and wildering fear

A veil of gloom have o'er me wove,

Then dost thou chide the falling tear,

And say that sadness is not love.

Yet others have lit the bloom,

And waked the smile thou'rt pleased to see:

But thou alone can'st spread the gloom,

And falls each anxious tear for Thee.

Unkind! thy steps no more delay,

But quiet to my breast restore:

Think, if I love thee much when gay,

When I am sad I love thee more.

Charlotte MacKenzie

In 1838 Maria shared with Charlotte a privately printed volume which included love letters and her translations of sonnets from Portuguese and Italian. Some of Maria and Charlotte's letters to each other, from the early 1820s to the late 1860s, were later published in separate volumes. The first of these by Maria herself in 1875 and the second four years later by Charlotte's friends and relations. Around the same time Maria, known as 'aunt Ben', helped her youngest niece Katherine to leave an unhappy marriage to William O'Shea, after which Katherine commenced a relationship with the politician Charles Stewart Parnell with whom she had several children.

After marrying Charlotte had moved to live in St Hilary where her husband Thomas Pascoe was the vicar. Charlotte's knowledge of parishioners and their circumstances derived partly from her interest in their children's education, commenting on the day school attached to the workhouse as well as being more closely involved in the organisation of the Sunday school. Like Catherine Phillips, Charlotte formed opinions on social and economic matters based on her observations in Cornwall. Nonetheless even in personal letters to a life long friend, whose husband was elected as a Whig MP for Southwark at a byelection in 1840, Charlotte wrote about the experience of individuals and their families without expounding political principles.

Maria missed the early springs in Cornwall noting in March 1830 'How beautiful must St Hilary now be'; and she observed of Charlotte's attachment to where she lived that 'Gulliver was not more pinned down to the earth than you are to your Land's End'.[467] In fact Charlotte divided her time between the vicarage at St Hilary and 'the Cove', regularly staying in a cottage at Bessy's cove, and walking rather than riding to call on parishioners. Charlotte counted the stiles walking cross country to Marazion, where St Hilary parish included the chapel on St Michael's Mount. She was generally accompanied on these walks and visits by her niece Kate Pascoe. The daughter of Nicolina and James Pascoe, Kate was living with her aunt and uncle at the time of the 1841 census, and married Lieutenant Edward Glover at St Hilary from the vicarage in the following year. The Glovers established their home in Penzance where by the time of the 1851 census they were living with their children on the same street as Jane and Eliza Jane Kingston, whom Charlotte may have met.

Maria printed her own letters, while Charlotte's were posthumously edited for publication by Charlotte Grenfell Bridgeman Rogers and Mary Rogers. This may be why Maria's seem more personally revealing, while Charlotte's focus on her observations on parishioners, or other social activities in the 1830s and 1840s. Because both collections were selectively edited and separately published it is difficult to follow their letters as replies to each other. Maria's printed letters were from the 1820s to the 1870s while those of Charlotte's which were dated in the published volume were from the 1830s-40s, and many were undated. Charlotte and Maria had been writing to each other for at least seven years when Maria told Charlotte

> In all that concerns you, immediately or remotely, I like that plenitude and liberality of communication with which the ' Edinburgh Review' reproaches Goëthe, saying he "not only strips himself stark naked, but turns his pockets inside out into the bargain," and therefore I will conclude that you like the same "turn out."[468]

When Charlotte died she asked for her manuscripts to be destroyed, which Louisa did. It was Maria who had retained Charlotte's letters which may not have been written with publication in mind. It is possible that other letters from Charlotte were retained by Maria but not published by the editors. Whose preface noted that they had taken on the task of transcribing and editing Charlotte's letters after Louisa stepped aside.

Charlotte MacKenzie

Charlotte's niece Kate was 15 years old in 1830; old enough to be aware of social

problems but without the life experience to talk these through fully with Charlotte, who

occasionally wrote frankly and uncompromisingly to Maria about the experience of

individuals in St Hilary. One that stood out was Charlotte's account of domestic violence

in April 1837. 'Jack Bawden' was identified as the man who assaulted his wife 'Betsey'

with a knife. This was a rare instance in which Charlotte wrote a four page account and

communicated her anger at what she heard had occurred. Nonetheless her casual

opinion that Betsey's survival was detrimental 'for society, who have thus lost a fine

warning, and retained a pernicious member' (meaning Betsey's husband Jack) revealed

the social gulf between Charlotte and those she visited, and in this case an empathy

gap. At the same time Charlotte's willingness to write frankly to her friend about what

she had heard, and the separate later decision by the editors to publish what Charlotte

had written, at length and with full names, confirmed that, like Anne Brontë, all three

women 'wished to tell the truth' about one woman's experience of domestic violence.

Charlotte had initiated her correspondence with Walter Scott by sending him her

'transcript of the very curious Cornish legend concerning the fairies'. Many years later

she corresponded with the novelist Charlotte Mary Yonge and on at least one occasion

sent her unusual dried flowers and seeds from Cornwall. Yonge forwarded another letter

to a friend noting without giving the name of the sender

> a clergyman's wife in Cornwall - has sent me on the principle of a delusion of
>
> which I have known other instances, that authoresses must know of governesses.
>
> ... The letter adds that the lady should be neither governess nor duenna but about
>
> 5 or 10 years the senior of the damsel who is about 20, and very silent. If you do

210

not know of anything likely to suit, pray burn the letter and do not trouble

yourself with answering it would be too bad to take up your time for nothing.

In the 1870s Mary Rogers sent a copy of Charlotte's printed letters to Yonge, who replied with thanks, and at the same time highlighted the generational gap between herself and their author by observing that her mother had always enjoyed them.[469]

Charlotte's letters to Maria reflected her strong awareness of Cornish folk memory and history. At 'the Cove' Charlotte assiduously recorded the occasions when she coincided with Captain Will Richards, who continued to live at Prussia Cove where he had been the executor and residuary legatee of the 'King of Prussia' John's widow Joan Carter in 1822. Charlotte also noted 'Cornishisms' she heard in conversations with parishioners. In 1861 Charlotte pseudonymously published *Wan an Aell, a Cornish Drawel, as Zung, Zold, and Spauken by Barzillai Baragweneth, proving to Juniversal Zatizfaction that Coarnwall is held the fust county in Ingleland (more 'special by those as enters it from the Westard, - and tarries there)*. An extant copy of this dialect verse was accompanied by manuscript musical notations for the 'Furry Dance' and 'One and All'. It was written as a song in which 'Wan an' aell' is repeated as a final chorus line of almost every verse. It may have been performed in home or parish entertainments.

The verses told an outline history of Cornwall through the achievements of notable men, mostly of the previous century and a half before 1861. It makes one claim that 'many a Newlyn Scould' or scold would 'bate' or beat college educated men. The history commemorated the scientific, creative, and political achievements of Cornish men regardless of their social origins, rather than celebrating military careers or victories. The verses were accompanied by notes providing historical identifications of individuals, and comments on language including the Cornish meaning of the word 'proper' with many examples of its use in a range of different contexts. What distinguished Charlotte as a writer and united all three of her publications was her continuous, conscious interest in Cornwall's distinctive characteristics and culture.

Notes

[1] Letter from Mary Wollstonecraft to William Godwin [15 February 1797] in Janet Todd (ed) *The collected letters of Mary Wollstonecraft* (London: Allen Lane, 2003), p.397.

[2] Letter from Eliza Fenwick to Everina Wollstonecraft, 12 September 1797.

[3] [Charlotte Champion Pascoe and Jane Louisa Willyams] *Coquetry* (Edinburgh: J Ballantyne and Co, 1818); National Library of Scotland (NLS) MS. 5317 15 letters of Walter Scott to Mrs Pascoe, letter 11 March 1817.

[4] Admiral Sampson Michell (1755-1809) was the son of the Truro physician Thomas Michell (1727-1811) of Croft West and his first wife Jane Spry (1728-59); Sampson Michell was married to Anne Shears (d.1838).

[5] Isaac Taylor *Memoirs and poetical remains of Jane Taylor* (London: B J Holdsworth, 1825).

[6] [Eliza Fenwick] *Secresy, or the ruin on the rock* (London: printed for the author and sold by William Lane; Knight and Co; Miller; Hodgson; E Harlow; and Scatchard, 1795); also printed in London by 'G Kearsley'.

[7] Lissa Paul *Eliza Fenwick. Early modern feminist* (University of Delaware Press, 2019) is a full biography of Eliza Fenwick; the chapter here focuses on Eliza's connections with Cornwall and her novel *Secresy*.

[8] Mary Wollstonecraft *Thoughts on the education of daughters* (London: Joseph Johnson, 1787), p.72.

[9] Charles Fisher printer and bookbinder in Penzance in the 1790s, married Margaret Branwell a sister of Maria Branwell who later married Patrick Brontë; Reverend John Fisher *The valley of Lanherne and other pieces of verse* (London: J Hatchard, 1801).

[10] Letter from Eliza Fenwick to Mary Hays 17 December 1802; Royal Institution of Cornwall (RIC) Eva collection, Penzance school memories of Grace Lucilla Boase.

[11] Hubert Penrose (ed) *Letters from Bath, 1766-1767 by the Rev. John Penrose* (Sutton Publishing Ltd, 1983), p.176.

[12] Charlotte MacKenzie 'Cruel Coppinger: the women's stories' *Royal Institution of Cornwall Journal* 2017, p.21.

[13] Francis Paget Hett (ed) *Memoirs of Susan Sibbald* (London: John Lane the Bodley Head, 1926), pp.3-83 described her time in Fowey and at the Lees' school; Kresen Kernow Archives and Cornish Studies Service (ACSS) AD2077/3/1-3 Letters to Louisa Willyams.

[14] *Bath Chronicle and Weekly Gazette*, 28 December 1780.

[15] Edward A. Bloom and Lillian D. Bloom *The Piozzi letters. Correspondence of Hester Lynch Piozzi, 1784-1821 (formerly Mrs Thrale)* volume 3 1799-1804 (University of Delaware Press, 1993).

[16] Charlotte Champion Pascoe, James Bridges Willyams, Jane Louisa Willyams were published authors; Humphry Willyams printed a catalogue of his art collection in 1871.

[17] Davies Gilbert *The parochial history of Cornwall* (London: J B Nicholls and son, 1838) volume 3, pp.33-4; and A. C. Todd *Beyond the blaze. A biography of Davies Gilbert* (Truro: D Bradford Barton Ltd, 1967) Part 3, pp.113-50 give an account of Thomasin Dennis' education and relationship with Davies Giddy who changed his surname to Gilbert in 1816. Throughout this book he is identified as Davies Giddy as that is the name by which he was known throughout his relationship with Thomasin Dennis.

[18] Benjamin Martin *The natural history of England* (London: W Owen, 1759) volume 1, p.3.

[19] ACSS AP/L/2019 Will of Mary Love, widow of Madron, 1812.

[20] George Clement Boase and William Prideaux Courtney *Bibliotheca Cornubiensis* volume 1, A-O (London: Longmans, Green, Reader, and Dyer, 1874) entry for Blanche Lean p.308.

[21] Dorothy Enys 'Address to simplicity' *Gentleman's Magazine* (October 1785) volume 55, p.787.

[22] Ann Thomas *Poems on various subjects* (Plymouth: printed and sold by M. Haydon and Son, 1784).

[23] Ann Thomas *Adolphus de Biron. A novel founded on the French Revolution* (Plymouth: printed by P Nettleton for the authoress, 1794).

[24] For Catharine Phillips see chapter 2.

[25] For Elizabeth Trefusis see chapter 3.

[26] National Archives (NA) PROB 11/989/290 Will of John Enys of Enys, Cornwall, 15 July 1773; PROB 11/1054/60 Will of Robert Cotton Trefusis of Trefusis, Cornwall, 8 June 1779.

[27] William Borlase, *The natural history of Cornwall* (Oxford: printed for the author, 1758).

[28] ACSS EN/2529 Accounts, expenses on journeys, John Enys, esquire 1766-1769.

[29] *Letters from Bath*, p.155.

[30] Elizabeth Cornetti (ed) *The American journals of Lieutenant John Enys* (Syracuse University Press, 1976).

[31] NA PROB 11/989/290 Will of John Enys of Enys, Cornwall, 15 July 1773.

[32] ACSS EN/889 Correspondence between Dorothy Enys and Thomas Warren, will of John Enys, 1778-81.

[33] Thomas Penrose *Flights of Fancy* (Newbury: J Walter and J Willis, 1775) pp.15-22.

[34] Richard Polwhele *Reminiscences in prose and verse; consisting of the epistolary correspondence of many distinguished characters* (London: J B Nichols and Son, 1836) pp.169-70.

[35] NA PROB 11/1114/347 Will of Dorothy Enys, spinster of Bath, Somerset, 22 March 1784.

[36] Anna Maria Wood *Letters addressed to Mrs Pascoe, of St Hilary vicarage, Cornwall: and on her death in the spring of 1874 returned to the writer* (London: printed by Taylor and Co, 1875) letter 13 June 1838, pp.132-3.

[37] Anne Batten Cristall *Poetical sketches* (London: Joseph Johnson, 1795); for Anne Batten Cristall see chapter 4.

[38] For Eliza Fenwick see chapter 5.

[39] ACSS AD1088/3 Mortgage Market Place, Penzance; AD1088/4 Lease and release, houses and shops in Market Place, Penzance.

[40] [Thomasin Dennis] *Sophia St Clare. A novel.* (London: Joseph Johnson, 1806).

[41] Elizabeth Trefusis *Poems and Tales* (London: Samuel Tipper, 1808).

[42] Letter from Mary Lamb to Dorothy Wordsworth, 9 July 1803.

[43] For Thomasin Dennis see chapters 6 and 7.

[44] Richard Polwhele *The unsex'd females* (London: Cadell and Davies, 1798).

[45] Richard Polwhele *Poems* (Truro: J Michell and Co, 1810) p.60; Richard Polwhele *History of Cornwall. A new edition corrected and enlarged.* (London: Law and Whitakker, 1816) volume 5, p.205; Richard Polwhele *Biographical sketches in Cornwall* (Truro: W Polyblank, 1831) unnumbered page listing 'The persons eminent. Poetry'.

[46] NLS MS. 5317 15 letters of Walter Scott to Mrs Pascoe.

[47] Charlotte Champion Pascoe *Walks about St Hilary, chiefly among the poor* (Penzance: Beare and Son, 1879), compiled by Charlotte Grenfell Bridgeman Rogers and Mary Rogers.

[48] *Wan an Aell, a Cornish Drawel, as Zung, Zold, and Spauken by Barzillai Baragweneth, proving to Juniversal Zatizfaction that Coarnwall is held the fust county in Ingleland (more 'special by those as enters it from the Westard, - and tarries there)* (Penzance: F T Vibert, 1861).

[49] Charlotte MacKenzie 'A 'new and strange conversation' Cornwall's eighteenth century connections with the African diaspora and the politics of abolition and reform' *Cornish Studies* (forthcoming 2021).

[50] William Godwin's diary, 9 February 1790.

[51] Ann Thomas *Adolphus de Biron* volume 2, p.77.

[52] [Eliza Fenwick] *Secresy*, letter XXXIX, Caroline Ashburn to George Valmont.

[53] James Lackington *Memoirs of the forty-five first years of the life of James Lackington, bookseller. Written by himself in forty-seven letters to a friend.* (London: printed for the author, Temple of the Muses, Finsbury Square, 1794) p.246.

[54] Richard Polwhele *The language, literature, and literary characters of Cornwall* (London: T Cadell and W Davies, 1806) p.97.

[55] Letter from Benjamin Disraeli to Sarah Disraeli, 1 June 1830, from Royal Hotel Falmouth, in Benjamin Disraeli *Letters 1815-1834* (University of Toronto Press, 1982) volume 1, p.89.

[56] *Bibliotheca Cornubiensis* volume 1, A-O (London: Longmans and Co, 1874); volume 2, P-Z (London: Longmans and Co, 1878); volume 3, a supplement (London: Longmans and Co, 1882). *Bibliotheca Cornubiensis* did not include Anne Brontë, Emily Brontë, or Eliza Fenwick; but included Charlotte Brontë and Eliza's father Peter Jaco. *Bibliotheca Cornubiensis* listed Ann Thomas' volume of verses but omitted her novel.

[57] [Joseph Batten] *Penzance; - a sketch* (Penzance: T Vigurs, 1815). Alexander Dennis *Journal of a tour through great part of England and Scotland in 1810* (Penzance: T Vigurs, 1816).

[58] [Robert Poltock] *The life and adventures of Peter Wilkins, a Cornish Man* (London: J Robinson and R Dodsley, 1750).

[59] [Edward Trelawney] *An essay concerning slavery and the danger Jamaica is exposed to from the too great number of slaves, and the too little care that is taken to manage them, and a proposal to prevent the further importation of negroes* (London: Charles Corbett, 1746)

[60] [Richard Williams] *A satirical poem on slavery* (Falmouth: E. Elliott, 20 December 1791).

[61] *Walks about St Hilary* p.147.

[62] Fortescue Hitchins *Visions of memory and other poems* (Plymouth: E Hoxland, 1803); Fortescue Hitchins *The seashore with other poems* (Sherborne: printed for the author by James Langdon, 1810); Fortescue Hitchins *The tears of Cornubia* (Penzance: T Vigurs , 1812).

[63] 'Supernatural appearance' *The Naval Chronicle* January-July 1812, volume 27, p.307. For the Branwell family and the Brontës see chapter 8.

[64] NLS MS. 5317 15 letters of Walter Scott to Mrs Pascoe, letter 4 August 1811.

[65] For Charlotte Champion Pascoe see Chapter 9.

[66] Alan M Kent *Wives, mothers and sisters: feminism, literature and women writers in Cornwall* (Penzance: The Patten Trust in association with the Hypatia Trust, 1998); Alan M Kent *The literature of Cornwall: continuity, identity, difference 1000-2000* (Bristol: Redcliffe, 2000).

216

[67] [Emily Trevenen] *Little Derwent's breakfast. By a lady.* (London: Smith, Elder and Co, 1839).

[68] *Memoirs of the life of Catharine Phillips to which are added some of her epistles* (London: James Phillips and son, 1797) pp.4 and 18.

[69] Jerry William Frost (ed) *The records and recollections of James Jenkins* (Lewiston, New York: E Mellen Press, 1984) p.260.

[70] Catharine Phillips *The happy king: a sacred poem. With occasional remarks addressed to George the Third.* (? printed for the author, 1794) p.51.

[71] Mary Neale *Some account of the lives and religious labours of Samuel Neale and Mary Neale formerly Mary Peisley* (Philadelphia, 1860) pp.131 and 135-6.

[72] Phillips *Memoirs*, p.68.

[73] Phillips *Memoirs*, p.206.

[74] *Records and recollections*, p.260. James Jenkins (1753-1831) referred to hearsay that Catharine more specifically wanted 'to avoid the transmission of a disease allied to insanity with which several of her family (as well as herself for a while) had been afflicted'. This claim is not supported by the evidence related to Catharine's family or personal experiences of ill health in her *Memoirs* or extant letters. There is evidence that Jenkins disliked Catharine, whom he saw as unfeminine and 'domineering', which was summarised in Gil Skidmore's *Presidential address to the Quaker Britain Yearly Meeting*, 4 August 2011.

[75] *Some discourses, epistles, and letters, by the late Samuel Fothergill. To which are added some discourses by the late Catharine Phillips, both of the Society of Friends.* (London: W Phillips, 1803).

[76] Phillips *Memoirs*, p.246.

[77] Catharine Phillips *To the principal inhabitants of the county of Cornwall who are about to assemble at Truro on the mining concerns of this county* (London: James Phillips, 1792).

[78] Catharine Phillips *Reasons why the people called Quakers cannot so fully unite with the Methodists in their missions to the negroes in the West India islands and Africa as freely to contribute thereto* (London: James Phillips, 1792).

[79] Catharine Phillips *Considerations on the causes of the high price of grain, and other articles of provision* (London: James Phillips, 1792).

[80] Catharine Phillips *To the lower class of people in the western part of the county of Cornwall* (London: James Phillips, 1792).

[81] Thomas Clarkson *The history of the rise, progress and accomplishment of the abolition of the African slave trade by the British Parliament* (London: Longman, Hurst, Rees, and Orme, 1808) volume 1, pp.129-30.

[82] David Clover 'The British abolitionist movement and print culture: James Phillips activist, printer, and bookseller' Society for Caribbean Studies (UK) Annual Conference 3-5 July 2013, University of Warwick; unpublished paper.

[83] Library of the Religious Society of Friends, Thompson-Clarkson manuscript collection, volume 2, letter from George C Fox to James Phillips, 22 February 1788.

[84] Charlotte MacKenzie *Merchants and smugglers in eighteenth century Cornwall* (Cornwall History, 2019) pp.190-96.

[85] Edwin Jaggard *Cornwall politics in the age of reform 1790-1885* (London: Boydell and Brewer, 1999) p.65.

[86] Morrab Library PEN/23 Penzance Ladies' Book Club.

[87] *Bury and Norwich Post* 28 March 1792.

[88] Charlotte MacKenzie *Merchants and smugglers in eighteenth century Cornwall* (Cornwall History, 2019) p.39.

[89] William Beloe *The sexagenarian; or, the recollections of a literary life* (London: F C & J Rivington, 1817), volume 1, pp.368-84 describe 'Ella'.

[90] Elizabeth Trefusis *Poems and Tales* (London: Samuel Tipper, 1808).

[91] Thomas Penrose *Flights of fancy* (London: printed by J Walter, 1775).

[92] Manuscript notebook of Elizabeth Trefusis' verses, inscribed 'HEP Colquhoun'.

[93] Elizabeth Trefusis *Poems and Tales* (London: Samuel Tipper, 1808) British Library (BL) copy [With copious MS. Additions] UIN BLL01003669373.

[94] Reviews *in Annual review* volume 7, 1808, pp.524-5; *Anti-Jacobin review* volume 30, 1808, pp.256-7; *British critic* volume 32, 1808, pp.126-30; *Critical review* volume 14, 1808, pp.442-3; *Monthly review* volume 57, 1808, pp.206-8; *Poetical register* volume 7, 1808-9, p.557.

[95] *Bibliotheca Cornubiensis* volume 2, entry for Robert Trefusis (1708-42).

[96] NA C 11/827/16 Pearse v. Carleton.

[97] The eight children born to Robert Cotton Trefusis and his first wife Anne St John were: 1762 Elizabeth (d. 1808); 1763 Anne St John m. 1792 to Thomas Maxwell Adams of Barbados; 1764 Robert George William (d. 1797) m. 1786 to Albertina Marianna Gaulis (d.1798); 1766 John (d.1771); 1769 Herbert Barlow (died young); 1772 John (d. 1841) m. 1801 to Elizabeth Cory; 1775 Barbara Crowley (d. 1851); 1776 Louisa (d. 1790).

[98] NA PROB 11/1054/60 Will of Robert Cotton Trefusis of Trefusis, Cornwall, 8 June 1779.

[99] Worcestershire Archive and Archaeology Service (WAAS) 705:73 BA14450/359/3 (1-7) Lady Barbara St John Countess of Coventry, verses.

[100] Charlotte MacKenzie 'Cruel Coppinger: the women's stories' *Royal Institution of Cornwall Journal* 2017, pp.15-32.

[101] Wedding of Mary Ann Trefusis and John Baptist Edward Collier, St Mary Marylebone 12 September 1798; NA PROB 11/1384/370 Will of Francis Mackworth Trefusis, 31 December 1802, gave his step-father's name as 'Jean Baptiste Edward Collier Starmer'.

[102] Hertfordshire Archives and Local Studies (HALS) DE/HCC 27449 Plan and particulars of manor of High Cannons, Shenley, Herts, May 1776. NA C 108/39 Trefusis v. St John 1778-93; C 12/1066/21 Trefusis v. Trefusis 1782; C 101/3178 Lord Clinton v. Earl of Coventry 1797-1803 in which Elizabeth Trefusis was the representative of her nieces and nephews who were minors.

[103] Bedfordshire Archives and Records Service (BARS) SJ 249-305 Trefusis trust 1777-1807; including payments for Louisa Trefusis 1779-90, and a letter to Humphry Hall of Manadon regarding the account.

[104] *Poems and Tales* BL copy [With copious MS. Additions] UIN BLL01003669373.

[105] *Poems and Tales* BL copy [With copious MS. Additions] UIN BLL01003669373.

[106] Find my past (FMP) Westminster rate books 1634-1900.

[107] William Beckford *Italy with sketches of Spain and Portugal by the author of Vathek* (London: Richard Bentley, 1834) volume 2, pp.5-22 describes his stay in Cornwall.

[108] Dr François Verdeil (1747-1832) a Swiss physician who was travelling with Beckford as his medical adviser and companion; and who assisted in preparing the publication of *Vathek* in French in December 1786, three months before they were in Falmouth.

[109] Beloe *Sexagenarian* p.370.

[110] FMP Westminster rate books 1634-1900.

[111] William Godwin's diary, 9 February 1790.

[112] Katharine C. Balderston (ed) *Thraliana. The diary of Mrs Hester Lynch Piozzi* (Oxford: Clarendon Press, 1951) pp.750-1, October to December 1792.

[113] *European magazine* 1787, 40, p.202.

[114] *Letters of Anna Seward* (Edinburgh: Archibald Constable, 1811) volume 1, pp.314-6, 336, and 391-2.

[115] WAAS 705:73 BA14450/288/11 (8) letter from Barry to Earl of Coventry, 9 August 1788.

[116] Diary of William Godwin, 9 February 1790.

[117] Maria and Harriet Falconar *Verses* (London, 1788).

[118] NA PROB 11/1457/30 Will of Sarah Barry, widow of St Peter Worcester, 2 March 1807.

[119] NA PROB 11/1653/397 Will of Elizabeth Barry, spinster of St Martin Worcestershire, 26 February 1822.

[120] Army officers were listed in NA WO 65 Army lists; and the *London Gazette*.

[121] NA WO 71/83 – 71/87 Marching regiments.

Charlotte MacKenzie

Charlotte MacKenzie

[122] Alexander Garden *Anecdotes of the revolutionary war in America* (Charleston: for the author by A E Miller, 1822) p.147; a tale which was later incorporated and retold by the novelist and pro-slavery historian of the American South William Gilmore Simms *Eutaw: a tale of the revolution* (New York: W J Widdleton, 1856) p.520.

[123] NA PRO 30/55/46/82 5291. Adjutant General J. Barry, New York, 14 August 1782.

[124] *Thraliana* p.756, entry for 6 February 1790.

[125] Charles Derek Ross (ed), *Correspondence of Charles, first Marquis Cornwallis* (London: J Murray, 1859) p.142, letter from Lieut General Sir William Fawcett, 26 July 1791; Edward A. Bloom and Lilian D. Bloom *The Piozzi letters 1784-1821* (University of Delaware Press, 1989) volume 1, p.337, letter to Penelope Sophia Weston, 12 October 1790.

[126] Nottingham University Library (NUL) Pw Ja 27 Letter from Colonel J. Barry to Lord William Bentinck, 17 January 1794.

[127] Garden *Anecdotes*, p.147.

[128] *The strictures on the friendly address examined, and a refutation of its principles attempted. Addressed to the people of America.* ('Printed in the year 1775'); *The advantages which America derives from her commerce, connexion, and dependance on Britain. Addressed to the people of America.* ('Printed in the year 1775').

[129] John Russell quoted in Marianne Eliot *Wolfe Tone* (Yale University Press, 1989) p.157.

[130] Edward A. Bloom and Lilian D. Bloom *The Piozzi letters 1784-1821* (University of Delaware Press, 1991) volume 2, p.144, letter from Penelope Sophia Pennington, 5 February 1794; and letter to Penelope Sophia Pennington, 5 May 1795.

[131] Henry Barry *Elegy to the memory of Miss Elizabeth Swift* ([no imprint]); Henry Barry *Sketches of modern improvement* ([no imprint]).

[132] *Thraliana* p.755.

[133] Garden *Anecdotes*, p.147.

[134] *Thraliana* p.868.

[135] NA PROB 11/1357/176 Will of Honourable John Knox, Major General of His Majesty's forces, of Grafton Street, Fitzroy Square, Middlesex, 16 May 1801.

[136] WAAS 705:73 BA14450/288/11 (8) letter from Barry to Earl of Coventry, 9 August 1788; 705:73 BA14450/287/8 (5) letter from Barry to Countess of Coventry, 16 June 1797.

[137] NA PROB 11/1454/59 Will of Thomas Maxwell Adams of St David's Exeter, 9 January 1807; PROB 11/1434/100 Will of the Right Honorable Susanna Louisa Baroness St John widow of Bath, Somerset, 29 November 1805.

[138] Edward A. Bloom and Lilian D. Bloom *The Piozzi letters 1784-1821* (University of Delaware Press, 1993) volume 3, p.145, letter to Penelope Sophia Pennington, 8 December 1800.

[139] Fanny Burney's diary, volume 9.

[140] Legacies of British slave ownership website entry for Thomas Maxwell Adams and Adams Castle, Barbados.

[141] Thomas Maxwell Adams *A cool address to the people of England on the slave trade* (London, 1788).

[142] Beloe *Sexagenarian* p.368

[143] Beloe *Sexagenarian* p.383.

[144] Index to death duty registers, Elizabeth Trefusis of James Street, Buckingham Gate.

[145] Anne Batten Cristall *Poetical sketches* (London: Joseph Johnson, 1795).

[146] Joseph Batten *An elegy on the death of Mr Thomas Vigurs* (Falmouth: Matthew Allinson, 1774); also printed in Bath by W. Gye.

[147] NA HCA 26/12/130 High Court of Admiralty, Prize Court, Register of declarations for letters of marque against France, 2 November 1761; *Lloyds List* 14 May 1762.

[148] *Lloyds List* 27 December 1763 and 6 January 1764, and October 1764.

[149] *Kentish Gazette*, 25 December 1770; the Cristall family's enterprises at Rotherhithe were listed in London trade directories 1776-1850s.

[150] NA IR 1/31 fol 121, 2 May 1782.

[151] Walter Wilson *The history and antiquities of dissenting churches and meeting houses in London, Westminster, and Southwark, including the lives of the ministers* (London: printed for the author, 1808) p.272.

[152] Mary Wollstonecraft to Joshua Cristall, 19 March [1790?] in Todd (ed), p.168.

[153] The Royal Cornwall Museum has one of Joshua Cristall's images of St Michael's Mount.

[154] Mary Wollstonecraft to Joshua Cristall 9 December [1790?] in Todd (ed), p.185.

[155] NA PROB 11/1218/272 Will of John Batten, merchant of Penzance, Cornwall, 25 May 1792.

[156] [Joseph Batten] *Penzance; - a sketch* (Penzance: T. Vigurs, 1815).

[157] *The British Critic* (1795) volume 5, pp.423-4; *New Annual Register* (1795) volume 16 p.278.

[158] *The Critical Review* (1795) volume 13, p.292; *The Monthly Review or Literary Journal* (1796) volume 20 pp.198-200.

[159] *William Godwin's diary*, 16 June 1796; Mary Wollstonecraft to William Godwin [15 February 1797] in Todd (ed), p.397.

[160] *William Godwin's diary*, 16 April 1796.

[161] George Dyer to Mary Hays, 6 February 1797, in Timothy Whelan (ed) *Mary Hays life, writings, and correspondence* online.

[162] Robert Southey to Joseph Cottle, 13 March 1797, in Linda Pratt, Tim Fulford, and Ian Packer (eds) *The collected letters of Robert Southey* electronic edition.

[163] George Dyer *Poems* (London: T. N. Longman and O. Reese, 1802) volume one, prefatory essay on lyric poetry, p.xxxviii.

[164] Anna Eliza Bray *Autobiography of Anna Eliza Bray* (London: Chapman and Hall, 1884) pp.324-5.

[165] NA PROB 11/1376/85 Will of Alexander Cristall, mast, block, and sail-maker of St Mary Rotherhithe, Surrey, 12 June 1802.

[166] NA PROB 11/2071/11 Will of Anne Batten Cristall, spinster of Blackheath, Kent, 20 March 1848.

[167] *Cary's new itinerary* (London: printed for J. Cary, 1810) pp.133-4.

[168] Frederick Charles Danvers and others *Memorials of old Haileybury College* (London: Archibald Constable and Company, 1894) listed those holding teaching or other appointments at the college since 1806.

[169] Harriet Martineau *Harriet Martineau's autobiography* (London: Smith, Elder & Co, 1877) volume one, pp.328-9.

[170] This print is one of the illustrations in Leland Lewis Duncan *A short history of Colfe's grammar school Lewisham* (London: printed by Charles North, the Blackheath Press).

[171] NA PROB 11/2166/217 Will of Elizabeth Cristall, spinster of Lewisham Hill, Blackheath, Kent, 5 February 1853.

[172] [Eliza Fenwick] *Secresy.* The radical publisher and bookseller George Kearsley, who had been briefly imprisoned in the Tower in the 1760s for publishing John Wilkes' *North Briton*, died in 1790. Kearsley was the publisher of Dr John Wolcot's satires using the pseudonym Peter Pindar. Eliza's book was printed while the business was being continued by Catharine, who was George's widow, and their son Thomas Kearsley born in 1775.

[173] Eliza included her parents' names in the christening record of her son Orlando. 'The life of Mr Peter Jaco, written by himself'; published in Thomas Jackson (ed) *The lives of early methodist preachers, chiefly written by themselves* (London, 1837), volume 1.

[174] *A dictionary of Methodism in Britain and Ireland* online.

[175] Samuel Warren and John Stephens *Chronicles of Wesleyan Methodism* (London, 1827).

[176] Letter from Eliza Fenwick to Mary Hays, Monday [no month stated, 1802]; Martha Jacca married William Burgess at Paul on 23 September 1773.

[177] NA PROB 11/1080/184 Will of Peter Jaco, hosier of St Leonard Shoreditch, Middlesex, 20 July 1781.

[178] NA PROB 11/2117/383 Will of Thomas James Fenwick clothier, taylor of Gravesend, Kent, 21 August 1850.

[179] London Metropolitan Archives (LMA) Will of Robert Mackaris of Enfield, Middlesex, 10 October 1735, MS 9172/140D, number 38; ACC/0801/0286 Mortgage for 1,000 years, 1791; ACC/0801/0288 Indenture of demise, 1793; ACC/0801/0289-290 Indentures of lease and release, 1793.

[180] Peter H. Marshall *William Godwin* (Yale University Press, 1984).

[181] *The Critical Review* (1795) series 2, volume 14, p.349; *The British Critic* (1795) series 1, volume 6, p.454.

[182] Letter from Eliza Fenwick to Everina Wollstonecraft, 12 September 1797.

[183] Charles Lamb *Last essays of Elia* (1833), p.247.

[184] Charlotte MacKenzie *Merchants and smugglers in eighteenth century Cornwall* (Cornwall History, 2019).

[185] Humphry Repton's 'red book' for Port Eliot is digitised and published in full online at www.EliotsofPortEliot.com

[186] Letter from Peter Jaco to Mrs Hall, London, 11 September 1776.

[187] ACSS AD1088/3 Mortgage Market Place Penzance.

[188] Charlotte MacKenzie *Merchants and smugglers in eighteenth century Cornwall* (Cornwall History, 2019).

[189] Letter from Eliza Fenwick to Mary Hays, Monday [no month stated, 1802].

[190] Letter from Mary Lamb to Dorothy Wordsworth, 9 July 1803.

[191] NA IR 1/68 board of stamps apprenticeship book 1794-9; *London gazette* 14 February 1807.

[192] ACSS DG 87/1-6 Correspondence between Davies Giddy and Thomasin Dennis, DG 87/1 Thomasin Dennis to Davies Giddy, 25 August 1798; *London gazette* 2 April 1816.

[193] NA PROB 11/1691/389 Will of Grace Dennis, spinster of Penzance, Cornwall, 19 November 1824.

[194] ACSS AD1088/3 Mortgage Market Place Penzance.

[195] John Rule *The labouring miner in Cornwall c.1740-1870 a study in social history* University of Warwick PhD, 1971, pp.139-40.

[196] Alexander Dennis *Journal of a tour through great part of England and Scotland in the year 1810* (Penzance: T Vigurs, 1816).

[197] John Rule *The labouring miner in Cornwall c.1740-1870 a study in social history* University of Warwick PhD, 1971, p.159.

[198] ACSS DG/16 Almanac 1796-1800, 19 December 1800.

[199] Exeter flying post 23 April 1801.

[200] ACSS DG 87/3 Davies Giddy to Thomasin Dennis, 23 April 1801.

[201] East Sussex Record Office (ESRO) GIL/4/8/296/7 An ode to night; the original pamphlet on houses of reception was reprinted in John Edmunds Stock *Memoirs of the life of Thomas Beddoes* (London and Bristol, 1811) appendix 3, pp.xxv – xxviii.

[202] Thomas Beddoes *Observations on the nature of demonstrative evidence* (London: J Johnson, 1793) and *Observations on the nature and cure of calculus, sea scurvy, consumption, catarrh, and fever: together with conjectures upon several other subjects of physiology and pathology* (London: J Murray, 1793) p.258.

[203] ACSS DG/40 correspondence and article to Dr Thomas Beddoes 1795-1803, letter from Davies Giddy to Thomas Beddoes, 7 January 1795.

[204] ACSS DG 87/1 Davies Giddy to Thomasin Dennis, 28 February 1799.

[205] ACSS DG/40 correspondence and article to Dr Thomas Beddoes 1795-1803, and DG/42 correspondence from Dr Thomas Beddoes to Davies Giddy 1795-1803.

[206] ACSS DG/16 Almanac 1796-1800, 29 November 1798 – 9 March 1799.

[207] John Skinner *West country tour. Diary of an excursion through Somerset, Devon and Cornwall in 1797* (Ex Libris Press, 1985) pp.55-6.

[208] Letter from James Watt to Dr Joseph Black, 7 February 1798.

[209] ACSS DG/16 Almanac 1796-1800, 28 November 1797.

[210] Barbara Wedgwood and Hensleigh Wedgwood *The Wedgwood circle 1730-1897: four generations of a family and their friends* (London: Studio Vista, 1980) p.101.

[211] ACSS DG 87/1 Thomasin Dennis to Davies Giddy, 23 June 1798.

[212] Christopher Upham Murray Smith and Robert Arnott *The genius of Erasmus Darwin* (Ashgate publishing, 2005) pp.168-9.

[213] Richard Buckley Litchfield *Tom Wedgwood, the first photographer* (London: Duckworth & Co, 1903) p.123.

[214] Christina de Bellaigue *Educating women: schooling and identity in England and France 1800-67* (Oxford University Press, 2007) pp.80-2.

[215] David V Erdman 'Coleridge, Wordsworth, and the Wedgwood fund' *Bulletin of the New York public library* (1956) volume 60, pp.425-43 and 487-507.

[216] The original prospectus was reprinted in John Edmunds Stock *Memoirs of the life of Thomas Beddoes* (London and Bristol, 1811) appendix 8, pp.xlix – li.

[217] Lisa Ann Robertson ' "Hints & speculation on education" Tom Wedgwood's materialist pedagogy' *Romantic circles*, May 2016.

[218] Letter from William Godwin to Mary Godwin, 10 June 1797.

[219] ACSS DG/16 Almanac 1796-1800, 17 March 1798.

[220] Eliza Meteyard *A group of Englishmen being records of the younger Wedgwoods and their friends* (London, 1871) pp.189-90.

[221] ACSS DG 87/1 Thomasin Dennis to Davies Giddy, 23 June and 17 July 1798.

[222] ACSS DG 87/1 Thomasin Dennis to Davies Giddy, 4 September – 4 October 1798.

[223] Henrietta Emma Litchfield *Emma Darwin a century of family letters 1792-1896* (Cambridge University Press, 1904) pp.14-6.

[224] Lisa Ann Robertson '"Hints & speculation on education" Tom Wedgwood's materialist pedagogy' *Romantic Education*, May 2016.

[225] ACSS DG 87/1 Thomasin Dennis to Davies Giddy, 25 August 1798.

[226] ACSS DG 87/1 Thomasin Dennis to Davies Giddy, 26 November 1799.

[227] ACSS DG 87/1 Thomasin Dennis to Davies Giddy, 23 June 1798.

[228] ACSS DG 87/1 Thomasin Dennis to Davies Giddy, 25 August 1798 and 2 June 1799.

[229] Henrietta Emma Litchfield *Emma Darwin a century of family letters 1792-1896* (Cambridge University Press, 1904) pp.8-9.

[230] *Gentleman's magazine* May 1799; I am grateful to Jacqui Howard for drawing my attention to this reference.

[231] ACSS DG 87/1 Thomasin Dennis to Davies Giddy, 2 June 1799.

[232] Letter from Humphry Davy to Davies Giddy, 18 April 1799.

[233] ACSS DG 87/1 Thomasin Dennis to Davies Giddy, 15 May 1799.

[234] Letter from Robert Southey to Thomas Southey, 12 July 1799.

[235] ACSS DG/16 Almanac 1796-1800, 27 July – 7 August 1799.

[236] Humphry Davy *Researches, chemical and philosophical, chiefly concerning nitrous oxide* (London: J Johnson, 1800).

[237] Humphry Davy 'An account of a method of copying paintings upon glass, and of making profiles, by the agency of light on silver nitrate. Invented by T. Wedgwood, Esq. with observations by H. Davy' *Journal of the Royal Institution* (1802) volume 1, pp.70-4. Davy remained at the Royal Institution until 1812 when he married Jane Apreece who had inherited a fortune including plantations in the West Indies from her father; which enabled Davy to give up his paid positions and concentrate on 'discovery'.

[238] ACSS DG 87/1 Thomasin Dennis to Davies Giddy, 12 December 1799.

[239] ACSS DG 87/1 Thomasin Dennis to Davies Giddy, 28 and 31 December 1799.

[240] ACSS DG/16 Almanac 1796-1800, 20 February 1800.

[241] Wedgwood Museum (WM) E2 1554 letter from Davies Giddy to Josiah Wedgwood, 25 March 1800.

[242] ACSS DG 87/2 Thomasin Dennis to Davies Giddy, 9 April and 6 May 1800.

[243] WM E2 1555 letter from Davies Giddy to Josiah Wedgwood, 16 May 1800.

[244] ACSS DG 87/2 Thomasin Dennis to Davies Giddy, 30 May and 23 June 1800.

245 Henrietta Emma Litchfield *Emma Darwin a century of family letters 1792-1896* (Cambridge University Press, 1904) p.16.

246 Mary Wollstonecraft *Thoughts on the education of daughters* (1787).

247 ACSS DG 87/2 Thomasin Dennis to Davies Giddy, 9 October 1800.

248 BL Add. MSS. 35345 Correspondence of Thomas Poole, letter from Josiah Wedgwood, 9 October 1800.

249 Letter from Samuel Taylor Coleridge to Josiah Wedgwood, 1 November 1800.

250 ACSS DG 87/4 Davies Giddy to Thomasin Dennis, 27 January 1805.

251 Letters from Samuel Taylor Coleridge to Robert Southey, February 1803.

252 ACSS DG 87/5 Thomasin Dennis to Davies Giddy, 10 April 1806.

253 [Thomasine Dennis] *Sophia St Clare. A novel.* (London: Joseph Johnson, 1806).

254 John Bugg (ed) *The Joseph Johnson letterbook* (Oxford University Press, 2016), p.lxxxvi.

255 *Anti-Jacobin Review* (1806) volume 25, pp.389-93.

256 *The Critical Review* (1807) series 3, volume 10, pp.402-3.

257 ACSS DG 87/1-6 Correspondence between Davies Giddy and Thomasin Dennis, DG 87/5 Davies Giddy to Thomasin Dennis, 27 March 1807; John Wolcot quoted in Tom Girtin *Doctor with two aunts, a biography of Peter Pindar* (London: Hutchinson, 1959) pp.182-3.

258 ACSS DG 87/3 Thomasin Dennis to Davies Giddy, 8 April 1801.

259 Lyndan Warner (ed) *Stepfamilies in Europe, 1400-1800* (London: Routledge, 2018) chapter by Tim Stretton 'Stepmothers at law in early modern England'.

260 Richard Polwhele *The unsex'd females* (London: Cadell and Davies, 1798).

261 Richard Polwhele *History of Cornwall. A new edition corrected and enlarged.* (London: Law and Whitakker, 1816) volume 5, p.205.

262 Thomasine Dennis 'To a screech-owl' *The weekly entertainer* (1803) volume 42, pp.259-60.

263 Davies Gilbert *The parochial history of Cornwall* (London: J B Nicholls and son, 1838) volume 3, pp.33-4.

264 Reverend John Fisher *The valley of Lanherne and other pieces of verse* (London: J. Hatchard, 1801).

265 Anna Eliza Bray's *Trelawny of Trelawne; or the prophecy: a legend of Cornwall* (London: Longman, Orme, Brown, Green & Longmans, 1837) volume 1, introductory chapter.

266 ACSS DG 87/4 Thomasin Dennis to Davies Giddy, 14 June 1805.

267 John Skinner *West country tour. Diary of an excursion through Somerset, Devon and Cornwall in 1797* (Ex Libris Press, 1985) p.55.

[268] A C Todd *Beyond the blaze a biography of Davies Gilbert* (Truro: D Bradford Barton, 1967) p.50.

[269] ACSS DG 87/6 Davies Giddy to Thomasin Dennis, 21 September 1808.

[270] ACSS DG 87/1 Thomasin Dennis to Davies Giddy, 16 March 1798.

[271] ACSS DG 87/1 Davies Giddy to Thomasin Dennis, 3 April 1798.

[272] ACSS DG 87/5 Thomasin Dennis to Davies Giddy, 17 March 1808.

[273] ACSS DG 87/1 Davies Giddy to Thomasin Dennis, 27 July and 29 September 1798.

[274] ACSS DG 87/3 Thomasin Dennis to Davies Giddy, 10 January 1804; DG 87/4 Thomasin Dennis to Davies Giddy, 29 March 1805.

[275] Tom Girtin *Doctor with two aunts, a biography of Peter Pindar* (London: Hutchinson, 1959) pp.182-3.

[276] ACSS DG 87/1 Thomasin Dennis to Davies Giddy, 25 August 1798.

[277] ACSS DG 87/5 Thomasin Dennis to Davies Giddy, 3 March 1807.

[278] Erasmus Darwin *Zoonomia or the laws of organic life* (London: J. Johnson, 1794).

[279] ACSS DG 87/1 Thomasin Dennis to Davies Giddy, 26 December 1798.

[280] ACSS DG 87/1 Davies Giddy to Thomasin Dennis, 12 January 1799.

[281] Davy notebook, 26 December 1799; Davy letter to Davies Giddy, 20 October 1800.

[282] ACSS DG 87/1 Thomasin Dennis to Davies Giddy, 19 February 1799.

[283] ACSS DG 87/1 Davies Giddy to Thomasin Dennis, 28 February 1799.

[284] ACSS DG 87/1 Thomasin Dennis to Davies Giddy, 15 May 1799.

[285] ACSS DG/16 Almanac 1796-1800, 27 July – 7 August 1799.

[286] WM E2 1550 letter from Davies Giddy to Josiah Wedgwood, 5 October 1799.

[287] ACSS DG 87/1 Thomasin Dennis to Davies Giddy, 28 and 31 December 1799.

[288] ACSS DG/16 Almanac 1796-1800, 15 January – 26 March 1800; Fortescue Hitchins *The sea shore with other poems* (Sherborne: printed for the author, 1810), pp.148-9.

[289] WM E2 1554 letter from Davies Giddy to Josiah Wedgwood, 25 March 1800.

[290] WM E2 1555 letter from Davies Giddy to Josiah Wedgwood, 16 May 1800.

[291] ACSS DG 87/2 Thomasin Dennis to Davies Giddy, 23 June 1800 and Davies Giddy to Thomasin Dennis, 23 June and 3 July 1800.

[292] R. Thorne, *The history of Parliament: the House of Commons 1790-1820* (London: Secker & Warburg, 1986) parliamentary biography of Giddy (afterwards Gilbert), Davies of Tredrea, Cornwall and Eastbourne, Sussex.

[293] I am very grateful to John Beddoes for sharing an October 2019 draft biography of Anna Beddoes prior to publication.

[294] WM E2 1550 letter from Davies Giddy to Josiah Wedgwood, 5 October 1799.

[295] ACSS DG 87/2 Thomasin Dennis to Davies Giddy, 9 October 1800.

[296] ACSS DG/16 Almanac 1796-1800, 12 November 1800.

[297] *Walks about St Hilary*, p.147.

[298] Letter from Henry Martyn to Reverend Malachy Hitchins, 23 July 1805.

[299] ACSS DG 87/2 Thomasin Dennis to Davies Giddy, 9 October 1800.

[300] ACSS DG 87/3 Thomasin Dennis to Davies Giddy, 4 November 1801.

[301] ACSS DG/89 Correspondence from Mrs Beddoes to Davies Giddy, Anna Beddoes to Davies Giddy, November 1803.

[302] ACSS DG/25 Scrap book about Catherine Davies by Davies Giddy, c.1800-20.

[303] DG/17 Almanac 1801-5, 1 December 1803.

[304] ACSS DG 87/4 Thomasin Dennis to Davies Giddy, 12 February 1805.

[305] ACSS DG 87/4 Thomasin Dennis to Davies Giddy, 20 August 1805.

[306] ACSS DG 87/5 Thomasin Dennis to Davies Giddy, 21 March 1806.

[307] *Sophia St Clare* volume 2, p.112.

[308] ACSS DG 87/5 Thomasin Dennis to Davies Giddy, 24 December 1806.

[309] ACSS DG 87/5 Thomasin Dennis to Davies Giddy, 2 February and 3 March 1807; Davies Giddy to Thomasin Dennis, 25 February and 27 March 1807.

[310] *Sherborne Mercury*, 6 August 1804.

[311] ACSS DG 87/5 Thomasin Dennis to Davies Giddy, July 1807.

[312] East Sussex Record Office (ESRO) FRE/2193 Letter from Mary Frewen to John Frewen, 11 Millbank Row, Westminster.

[313] NA PROB 11/1580/284 Will of Charles Gilbert of Eastbourne, Sussex, 15 May 1816.

[314] *London Gazette* 20 September 1808.

[315] ACSS DG 87/6 Thomasin Dennis to Davies Giddy, 15 August and 11 September 1808; DG 87/6 Davies Giddy to Thomasin Dennis, 8 July and 21 September 1808.

[316] ACSS DG 87/6 Davies Giddy to Thomasin Dennis, 16 May 1809.

[317] Davies Gilbert *The parochial history of Cornwall* (London: J B Nicholls and son, 1838) volume 3, pp.33-4; *Bibliotheca Cornubiensis* volume 1 entry for Thomasin Dennis.

[318] Alexander Dennis *Journal of a tour through great part of England and Scotland in 1810* (Penzance: T Vigurs, 1816).

[319] Beddoes *Observations on the nature of demonstrative evidence* p.68.

[320] R. Thorne, *The history of Parliament: the House of Commons 1790-1820* (1986), parliamentary biography of Giddy (afterwards Gilbert), Davies of Tredrea, Cornwall and Eastbourne, Sussex.

[321] Davies Gilbert *The parochial history of Cornwall* (London: J B Nicholls and son, 1838) volume 3, pp.33-4.

[322] Joseph Hambley Rowe 'William Bottrell and some of his characters' *Old Cornwall*, October 1929, p.5.

[323] [Charlotte Brontë] Currer Bell *Villette* (London: Smith, Elder & Co, 1853) volume 1, pp.261-2.

[324] Edward A. Bloom and Lilian D. Bloom *The Piozzi letters 1784-1821* (University of Delaware Press, 2002) volume 6, p.418, letter to John Salusbury Piozzi Salusbury, Friday 28 July 1820.

[325] Elizabeth Gaskell *The life of Charlotte Brontë* (London: Smith, Elder & Co, 1857) p.62

[326] Ellen Nussey 'Reminiscences of Charlotte Brontë' *Scribners Monthly* (1871) volume 2, p.26.

[327] Joseph Hambley Rowe 'The Maternal Relatives of the Brontës' *Brontë Society Transactions* (1923) volume 6, pp.135-46.

[328] Ivy Holgate 'The Branwells at Penzance' *Brontë Society Transactions* (1960) volume 13, pp.425-32.

[329] Margaret Newbold 'The Branwell Saga' *Brontë Society Transactions* (2002) volume 27, pp.15-26.

[330] Melissa Hardie *Brontë Territories Cornwall and the unexplored maternal legacy 1760-1860* (Edward Everett Root Publishers, 2019).

[331] Sharon Wright *The mother of the Brontës* (Pen and Sword Books, 2019) p.156.

[332] Nick Holland *Aunt Branwell and the Brontë legacy* (Pen and Sword Books, 2018) pp.105-7.

[333] Hambley Rowe, *Old Cornwall*, October 1929, pp.1-5.

[334] [Anne Brontë] Acton Bell *The Tenant of Wildfell Hall* (London: T. C. Newby, 1848) second edition preface dated 22 July 1848; *Villette* volume 3, pp.290-1.

[335] Hambley Rowe, *Old Cornwall*, October 1929, p.5.

[336] Robert Hunt *Popular romances of the West of England* (London: John Camden Hotten, 1865) volume 1, p.xxiii.

[337] Hambley Rowe, *Old Cornwall*, October 1929, pp.1-2.

[338] Ellen Nussey *Scribners Monthly* (1871) volume 2, p.21.

[339] ACSS AP/B/5137 Will of Thomas Branwell, merchant, of Madron, 1808.

[340] [Anne Brontë] Acton Bell *Agnes Grey* (London: Thomas Cautley Newby, 1847); [Charlotte Brontë] Currer Bell *The Professor* (London: Smith, Elder & Co, 1857) was published posthumously.

[341] Letter from Patrick Brontë to John Buckland, 27 November 1821.

[342] Letter from Branwell Brontë to Francis Grundy, 25 October 1842.

[343] [Charlotte Brontë] Currer Bell *Shirley* (London: Smith, Elder and Co, 1849) volume 2, p.22.

[344] NA PROB 11/1971/382 Will of Elizabeth Branwell, 12 December 1842.

[345] RIC William Borlase costs book 19 December 1734 – 29 August 1772, entry 17 May 1754.

[346] C W Boase, G C Boase, and F Boase *An account of the families of Boase or Bowes* (Exeter: privately printed for Charles William, George Clement, and Frederic Boase, 1876) p.5.

[347] ACSS DCPEN/306 Mayors accounts and resolutions Penzance Borough 1747-93.

[348] NA PROB 11/1367/165 Will of Elizabeth Stone, widow of Penzance, Cornwall, 16 December 1801; *Sherborne Mercury* in 1800 referred to Elizabeth Stone's house on Chapel Street.

[349] ACSS AD 350/1 Circuit book west Cornwall Methodist circuit June/July 1767.

[350] Thomas Longley *Some account of Thomas Longley written by himself* (1803).

[351] Letter from Eliza Fenwick to Mary Hays, Monday [no month stated, 1802]

[352] Quoted in Samuel Smiles *Josiah Wedgwood FRS his personal history* (1895) p.201.

[353] Morrab library (ML) RefHIS/21 Ludgvan female friendly society, printed rules published 1796.

[354] ACSS CN/3533 Notices of anniversary meeting of Powder Literary Society at Queen's Head, Tregony with lists of books to be disposed of, 1798-9.

[355] Boase et al *An account of the families of Boase or Bowes* p.5; RIC Borlase costs book.

[356] ML MS PEN/23 Penzance ladies' book club.

[357] *The Cornwall Gazette and Falmouth Packet*, 30 May 1801.

[358] NA IR 1/69 p.45 10 May 1797 apprenticeship of Samuel M Harris to Charles Fisher, printer of Penzance.

[359] NA IR 23/9 and 10 Land tax assessment 1798 and 1799.

[360] ACSS TM 179 Penzance tithe map, 1844; TA 179 apportionment book, 1844.

[361] *The Cornish Telegraph*, 24 December 1878.

[362] G. C. Boase *Reminiscences of Penzance. Reprinted from the 'Cornishman' newspaper, Penzance, 1883-4.* Edited by Peter Pool (Penzance Old Cornwall Society, 1976) pp.53-7.

[363] Edward A. Bloom and Lilian D. Bloom *The Piozzi letters 1784-1821* (University of Delaware Press, 2002) volume 6, pp.418-9, letter to John Salusbury Piozzi Salusbury, Friday 28 July 1820.

[364] Letter from Peter Jaco to Mrs Hall, 11 September 1776.

[365] J. Cambry *Voyage dans le Finistère ou État de ce département en 1794 et 1795* (France: Imprimerie-Librairie du Cercle Social, 1799). G. Le Bouédec 'Les négociants lorientais 1740-1900' Marzagalli, S. and Borin, H. (eds) *Négoce, ports et océans, XVIe-XXe siecles: mélanges offerts a Paul Butel* (Pessac: Presses universitaires de Bordeaux, 2000), p.104.

[366] P.Pourchasse 'Roscoff un important centre de contraband entre la France et l'Angleterre a la fin du xviiie siecle' in M. Figeac-Monthus and C. Lastécouères (eds) *Territoires de l'illicite, ports et îles, de la fraude au contrôle XVIe-XXes* (France: Armand Colin, 2012) p.25.

[367] William Bottrell *Traditions and hearthside stories of west Cornwall* (Penzance: printed for the author. 1870) p.72.

[368] Charlotte MacKenzie *Merchants and smugglers in eighteenth century Cornwall* (Cornwall History, 2019).

[369] Letter from Maria Branwell to Patrick Brontë, 18 November 1812; *Lloyd's List* October 27, 1812.

[370] Elizabeth Sparrow *The Prices of Penzance. The influence of 18th century Jamaican sugar plantation owners on west Cornwall* (The Penzance Library, 1985).

[371] Michael Craton and James Walvin *A Jamaican plantation: the history of Worthy Park 1670-1970* (University of Toronto Press, 1970).

[372] Ray Costello *Black salt: seafarers of African descent on British ships* (Liverpool: Liverpool University Press) pp.32-3. David H. Luker *Cornish Methodism, revivalism, and*

popular belief, c.1780-1870 University of Oxford PhD, 1987, pp.97 and 104; Bernard Deacon *The reformulation of territorial identity* p.280.

[373] Charlotte MacKenzie 'A 'new and strange conversation' Cornwall's eighteenth century connections with the African diaspora and the politics of abolition and reform' *Cornish Studies* (forthcoming 2021).

[374] *List of the society instituted in 1787, for the purpose of effecting the abolition of the slave trade* (London, 1788).

[375] ML MS PEN/23 Penzance ladies' book club; Olaudah Equiano *The interesting narrative of the life of Olaudah Equiano, or Gustavus Vassa, the African* (London: T Wilkins, 1789).

[376] *Bury and Norwich Post* 28 March 1792.

[377] ACSS P133/16b/2 Register of inmates, paupers, apprentices and bastardy bonds, Madron, 1723-95, bastardy bond. 9 December 1789.

[378] NA PROB 11/1839/55 Will of Sir Rose Price of Madron, Cornwall, 24 November 1834.

[379] Letter from Eliza Fenwick to Mary Hays, 17 December [1802].

[380] [Charles Valentine le Grice] *The petition of an old uninhabited house in Penzance to it's master in town* (Penzance: T Vigurs, 1811) pp.18-19,

[381] Fortescue Hitchins *The tears of Cornubia* (Penzance: T Vigurs, 1812) p.24.

[382] [Joseph Batten] *Penzance; a sketch* (Penzance: T Vigurs, 1815).

[383] Boase *Reminiscences of Penzance*, p.12.

[384] Elizabeth Gaskell *The life of Charlotte Brontë* p.90; *Shirley*, volume 2, p.105.

[385] Charlotte Brontë draft letter to Hartley Coleridge, December 1840.

[386] Thomas Longley *Some account of Thomas Longley written by himself* (1803).

[387] University of Leeds Digital Library, Maria Brontë letter and manuscript 'The Advantages of Poverty in Religious Concerns'. This item includes part of an envelope addressed to Patrick Brontë at Hartshead.

[388] Letter from Charlotte Brontë to Branwell Brontë, 17 May 1832.

[389] ACSS AP/C 3485/1 Will of Philip Carne of Penzance, 4 September 1746.

[390] ACSS AP/C 3485/1 Will of Philip Carne of Penzance, 4 September 1746.

[391] P A S Pool *The history of the town and borough of Penzance* (Penzance: published by the Corporation, 1974) pp.57-69.

[392] NA C 11/458/16 Carveth v. Borlase, 1739.

[393] ACSS AP/C 3573/1 Will of John Carveth, 17 May 1750.

[394] LMA Sun fire insurance policy register 1777-86, policy number 394353. ACSS AP/B/5137 Will of Thomas Branwell, merchant, of Madron, 1808.

[395] NA CUST 68/11 Penzance collector to board 8 January 1778 – 14 March 1782, letter 10 December 1778.

[396] Charlotte MacKenzie *Merchants and smugglers in eighteenth century Cornwall* (Cornwall History, 2019).

[397] NA CUST 68/11 Penzance collector to board 8 January 1778 – 14 March 1782, letter 12 December 1778.

[398] ACSS AD 350/1 Circuit book west Cornwall Methodist circuit June/July 1767.

[399] ACSS DCPEN/322 Accounts, specifications and contracts, Penzance quay 1785-6; DCPEN/323 Note of survey made of Penzance quay, 23 November 1786.

[400] LMA Sun fire insurance policy register 1777-86, policy number 93057.

[401] ACSS MSR/PENZ/1 Shipping register 1786-1823.

[402] NA ADM 7/110 Register of passes 1790-2 number 1638.

[403] NA CO 142/19-22 Jamaica shipping returns.

[404] ACSS MSR/PENZ/1 Shipping register 1786-1823.

[405] ACSS DC/PEN 895 and 1083 Bond and lease on schoolground plot Todman Gear, Penzance.

[406] ACSS PD 1790 poll book.

[407] NA IR 23/9/38 Penzance land tax assessment 1798 and IR 23/10/124 Penzance land tax assessment 1799.

[408] Miniature portraits at Haworth parsonage.

[409] John Rule *The labouring miner in Cornwall c.1740-1870 a study in social history* University of Warwick PhD, 1971, pp.139-40.

[410] *Cornwall Gazette*, October 1803.

[411] *Sherborne Mercury*, 6 August 1804.

[412] *Sherborne Mercury* advertisements 1804.

[413] ACSS AD1088/3 Mortgage Market Place, Penzance; AD1088/4 Lease and release, houses and shops in Market Place, Penzance.

[414] NA IR 26/341/264 Abstract of will of Thomas Branwell, merchant of Penzance, Cornwall, 1808.

[415] ACSS AP/B/5137 Will of Thomas Branwell, merchant, of Madron, 1808.

[416] ACSS AP/B/5270 Will of Richard Branwell, innkeeper, of Penzance, 1812.

417 Peter S. Forsaith '...*too indelicate to mention...' transgressive male sexualities in early Methodism* (unpublished paper). University of Manchester Library GB 133 MAM/FL/4/9/8 Letter from George Lowe to Mary Fletcher, 28 July 1807.

418 *Federal Gazette & Baltimore Daily Advertiser* Saturday 5 September 1807.

419 NA IR 23/9 and 10 Land tax assessment 1798 and 1799.

420 As Jane was in America when Thomas Branwell made his will he appointed 'John Batten the younger' as trustee to manage payments of her annuity, ACSS AP/B/5137 Will of Thomas Branwell, merchant, of Madron, 1808.

421 See acknowledgements. I have read Fannie Ratchford 'Letters from Courtland 1829-35', *The Alabama Review* (July and October, 1949); 'Brontë cousins in America', *The Library Chronicle of the University of Texas* (Fall, 1952); and 'The loneliness of a Brontë cousin' *Brontë Society Transactions* (1957). Here I have chosen to give primacy to the historical evidence which is accessible, including authenticated letters of Charlotte Brontë to her relations in Cornwall, and not all of which was known or referred to by Ratchford.

422 *Baltimore patriot and evening advertiser*, patent medicine advertisements appearing throughout 1813-1816.

423 *American and commercial daily advertiser*, 15 May 1819. The sequence of Baltimore newspaper advertisements for John Kingston's retail activities up to and including 1816, and notices of the law suit in 1819, do not preclude the possibility that he had decided to leave Baltimore, and returned to or visited Britain before moving to New York, voyages for which contemporaneous extant evidence appears to be lacking.

424 Eliza Jane Kingston died in 1878, within the living memory of some of Joseph Hambley Rowe's Penzance family contacts in 1923. He referred to one of Eliza's sisters going to America where she married, and did not refer to her parents living in America, Joseph Hambley Rowe 'The Maternal Relatives of the Brontës' *Brontë Society Transactions* (1923) volume 6, pp.135-46. This followed a conflated query in the *Cornish Telegraph* on 27 February 1908 'Kingston Family of Penzance. I should be glad to know the name of the sister of a Miss Elizabeth Jane Kingston who died at Penzance in 1878. The sister was married and went to America. I should be glad also to know if Thos. Kingston solicitor, brother of the above, who died in London about 1855, left any descendants. GREGORY GRUSELIER.' The earliest reference I have found to Jane returning to Penzance in 1809 and then continuing to live there is in Fannie Ratchford's July 1949 article in the *Alabama Review*. This was later followed by many others including Peter Pool's published typescript lecture *The Branwells of Penzance* (1990) which Pool stressed was not definitive.

[425] New York probate letters volume 18, John Kingston bookseller of New York, administration granted to his son Thomas B. Kingston, 28 April 1824.

[426] NA PROB 11/1971/382 Will of Elizabeth Branwell, 12 December 1842. ACSS TM 179 Penzance tithe map, 1844; TA 179 apportionment book, 1844.

[427] Wright *The mother of the Brontës* p.37. Holland *Aunt Branwell and the Brontë legacy* p.63.

[428] *The Cornish Telegraph* 12 October 1864.

[429] *Coulson's directory* 1864 listing for 10 Morrab Place.

[430] *The Cornish Telegraph* 17 September and 24 December 1878.

[431] Margaret Smith (ed) *Letters of Charlotte Brontë* 1829-55, Oxford scholarly editions online.

[432] ACSS AP/B/5270 Will of Richard Branwell, innkeeper, of Penzance, 1812 did not give the names of his nieces who were resident at 25 Chapel Street when he made his will in February 1811.

[433] 'Supernatural appearance' *The Naval Chronicle* January-July 1812, volume 27, p.307.

[434] ACSS AP/B/5270 Will of Richard Branwell, innkeeper, of Penzance, 1812.

[435] ACSS TM 179 Penzance tithe map, 1844; TA 179 apportionment book, 1844.

[436] ACSS AP/B/5270 Will of Richard Branwell, innkeeper, of Penzance, 1812.

[437] ACSS AP/B/5370 Will of Richard Branwell, yeoman, of Penzance, 1815.

[438] RIC Eva collection, memoir of Grace Boase.

[439] E C Edwards *A history of the west Cornwall hospital, Penzance* (Truro: Oscar Blackford, 1946) chapter 3.

[440] NA PROB 11/2213/2 Will of Elizabeth Anne or Ann Stone, spinster of Penzance, Cornwall, 1 May 1855.

[441] [Emily Brontë] Ellis Bell *Wuthering Heights* (London: Thomas Cautley Newby, 1847); [Charlotte Brontë] Currer Bell *Jane Eyre* (London: Smith, Elder and Co, 1847).

[442] *Wuthering Heights*, chapter 3. Simon Young 'Five notes on nineteenth-century Cornish changelings' *Journal of the Royal Institution of Cornwall* (2013) pp.87-116 summarises these folktales.

[443] ACSS AP/B/5370 Will of Richard Branwell, yeoman, of Penzance, 1815; AP/B/6231 Will of Richard Branwell, innkeeper, of Penzance, 1845.

[444] 'Supernatural appearance' *The Naval Chronicle* January-July 1812, volume 27, p.307.

[445] Thomas Longley *Some account of Thomas Longley written by himself* (1803).

[446] Erasmus Darwin *Zoonomia or the laws of organic life* (London: J. Johnson, 1794). Erasmus Darwin *The Temple of Nature* (London: J. Johnson, 1803) Canto 3, pp.72-3.

[447] *Agnes Grey*, volume 1, chapter 1.

448 *The Tenant of Wildfell Hall* second edition preface dated 22 July 1848. Hambley Rowe, *Old Cornwall*, October 1929, pp.1-5.

449 Admiral Sampson Michell (1755-1809) was the son of the Truro physician Thomas Michell (1727-1811) of Croft West and his first wife Jane Spry (1728-59). Anna Maria Wood *Letters addressed to Mrs Pascoe, of St Hilary vicarage, Cornwall: and on her death in the spring of 1874 returned to the writer* (London: printed by Taylor and Co, 1875) letter 8 February 1866, p.227.

450 [Charlotte Champion Pascoe and Jane Louisa Willyams] *Coquetry* (Edinburgh: J. Ballantyne and Co, 1818).

451 William Lemon was James Willyams' first cousin once removed.

452 *London Gazette*, 3 July 1781.

453 ACSS AR/3/318 Notice of sale by auction of reversion of properties in Truro, 24 May 1785.

454 John Atkins *A voyage to Guinea, Brasil, and the west Indies* (London: Ward and Chandler, 1735) p.95.

455 TNA C 113/281 Letter from Thomas Phipps to James Phipps, 24 June 1715; C 113/272 Letter from Seth Grosvenor to James Phipps, 28 January 1721.

456 Charlotte MacKenzie 'A 'new and strange Conversation' Cornwall's eighteenth century connections with the African diaspora and the politics of abolition and reform' *Cornish Studies* (forthcoming 2021).

457 NA PROB 11/970/139 Will of William Bridges Champion, gentleman of Bristol, Gloucestershire, 9 August 1771.

458 *Letters addressed to Mrs Pascoe* letter 12 May 1841, p.146.

459 ACSS AD2077/3/1 Letter, James Willyams, Truro to Louisa Willyams, 21 April 1801; AD2077/3/2 Letter, James Willyams, Clifton to Louisa Willyams at Miss Lees, Bath, 19 February 1802.

460 *Bath Chronicle and Weekly Gazette*, 28 December 1780.

461 Francis Paget Hett (ed) *Memoirs of Susan Sibbald* (London: John Lane the Bodley Head, 1926), pp.3-83 described her time in Fowey and at the Lees' school.

462 Anna Eliza Bray had visited Trelawne where she later confirmed she saw 'three or four love-letters ... but though feeling letters, they were too antiquated in style ... having read with attention many old books .... It was on such materials that I ventured to build my story.' *Autobiography*, pp.270-1.

463 NLS MS. 5317 15 letters of Walter Scott to Mrs Pascoe, letter 10 August 1811.

464 Charlotte Champion Pascoe *Walks about St Hilary, chiefly among the poor* (Penzance: Beare and Son, 1879), compiled by Charlotte Grenfell Bridgeman Rogers and Mary Rogers, undated letter p.15.

[465] NLS MS. 5317 15 letters of Walter Scott to Mrs Pascoe, letters 11 February 1817, 11 March 1817, and 15 June 1817.

[466] NLS MS. 5317 15 letters of Walter Scott to Mrs Pascoe, letter 7 January 1814.

[467] *Letters addressed to Mrs Pascoe* letters 2 March 1839 and 27 April 1831, pp.17 & 29.

[468] *Letters addressed to Mrs Pascoe* letter 25 June 1829, p.12.

[469] Letters of Charlotte Mary Yonge to Elizabeth Missing Sewell, Easter Eve [c. 1853-1862]; to Charlotte Champion Pascoe, 31 August 1860; and to Mary Sophia Rogers, 22 October [1879?].

Printed in Great Britain
by Amazon

26451144R00137